JACK RUSSELL

JACK RUSSELL

UNLEASHED

CollinsWillow

An Imprint of HarperCollins*Publishers*

First published in 1997
by CollinsWillow
an imprint of HarperCollins*Publishers*
London

© Jack Russell 1997

3 5 7 9 8 6 4

A CIP catalogue record for this book
is available from the British Library

ISBN 0 00 218768 X

Origination by Saxon Photolitho, Norwich, UK
Printed and bound by Caledonian International Book
Manufacturing Ltd, Glasgow

Publishers' Acknowledgements
The publishers would like to thank the following for their
permission to reproduce copyright photographs: Allsport,
Patrick Eagar, Empics, Hallawell Photos, Graham Morris,
David Munden, and Chris Turvey. Thanks also to Jack Russell
for providing photographs from his private collection, and to
the late Willie Rushton for his portrait cartoon of Jack.

To my late brother David,
whom I miss terribly. I would love to have
had you alongside me to share all the memorable
adventures in this book.

CONTENTS

ACKNOWLEDGEMENTS

I hope no one is offended by my opinions in this book. I hold no grudges against anyone in my life or my cricket career, and I hope nobody holds anything against me. I've faced up to everything as honestly as I can in my autobiography; my views are sincerely held and not designed to hurt anyone.

I would particularly like to thank the following:

Mum and Dad for bringing me into this world and tolerating my idiosyncrasies; Aileen, my dear wife, for bumping into me at the right time, and for asking me out on a date; and my children Katherine, Elizabeth, Victoria, Marcus and Charles for changing my priorities in life.

Alan Knott and Bob Taylor – two master craftsmen who have been inspirations to me and continually generous in their support and guidance.

My agent, Jim Ruston, for totally understanding my various eccentricities (he's just the same as me), and my support team at the Jack Russell Gallery in Chipping Sodbury.

The legends of the St Nazaire Society, for enriching my life.

The Lord's Taverners, for the endless fun and entertainment they've given me through their love of cricket.

And, finally, the Imperial War Museum, for allowing me to lose myself in their outstanding military exhibits, which will always be an inspiration to me.

Jack Russell
Chipping Sodbury

1
THE RECURRING NIGHTMARE

My ninth England tour proved to be a disaster on a personal level. Of course I was pleased to be part of the squad that turned round a lacklustre effort in Zimbabwe with a more committed, positive performance in New Zealand, enabling us to win an overseas series for the first time in five years. Yet I was desperately frustrated at missing out on the big games, being restricted to just eight days of cricket in the three and a half months from November 1996 to early March 1997.

Only a year before, I had been a hero in the eyes of many, helping Mike Atherton save the Johannesburg Test, as well as setting up a world record for wicket-keeper's dismissals in the same match, and going on to play in the World Cup for the first time. Now I was sidelined, getting sympathy from all quarters and being told by the management that I had done nothing wrong and my exclusion was purely in the interests of the side to get a better balance. That is code for 'We don't think we can win a Test on a good pitch without five main bowlers, rather than four, because our bowling isn't quite good enough. So we need to sacrifice the specialist keeper to get another front-line bowler in.' I under-stood the cricketing reasons, but that didn't make it any easier for me. I was determined not to moan publicly or to mope around and when I came home early in March, I was at ease with my contributions off the field and my general supportiveness to the rest of the squad. Yet Alec Stewart's excellence throughout the tour as our main all-rounder meant I was on the periphery, because he had produced his most consistent performances yet for England as batsman and keeper. Alec's comeback over the past year has been the best news for England supporters, and I was delighted for a guy who has always been great to me, and whom I admire for his dedicated professionalism. His continued success, though, meant I was out of the side for the time being. This seemed to take more out of me than when I was playing; it was difficult getting the adrenalin flowing when carrying drinks.

I admit I feared the worst as I prepared for Zimbabwe. The events of late summer of 1996 had prepared me for the possibility that Alec might get the gloves ahead of me. I was dropped for the last Test of the summer, at the Oval against Pakistan. We were 1–0 down in the series, and the chairman of selectors Raymond Illingworth had been slipping lines to the press, hinting that our best way of getting back in the series was to play an extra bowler. When Mike Atherton phoned me at home on the Sunday morning before the Test, I was mentally prepared. He told me that he hoped to win the Test with another bowler – hadn't he been trying to win it with me in the side? – then came out with the same old story that all this was no reflection on me, and that I would be going on the winter tour to Zimbabwe and New Zealand.

I was cheesed off, as I always am when dropped by England, especially as this had been a good summer for me. By now, I have to admit, I was very tired, physically and mentally. The World Cup earlier in the year had taken a lot out of me, and I had burned myself out trying to get super-fit for the start of the English season. That only made me feel shattered; I had over-trained and that meant my sharpness behind the stumps had slipped slightly. I don't know how I got through that 1996 season. Somehow I got away with it, keeping wicket well, but I was worried that Atherton and Illingworth might have spotted I was just a little flat at times. 'Athers' liked me to impose myself on the batsmen, to shout and encourage the rest of the side, yet I was about five per cent down on my best performances towards the end of the summer. I know I would have raised my game for the Oval Test – it would have been my fiftieth Test, and I felt sure I'd be able to celebrate in a satisfying manner. At this stage of my career, experience and pride in performance can pull you through when you're a shade below par physically, and playing for my country for the fiftieth time would really have inspired me.

As it turned out, I remained stuck on 49 Tests. I took no consolation from the fact that our lower batting order was twice swept away by the Pakistani bowlers at the Oval, giving them a 2–0 series victory. I never want England to lose in any sport, but anyone who has studied my career will tell you that all my runs for England have come at number seven and eight (except as nightwatchman), and I'd like to think that my experience of backs-to-the-wall innings might have helped the cause at the Oval. Unfortunately, I didn't get the opportunity.

We had started the 1996 season under a new England coach, with Ray Illingworth reverting to chairman of selectors after failing to impress the players in South Africa and the World Cup. David Lloyd succeeded Raymond, and immediately got us going with his infectious enthusiasm, innovative training ideas and emotional sense of patriotism. I thought it a great idea of his to have uplifting music, such as 'Jerusalem', on a specially compiled tape in our dressing-room, plus some inspirational words from my all-time hero, Winston Churchill. We couldn't wait to get at India, then Pakistan. We owed it to ourselves and the British public to be more dynamic and successful than in the World Cup, where we started badly and just faded away so disappointingly.

The new regime started well, with England winning the one-day series and then beating India in the Edgbaston Test. Yet I left Birmingham worried about my England future. I had made nought in my only innings, and the new coach told me he thought I'd batted too negatively. A few months earlier, in South Africa, I had batted well all tour, at times deploying a 'leave alone' stroke that frustrated bowlers and made them alter their line, to my advantage. In this innings at Edgbaston I had set myself to bat for a long time, just getting used to the pace and bounce of the wicket, before I could have a go at anything loose from the bowlers. Then I was yorked by Prasad and I was on my way. One of those things, I thought – except David Lloyd told me I should have been more positive. He added that he didn't like the 'leave alone' stroke that had been so productive for me in South Africa. Geoffrey Boycott, whose advice I respect, said more or less the same to me at Edgbaston; he felt it was right to play tightly, but said I should have been in a position mentally to punish a full toss early on. He felt there should always be a positive element in a batsman's head, so that he doesn't miss out on the chance to score when the opportunity comes along.

All of a sudden, the doubts started to flood in on me. 'They don't like the way I'm batting … my place is in danger.' I knew how important it was for the wicket-keeper to get runs, I couldn't rely any longer on doing the job behind the stumps to the best of my ability. When the side was picked for Lord's, I told myself I was on trial, playing for my England career. Again I felt exactly the same as I did seven years earlier, after being heavily criticised for the way I had batted during our defeat at Leeds by the Australians. I had gone into the 1989 Lord's Test determined to take the fight to the Aussies. The strategy had worked, and I survived. For the 1996 Lord's Test, Alec Stewart was reinstated after opener Nick Knight broke a finger, so I saw Alec as a rival for my role in the side. I psyched myself up for a battle. No one was going to get my England place without an almighty struggle.

In the nets on the afternoon before the Test, Mike Atherton came up to me and said, 'You're not worried, are you?' I said I wasn't. I was more frustrated that one nought from a simple misjudgement had led to the vibes from David Lloyd about the way I was batting. On the Tuesday night, some of the players went to Wembley to see England beat Holland 4–1 in the Euro '96 competition and I would dearly love to have gone with them, but I was worried and confused. Instead, I spent three hours in the company of Alan Knott, a genius among keepers who has been massively supportive to me for years. We worked out how I was going to approach the Indian bowlers, and decided that I'd get after them.

We batted first, got into trouble and when I walked out to join Graham Thorpe I was really pumped up, more than I've ever been when going out to bat. Lord's has always given me an extra buzz but this day was special. My England place was on the line as far as I was concerned. As I walked onto the outfield after coming down the pavilion steps, I thought of my brother, David. Ten years earlier, he had died tragically in an accident outside a pub. He was only twenty-one. Not a day went by without me thinking of him and wishing he'd been there to share in my successes. This time at Lord's, I said out loud, 'David, I need you here with me today, help me show them!' I walked straight past 'Thorpey' in the middle, not hearing a word he said to me, I was in a trance. Dickie Bird was waiting at my end and I was soon gibbering away at him. 'Dickie,' I said, 'today they've come to watch you and me perform – no one else. They're going to drop me if I don't make runs here.' I had never said anything like that before to an umpire, but I was so fired up. The wicket was helping the Indian seamers, and I played the 'leave' early. I continued to play it when necessary, and it worked, frustrating their bowlers. I also played a few shots and by the close, I'd passed my fifty and was game for a lot more.

Next day, I managed to get a hundred, my second for England, and the fuss I made when I got to three figures, punching the air and shouting my head off, made it clear to everyone how vital this innings was to me. I hadn't planned it, the jump and the punch just came out. It must have been all that pent-up anger unleashing itself. I shall always remember the roar from the full house when I did it. I don't care what the management said about my place not being in jeopardy at that stage of the summer – I just felt I had to regain their confidence in me with a big innings. On the final day, I was involved in another crisis, in company with Ronnie Irani, after a flurry of wickets fell. Ronnie played his shots while I hung around, annoying the bowlers with the 'leave' stroke and concentrating hard. We managed to do a lot towards saving the situation. So by the end of that Lord's Test, I felt tired after being out in the middle for so long – but vindicated. I had got runs playing in my own preferred way, rather than following the suggestions of others.

There was an amusing postscript to that hundred on the second day. My agent, Jim Ruston, had been chatting to me about my prospects a few days earlier, and I had rashly forecast that I would get a hundred. 'I can feel a hundred in me,' I told Jim. He promised he'd be there to see me try, but he also had his eye on another challenge. He had heard that, at an auction in London on the Friday, the blazer and gloves of Keith Andrew were to come under the hammer. Now Keith had been a marvellous keeper for Northants and England in the fifties and sixties. The gloves were also signed by Bertie Oldfield, the legendary Australian keeper between the two World Wars, who was another all-time great. Jim and I agreed that it would be wonderful to get the blazer and gloves and he agreed to go and bid for me. He just had time to see me reach my hundred before rushing off across London in a taxi. He was successful in his bid and couldn't wait to tell me when he got back to Lord's. Jim bumped into Sir Colin Cowdrey at the back of the pavilion who kindly offered to take the prized possessions to me in the England dressing-room. Sir Colin was just as excited at our capture, and marched into the England dressing-room only to fall over somebody's gear and find himself in the middle of one of David Lloyd's most impassioned team talks. David's style in these team meetings is to concentrate on our strengths and the opposition's weaknesses. His whole aim is to be upbeat, positive and aggressive, to make us feel better than the guys in the other dressing-room. So there was Sir Colin Cowdrey, listening to our new coach getting into his passionate stride. As David was telling us about the need for early wickets, that England expects us to give everything to the cause, I stood there in my jockstrap and vest, clutching a plastic bag thrust towards me by Sir Colin. The jaws of the players almost hit the floor – but the coach kept on talking! The lads must have thought, 'What's Russell up to now?' That game was also notable as the last time Dickie Bird stood as a Test umpire. He gave Mike Atherton out lbw in the first over of the game, after Athers had joked he'd do just that. It was plumb, and so was my lbw dismissal on the final afternoon, the last Dickie gave in Test cricket. Now I never like getting out, but on this occasion it was an honour to depart to his decision. Dickie has been a great character and servant of the game. He has been a great support to me and I thank him for that.

It would have been reassuring to think that my efforts at Lord's would have set me up for the rest of that international summer, but I only lasted another three Tests before I was dropped. By the time we got to Leeds, we were 1–0 down to the Pakistanis, and I had to ask the captain on the morning of the match if I was actually playing! Unfortunately, I got out cheaply to Wasim Akram; Alec Stewart made a marvellous hundred, the game was drawn, and Alec took over the gloves at the Oval. That made it six times now that I had been dropped by England, starting at Adelaide in 1991. Each time I had been reassured about my future, but with my 33rd birthday approaching, I was no longer taking anything for granted. As I prepared for Zimbabwe and New Zealand, I seriously wondered if my career would be stalled permanently on 49 Tests.

I heard Mike Atherton say in an interview on BBC's highlights programme at the end of the series that he was happy with six batsmen, which left little scope for me if he wanted to play five bowlers, and that was soon confirmed to me when we got to Zimbabwe. Alec Stewart and I had a game each on the first weekend, and I knew that whoever got the nod for the first big game, the four-dayer against Mashonaland, was set for the rest of the tour. On the eve of that match, there was a knock on my hotel door. I looked through the spyhole and my heart sank. It was Mike Atherton. He wasn't coming to see me to talk about my painting and he got straight to the point. Alec would have the gloves for the Zimbabwe section of the tour, but I knew deep down that meant for New Zealand as well. 'You don't expect me to be happy with that, do you?' I said, then continued, 'On the outside, I'll be lively and bubbly and will support you all I can – but don't think I'll ever accept the situation totally.' Athers agreed, saying he wouldn't want me to be happy about something that wasn't down to any inadequacies on my part. I was half expecting the news, but it still came as a hammer blow. That night, I had to put on a brave face for a couple of media interviews, standing behind the captain whether he was right or wrong. It was hard to put on the philosophical facade. David Lloyd later came up to me and said, 'Hard luck' but nothing else. Why didn't he take the time to talk to me about the situation? To me, that was confirmation he was in the same stable as Athers and another England selector, Graham Gooch. Both had dropped me for England when they weren't happy about playing only four main bowlers. To them, I was expendable and it hurt. I was surplus to requirements before we had played a meaningful game on what was to be a long tour – exactly a year since I had been a national hero with Mike Atherton after the Johannesburg Test.

Athers told me that he valued my input and that he would expect me still to offer my thoughts at team meetings, no matter how disappointed I felt at being sidelined. There was never any danger of me not offering anything; it's called professionalism. I was determined not to appear miserable on the surface, I stayed upbeat with the boys, and did all the fetching and carrying of drinks out to the middle whenever necessary. My frustrations were eased to a certain extent by the hard work I put in under the supervision of our fitness trainer, Dean Riddle. I reckon Dean's ideas will help to add another five years to my career, so it wasn't all unproductive time spent on that tour. My painting kept me occupied on days off. In Bulawayo, I went to Matopos National Park, to paint the grave of Cecil Rhodes, and that was a fascinating experience. There were so many rocks around his grave that it must have been almost like painting on the moon. I went to Matopos as often as I could, and at the ground managed a few sketches of some team-mates. It passed the time, but there's no substitute for playing when you're on tour.

It was important to get my mind around what lay in store, at the same time being mentally ready to step into Alec Stewart's place at the last moment. I had to tell myself that things could easily change, otherwise there was no point in being out there. This was not to wish ill-fortune on 'Stewie', merely a way of finding the self-motivation and drive to keep up my spirits. It had to come from within me – no amount of understanding words from my team-mates or the management would compensate. So when I woke up on the morning of a match on that tour, it was a case of steeling myself to expect that I might play. That made the inevitable disappointment and anti-climax harder to bear, but at least the competitive juices were still bubbling.

Inevitably, comparisons were made between Alec Stewart and me, and some sections of the media wondered how intense was our rivalry. Well, Stewie and I have had a great relationship since we played against each other at the age of fifteen, me for West of England Schools and Alec for South of England. It was a trials match, and I got the nod ahead of him for England Schools; all these years later, he's paying me back! Over the years, we have roomed together, and gone out of our way to help each other. As room-mates, I would tolerate his habit of falling asleep with the television on, and he'd accept I needed all the tea bags to fuel my passion for draining countless cups. He also turned a blind eye to me stealing all the chocolate biscuits! I would go so far as to say that our relationship has been as close and supportive as that between Bob Taylor and Alan Knott on their various England tours, when Knotty's genius kept out Bob, a great keeper. For me, Alec gets maximum marks for his fitness, dedication and commitment in taking on the two roles of top-order batsman and wicket-keeper. He's getting better and better as a keeper, because he's doing it more now for Surrey. With the tragic death last December of Graham Kersey, that means Alec will probably take over the gloves for Surrey in almost all the first-team games, so it was wise of him to resign the county captaincy in case too many tasks reduced his effectiveness. I know that deep down Alec would prefer to concentrate on his batting, but he was justified in hanging onto his keeping, because it was another string to his bow. It's tiring having to do both jobs, though, when you're a top-order batsman, and just at the end of the New Zealand tour, Alec was struggling just a little. He wasn't moving his feet quite as well as he should, but you can't blame him for that, because he worked so hard at both disciplines while still finding the time to help and encourage me. When I played in the one-day international at Wellington, Alec was there to tell me where to stand, who would be bowling from what angle and all the other various tricks of the trade that keepers pass on. This tour was the first time that Alec had made runs consistently while keeping wicket, and that's because he has learned more about how to cope mentally with the two demands. Practical experience has been the making of him, as well as his attitude. I think Alec is a fantastic role model for young cricketers, he's always keen and smart, with a terrific competitive instinct. In my opinion, he's been unlucky to miss out on captaining England on a regular basis.

So when Stewie was confirmed early on tour as the first-choice keeper, we didn't need to say anything to each other, we both knew the score. Exchanging glances and smiles was enough; we knew that our friendship and working relationship would never be affected. After a month on the tour, the die was cast. Alec had batted very well in the Bulawayo Test, almost nailing down a win for us in the run chase, and his wicket-keeping couldn't be faulted. So I just had to keep working hard. I had to smile at Geoffrey Boycott's typically forthright advice to me: 'I'd send you home for Christmas, lad. You'll not be getting a game out here. Better to send you home to recharge your batteries, and have you fresh for New Zealand. You're wasting your time here.' Thanks, Geoffrey.

Christmas was a difficult time for me. Our daughter Katherine had been born in the first week of the tour, and I found myself thinking all the obvious thoughts of a proud dad when he's thousands of miles away from home. Not having a meaningful role to play on the tour made it worse. The highlight of Christmas Day for me came when my wife, Aileen, rang my hotel room and played the Queen's Speech down the phone line from the television back home. As an unashamed patriot, hearing the Queen from so far away was a consolation. After all, I was serving my country in one capacity, even if it was to be just carrying the drinks.

By this time in Harare, a siege mentality had settled on some members of our squad, and I couldn't see why. Some of our lads moaned about the standard of hotels, that there was nothing to do at night, and that the practice facilities were poor. It's true that the facilities at the grounds were below par, but you just get on with that on tour and concentrate on essentials. As for the hotels, they were fine in my opinion and I told some of those complaining that I'd been in far worse elsewhere in the world while on England duty. That didn't seem to make an impression and I ended up a little disappointed at the negative attitude of some of the England players. It rained a lot, sure – as it does in the Caribbean, South Africa and New Zealand, not forgetting England. You just have to accept that, it's part of cricket. The chemistry just wasn't right between the country and some of our players and I was sorry about that. Perhaps the fact that New Zealand had more in common with England cheered them up when we left Zimbabwe.

I'm sure the media criticism of our efforts in Zimbabwe helped develop an inward-looking attitude in our tour party, but our generally below-par displays were nobody's fault but our own. I couldn't see why the media were being blamed when we were deservedly copping the flak. I believe we were subconsciously complacent in Zimbabwe, taking far too long to come to terms with the slow pitches, the need to graft for runs and to bowl a consistent line. We were adrift in cricketing awareness early on, and although we talked about the opposition in team meetings, I got the feeling that their players weren't rated all that highly by us, especially at Test level. After we had lost inside three days to Mashonaland, a poor performance in anyone's book, I asked two important questions at our team meeting – 'Do we think we've practised properly?' and 'Don't we rate their bowlers?' I felt we weren't bowling with enough discipline and we batted at times with too much freedom when it was a time to graft. Those observations were brushed under the carpet by everyone, management and players. Maybe I should have put my points in a different way, because no one in the team meeting seemed to understand what I was getting at. That annoyed me.

A few weeks later, we showed we still hadn't addressed ourselves to the best way of playing cricket in Zimbabwe, as our batsmen played a series of cavalier shots to get bowled out cheaply in the first innings of the Harare Test. To me, there was still an air of complacency in the England camp, the feeling that the opposition couldn't bowl and that it would all come right for us if we played our natural game. With rain washing out the final day of that second Test, we clung to the belief that we might have come close to victory by a well-timed declaration, and then bowling out Zimbabwe. To me, their lower order seemed more difficult to budge, which seemed strange, and they were no pushover. To have beaten them in their own backyard, we would have needed to play well. Honours were even, and there was no point in pretending otherwise.

We could and should have won the First Test. On that final day in Bulawayo, Nick Knight and Alec Stewart batted marvellously in a run chase that saw us fail to win by three runs. Another delivery would probably have brought us victory. But it didn't happen, because the opposition fielders found inspiration at the crucial time, we lost wickets in an effort to force the win and then they frustrated us in the final hour with negative tactics. The bowling was concentrated outside the stumps, but they weren't all called wides by the umpires, and we had to live with that, no matter how disappointed we felt. Afterwards, our dressing-room was a very sombre place, just like the one in South Africa when Athers and I had thwarted the opposition in Johannesburg a year earlier. It was almost as if we had lost, having come so close to winning. We failed to appreciate the resilience of the Zimbabweans, and their tactical awareness in throttling us with some legitimate, negative bowling near the end. It was a time to lick our wounds, have as sporting a word as we could find with the opposition, then regroup back in the team hotel, finding consolation from our performance, resolving to go one better next time. Unfortunately, David Lloyd, our coach, allowed his emotions to get the better of him. Just after the game had ended so frenetically in a draw, I saw him wagging his finger angrily at some local officials outside the VIP tent, and I wondered what all that was about. Was he having a go at them about the quality of umpiring in the Test, and the allegedly unsporting bowling near the end? It shows how passionate he was for the success of English cricket. When David spoke on the record to the media, he went on in a similar vein, claiming 'We flippin' murdered 'em, and they know it.' The fact is that the match was drawn. We were only in charge for a couple of hours on that final afternoon, and when the emotions had cleared, we ought to have looked closely at a period in our first innings, when we should have pushed on more positively, and built a bigger lead more quickly, giving us more time towards the end of the game. The object for them was not to lose the match in such a situation. Zimbabwe should be given credit for hanging on in there.

The fall-out from David Lloyd's remarks meant he got a fair amount of stick from the British media, both on the tour and back home. That led to further deterioration in our relationship with the media corps on the trip. Some of our party thought they'd had too much criticism that was personal and, with the traditional press pantomime looming at Christmas, we had a meeting to decide whether we should attend it. Now this is a traditional way of passing twenty minutes on Christmas morning, when the press give us a drink, then put on a short show that's full of in-house observations about both players and reporters. It's always been an amusing distraction when you're on tour and so far from home. But the mood in our squad had soured towards the press, because some felt we had been getting an unfair amount of stick for our performances in the first month. At the meeting, around eighty per cent voted against attending the press panto because the criticism had been too wounding; the general feeling was that we shouldn't be hypocritical and have a drink with someone who had slagged us off in print. I thought that a short-sighted attitude and after the vote was taken, I said to the players, 'Are you sure we're doing the right thing?' To me, press–player relations are important in all aspects. If you get the press on your side, it does you no harm as an individual and by extension, the team. That also pleases the sponsors of the team and improves the game's overall image. I admit that ninety per cent of my press coverage throughout my career has been favourable and that I might appear biased, but I believe you need to keep the lines of communication open even if you are getting stick. As players, we're always happy to take the plaudits, so we have to accept the other side of the coin when it's going badly. It was naive to cut ourselves off from the travelling press contingent, because that breakdown would come back and haunt us at a later date. My views were in a substantial minority at that meeting, though, and the drawbridge stayed up. That only increased the pressure on Mike Atherton and David Lloyd to get it right for the rest of the tour, which to me was an extra hassle that should have been avoidable.

So when the Zimbabwe leg of the tour ended with us losing 3–0 in the one-day internationals, the press climbed into us, and we couldn't complain about the lack of goodwill, nor the criticisms about the way we had played, which to me seemed burdened by the fear of failure. We were in a mental hole, worried about being bold, concerned that it would rebound in our faces, leading to the inevitable flak. I also believe we were still underestimating Zimbabwe, thinking that our experience of one-day cricket would see us through. After all, we play that form of cricket all the time back home, don't we? Yet we showed we had learned nothing from the World Cup debacle nine months earlier. We were going backwards, after being one of the best one-day sides in the world a few years before. We lacked purpose, imagination and flair. There were no excuses, we'd been long enough in Zimbabwe to adapt to the conditions.

The pressure was certainly building on Mike Atherton and David Lloyd by the time we settled into the New Zealand leg, and although our lads soon showed they were happier to be there rather than in Zimbabwe, we were still on thin ice after a month. The warm-up games had gone well for us, but it was a huge disappointment only to draw the Auckland Test after playing well during periods of the match. All credit to Nathan Astle and Danny Morrison for defying us so long to get the draw, but if we'd batted more positively in our second innings, the extra time gained would have stood us in good stead and surely we would have bowled New Zealand out. It got even worse after the Auckland Test, when we lost badly to New Zealand 'A' in Wanganui. Athers was under strain, you could see it in his face and I asked him if he'd considered having a game off. I wanted to have a chat with him about my own thoughts, but he said he had already decided to play. The conversation went no further. He did need time in the middle to get his footwork sorted out, but I felt he's a good enough player to have a game off, do some fishing, recharge and come back refreshed, firing on all cylinders. I know everyone in the tour party would have understood, but Athers always wants to lead from the front. He can be rather too stubborn for his own good at times, but that's why he's so tough. He elected to captain us at Wanganui, and that did him no good at all. He also failed again with the bat, which only made things worse. I got a game, kept wicket well after a few early overs of acclimatisation, although I was out second ball in the first innings, a rash shot full of eagerness and desire. I'd lost my tightness trying to be too aggressive too early on, on a wicket that wasn't suitable for first-class cricket. I'd made myself look a bit of a fool that day. Somehow the local press had heard that I would love to win a professional horse race as a jockey, because horses fascinate me as characters. So I had my photo taken, sat on a chair, with riding gear, a whip and my keeper's pads on. That morning, the photo appeared in the local paper, and after getting nought, I was left with egg on my face. Our whole performance in that game was downbeat and negative. In the field, I kept tugging at my England shirt, shouting 'Remember the three lions, lads,' but I didn't get much response. It was understandable to a degree. Not winning in Auckland a couple of days earlier had really knocked the stuffing out of those who'd just played. I was lucky enough to make 61 not out in the second innings, but we still lost by ninety runs. When it was all over, David Lloyd told the press that, I quote, 'I was proud and pleased with the way we approached this game.' He said the defeat wasn't at all damaging, even though we had been bowled out for 107 in the first innings by New Zealand's second string attack, a great psychological boost for them, I would have thought. Our coach may have been philosophical, but I was angry at our defeat. I hate losing at the best of times, but it's even worse for me when I know we ought to have done better with a more positive approach. I sat in the dressing-room afterwards, thinking, 'It could go seriously downhill from here. We're in trouble.'

That proved to be the low point of the tour, but credit to the management, we did manage to pull things round in time. I honestly didn't think it was possible, but I didn't make my feelings known. We won the next Test, at Wellington, after we had batted well, taken the game by the scruff of the neck and not let go. We were excellent. Mike Atherton's personal example brought us victory at Christchurch and the series by 2–0. Significantly, we played an unchanged side at Christchurch, the first time in a Test since Antigua in 1994 – one of the reasons why we don't do ourselves justice sometimes. With too many changes, a lack of collective confidence often results. You don't see West Indies,

Australia or South Africa ringing the changes so often; they back what they feel are the class players. Our guys feel on trial too often. It's been a hard slog for Athers, and I was full of admiration for the way he led from the front in New Zealand, when it could have turned out disastrously. His inner reserves of stamina and mental steel are remarkable, and he is hugely respected in the England dressing-room. Just when it looked as if his poor batting form and the team's under-achievement were going to overwhelm him, he showed his strength of character. On the eve of the second Test, when we were lacking confidence after the Wanganui defeat, he struck just the right note at the team meeting. He told us to forget about previous results and performances, that the next two Tests would shape the destiny of the whole tour. Win them and we would be judged a success. He'd used a similar, positive approach after previous bad defeats – after Trinidad in 1994, then Melbourne a year later, and Edgbaston in 1995 – and we had bounced back. Again, Athers had been vindicated. In the Auckland dressing-room, after we had been held to a draw by the last-wicket pair, we were all very low. It felt as if we had lost, just like it felt in Bulawayo. It was a hell of an achievement by the captain to turn things round after Auckland and Wanganui.

The team's fortunes may have changed in New Zealand, but mine didn't. Alec Stewart's continued excellence saw to that, and he ended up as the outstanding player of the tour. I managed to get a couple of games with Takapuna, my old club side whom I had played for in the early eighties, just over the harbour bridge in Auckland, and it was good to see some familiar faces there again. My competitive instincts hadn't been dulled by my inactivity, I'm glad to say. I got a big kick out of my unbeaten 70 that helped win a close game. It was good to be taxed mentally, rather than just going to the nets every morning. That was honestly one of the highlights of the tour for me, and it was even better in the second game, when I scored 50 and 80 (I should have scored a hundred and fifty!) and, chasing 304 to win in two sessions, we won by one wicket with just a ball to spare, after it looked as if we'd lose. It was great to be involved again in a match situation. When I wasn't playing, I tried to keep a hold on my perspective. Surrey wicket-keeper Graham Kersey's tragic death in a road accident at Christmas in Australia did that, with the grief of his county colleagues, Alec Stewart and Graham Thorpe underlining the sense of waste. A blind man called Fred Raffle was also an inspiration to me in Zimbabwe. Fred would sit in the BBC Radio box, listening to the commentaries, enjoying the banter and the gossip, and I spent a fair amount of time in the box as well, relishing the change of scenery and different conversations. When a man who was been blind from birth can get so much out of the game that he loves, and is willing to travel from Birmingham to New Zealand just to experience the atmosphere, the cricketing frustrations of Jack Russell don't appear all that important.

At the end of the tour, Mike Atherton told the media that my attitude had been excellent throughout, and that I was still very much part of the England framework. They were nice words. The longer the New Zealand tour progressed, the more I felt David Lloyd had come to value me and what I could bring to the team. Conversely, I felt that Athers had blocked me out a little, but I guess he had enough on his plate. Anyway, I was old enough to look after myself and hopefully keep things in perspective. Some of the other guys, who hadn't much experience of long periods without playing in this sort of set-up, found it difficult to handle. They needed a little help – it's all too easy to fall away mentally. David Lloyd appeared more receptive than the captain, and he reassured me that my age would not count against me in future selection policy. Athers had gone on record saying that anyone over the age of 32 could be considered old for Test cricket, and that worried me, but the coach was less dogmatic. I told him that I felt fitter and stronger than at any stage of my career, that I was determined to get back in the England team, and that disregarding me purely because I was in my 34th year would be unfair. David reassured me that the policy is that the best players are picked, irrespective of their age. I told him I'd hold him to that, because I genuinely felt I had another five years in me at international level. We shall see.

I'm not looking at the wicket-keeping berth for just my own selfish reasons. Sooner or later, Alec Stewart will retire, and we'll be back with the problem of finding an all-rounder. When are we going to unearth an all-rounder good enough as bowler and batsman at Test level? At the moment, we don't have one, but I believe the potential is there. If Craig White could be encouraged to believe in himself, he could grow into the job. Mark Ealham and Adam Hollioake could make it, but what is needed is careful nurturing of that player, the support and conviction that the particular guy has the ability to nail down the all-rounder's role. Then stick with him. That would then leave you with more options. It would also help if England could find some batsmen capable of competent bowling. The other countries seem to manage it – Carl Hooper, Hansie Cronje, Jacques Kallis, Michael Bevan and the Waugh brothers spring to mind – but in recent years, only Graeme Hick has hinted at filling such a valuable role. Graeme is an effective off-spinner, who may lack control and consistency, but something seems to happen when he comes on to bowl. Perhaps he ought to bowl more. The other England batsman underrated as a bowler is Mark Ramprakash. He gives his off-breaks a real rip, and if he could have worked a little more on his bowling, he would have performed a very useful role for England. I believe he still has time to blossom internationally, as batsman and off-spinner. With Alec Stewart doing so well now as the all-rounder, England are just storing up trouble for the future balance of the side. The problem has to be tackled as a priority, for the sake of English cricket.

Wicket-keeping has become more demanding in recent years, but that applies to all aspects of the game, particularly in relation to increased fitness. I need to stay ahead in fitness terms as I get older, because you can't rely on being as naturally fit as a young player. From a keeper's perspective, Alan Knott tells me that the wickets have got more uneven, so that there's less room for error, but I grew up on the slow pitches at Bristol, so I was used to standing up closer to the stumps to accommodate the low bounce. The problem with low bounce is that you can't get your feet and body moving quickly enough when you have to stand closer. The ball doesn't come through at a nice pace, when you can judge it early and get your body in the right position. You need to get your timing absolutely right, otherwise the ball will hit you on the chest or arms, rather than the gloves. In England, I try to take the ball around my knees, rather than my waist, giving me more time. Knotty used to take it around his ankles, which also allowed him to take off for those spectacular one-handed diving catches. It's now a bit of a lottery, because of the uneven bounce of so many pitches.

The extra variety used by bowlers these days also adds to the challenge. In one-day cricket, in particular, bowlers are now expected to mix it up, with a slower, looping delivery followed by a quicker, shorter one. Someone like Darren Gough is always thinking, ready to try something different – and the keeper has to get inside the mind of such a bowler, trying to anticipate what's next. So the keeper can't expect anymore to be in a groove, instinctively aware of where the next ball will pitch, and its speed. The ball also tends to swing around after it pitches and passes the batsman, something Knotty says never used to happen in his day. I wish I knew why the balls swing more from one season to the next, but they don't seem to have a regular pattern of swing. So you can be made to look a fool, as you try to make what appears to be a routine 'take', only to find the ball swerving away from your flailing grasp.

Of all the bowlers I've kept to, the one who's always troubled me most is my Gloucestershire team-mate, Courtney Walsh. I still have trouble working him out. He's so deceptive. Ambling in off his smooth run, you just don't know when he'll produce that 'effort' ball, the one that appears to be bowled with the same action, but picks up pace, angling in at the batsman, sending the keeper off balance as he tries to get near the ball jagging back. I broke my right thumb – a rare injury for me – early in my career courtesy of Courtney, and he remains very difficult to judge. The bowler I'd love to work with is Shane Warne. He spins it so much from wherever he bowls it, and he has so much variety that it would be a real challenge to pick him. He's also remarkably accurate for a leg spinner, and still maintains his control even if you get after him. That's the main difference between Warne and Mushtaq Ahmed, another leggie I rate very highly. 'Mushy's' such a clever box of tricks, and if he gets one wicket, it can snowball with him, whereas Shane Warne seems to thrive on that control, and he still keeps coming at you. I envy Ian Healy his experience of keeping to Warne, it must be fantastically challenging. You've got to put Ian up there with the top keepers in recent years, not just because of his consistency, and the way he has improved year after year – but because he has kept so well to Shane Warne.

I regret not having the opportunity to keep consistently to a leg spinner. At Gloucestershire in my early days, there was Sadiq Mohammed for a time, then Vyvian Pike over a couple of seasons, and a few times to Mike Atherton with England, and of course, Ian Salisbury. The way leg spinners bowl these days is a real test for the keeper, because they all bowl around the wicket into the rough. Sometimes, that's a defensive measure, trying to tie the batsman down; on other occasions, you're looking for turn out of the rough, outside leg stump, created by the follow-through of the various bowlers. Your vision as a keeper is impaired for a split second in such cases, because the batsman's body is in the way. The ball could go anywhere, so you have to get ready to spring either side of the wicket when it takes a deflection. It's the same situation when a left-arm spinner goes over the wicket, aiming for the rough outside the right-hand batsman's leg stump. It's definitely a taxing situation for the modern wicket-keeper.

I fear for the future of the specialist wicket-keeper, both at county and England level. The attitude in recent years has been one of neglect, as the specialist keeper gets sacrificed. When Colin

Metson was dropped by Glamorgan last season, that was another nail in the coffin; Colin has been a very classy keeper over the years, but not all that productive with the bat. Yet he has the ability to dismiss the best batsmen with a dazzling piece of skill that's beyond the batsman/keeper. Sadly, that doesn't seem to matter so much now. Selectors don't seem to appreciate that Alan Knott was a genius, scoring five Test hundreds, averaging almost 33, as well as keeping wicket brilliantly. Knotty's scale of achievement means that his successors are expected to get near to his remarkable consistency, but that's not feasible, he was a one-off just like Ian Botham. The more productive the keeper, the less you can expect from him in batting, and vice-versa. The statistics show that there are only so many runs you can expect from a top-class keeper: just look at how few average over thirty in Test history. The demands of concentration and fitness, plus the need for consistency with the gloves all contribute to the difficulty in getting somewhere near Knotty's standard. It seems odd to me that selectors are persistent in encouraging wicket-keepers to improve their batting – rightly so – yet specialist bowlers and top-order batsmen never appear to be under serious pressure to develop another string to their bow. Too often, it's down to the individual himself to work hard at developing another skill. With the wicket-keeper, there isn't now an option.

We're getting close to the keeper being judged as just another fielder, rather than a specialist. It's so difficult between Tests to get proper wicket-keeping practice. If it wasn't for Alan Knott's guidance and presence in my time with England, I would really struggle. Yet when the keeper misses a crucial chance, everyone is looking hard at him. The keeper ought to be given some priority. That applies in tour selections as well. There should be two front-line keepers on senior and 'A' tours as an investment for the future, but too often it's a case of giving the reserve job to a batsman. In the long run, we'll lose out, something I try to impress all along.

I've no chance of getting back into the England side in the near future, unless Alec Stewart breaks a finger, or the management decide to change policy and settle on a conventional all-rounder. The writing was on the wall for me in the summer of 1996, when I was eventually dropped after scoring a hundred at Lord's, batting at number seven. Yet I won't accept the fact that I'll have to settle for 49 caps. I'll gladly tour for England again as the number two, even if I don't get a chance. It would be far worse, sitting at home wondering about the possibilities. That happened to me in 1993, when I was passed over for the India tour, and I never want to experience that frustration again. So the short-term target for me is to win my 50th cap and in the long run, to beat Bob Taylor's world record total of first-class dismissals. To manage that, I would need to get around sixty first-class dismissals for the next ten seasons. That's something to aim for. I always say that I get there in the end, even if it takes me ten years!

As for the future of England, I'm more optimistic than I was this time last year. For too long we buried our heads in the sands, after beating Australia in three series in the mid eighties. We should have used that success as a springboard, not as a sofa. We thought it would all come right, but most of the other countries have overtaken us and it's going to be a long haul to climb up that ladder. We need vision and determination at all levels from those in the game, and we need intelligent leadership. That's why I'm more upbeat than I was about our prospects. The new chairman of the English Cricket Board, Lord MacLaurin, came out to Zimbabwe and New Zealand and we were all very impressed by his dynamic approach and readiness to listen. He was terrific in the dressing-room in Harare, just after we had lost badly in the one-dayer to go 3–0 down in the series. It wasn't the time for recriminations, and he struck exactly the right note, telling us he was proud to be associated with the England side, that we were his priority, and that he'd do everything in his power to help get it right. I had an hour with him in Wellington, and he was very receptive. I said that man-management had been poor on most England tours I'd been on, and that was the main reason for me

2
THE DREAMER

For a grubby-haired little kid born in 1963 and from a council house in Stroud, I don't think I've done too badly in life. That's because I've always been stubborn. I truly believe you can do anything you want to do, and that's always been my philosophy for as long as I can remember.

Now, after all my years in cricket, people say I'm crackers, barking mad, because they look at my mannerisms on the field and they hear about my superstitions and my eating habits. I prefer to call my ways mildly eccentric, not mad. It suits me to drink thirty cups of tea a day, to eat a packet of wholemeal chocolate digestive biscuits or Jaffa cakes, and have my Weetabix soaked in milk for precisely twelve minutes. That's just the way I am. Why be the same as others if your own way suits you, as long as it doesn't disrupt team spirit? I didn't suddenly become an eccentric when I started playing for England, it's just that very few people were interested in my little quirks back then.

My Mum tells me I was strong-willed even as a baby. Apparently, I hardly slept and when I could walk, I was on the go all the time, fighting to do my own thing. Mum taught me to read and write, because I hated school and would do anything to get out of going there. On my first day at primary school, I clung to Mum's skirt and cried my eyes out when she left me. The school was only three minutes away from our home and, time and again, I'd run back to the house during the day, because I couldn't stand it – especially when we had dancing classes! I had nothing against my classmates, it's just that I was a little shy, and basically wanted to do my own thing. I was solitary, preferring my own company, unless sport was involved. Once, I hit on a brilliant ruse to get out of school. I'd had a dodgy ankle for a time from playing sports and so I knew the areas where I could point to pain convincingly. I went to hospital and told the doctor that I had turned my ankle during a cross-country run. He put a big bandage on the ankle and whenever I asked my parents to touch it in certain areas, I would wince and cry out in pain. It seemed to do the trick – I must have sounded very convincing – and the result was a week away from school. Brilliant! What did I want with going there? It wasn't as if I was hopeless with my classwork, I took a lot of pride in what I was doing, but I saw no point in being at school, and most important of all, I wanted to be on my own. Visiting the relatives at Christmas didn't appeal to me. I've never enjoyed having meals in other people's homes. I've always been a fussy eater – Mum must have spoiled me early on – and I just couldn't face conventional food. It was always a nightmare. I remember I would volunteer for extra paper deliveries or milk rounds just to get out of those visits, but usually my parents would drag me along.

For most of my childhood, I lived in a world of my own. I was happy enough, because my parents seemed to understand that I usually preferred my own company, and that I liked taking refuge in a fantasy land of my own making. I was practical with my hands early on, and my bedroom used to take on different characteristics, depending on my imagination. I would make Airfix models of soldiers, I would have planes hanging from the ceiling, and re-create battles. Sometimes, I would construct a railway, and in my determination to get every aspect right, I would go downstairs to the coal bunker, bring up some lumps and put them in the wagons. There would be coal dust everywhere, but my parents must have thought at least I was coming to no harm, so they left me alone to dream my dreams. I still have a lot of the toys from my childhood, especially the ones I made, like my lorries, diggers and trucks, because they remind me of the happy times I spent with my grandfather. He drove a lorry for Cullimore's, a gravel company near Cirencester, and he was one of the few people I was close to when I was a kid. I loved being in that lorry. Grandad died when I was about eight – I remember being devastated at the time. I thought the world of him and I wish he could have seen my career develop.

I used to fantasise about being a soldier regularly when I was a kid. There's a place a couple of miles out of Stroud called Swift's Hill, where I would sit for ages, imagining I was a member of the SAS – who dares, wins and all that. I would imagine that I'd climbed massive rocks and had to defend the position against the enemy. How would I do that? I'd just sit and observe, allowing my imagination to run wild. Sometimes, when I'd allow other kids to be involved in my fantasies about being a soldier, we would go off to Blackberry Wood, and stay out till ten o'clock at night, making dens, planning ambushes. We would have secret hiding places everywhere, just like Enid Blyton's Famous Five, and we'd talk about setting up a base camp and blowing up dams. All those war films on the telly were ideal at fuelling our imagination! We were so lucky, though, to have the countryside around Stroud to roam freely. In those days, parents didn't have to worry too much about their kids wandering off and being hounded by nutters. I don't know how I would have coped with growing up in a city.

This obsession of mine to try different things landed me in trouble with my parents when I was twelve. I decided I was going to stay out all night, re-creating the soldier on duty, lying in wait for the enemy. All very exciting to me but my parents were scared out of their wits. Mum came home from work at teatime, to find me standing in the kitchen, with my army jacket on, covered in military badges, wearing my camouflage hat, with a tin plate, a cup, blue sleeping bag and backpack all tied up with string, ready for action. She wouldn't let me go but that cut no ice with me, because in my vivid imagination I was setting out on an important mission. So off I went anyway. Apparently, Dad was convinced I would come back when it was dark, but Mum was worried sick and went searching for me in the nearby playing fields, calling out for me. No joy. I had gone off to a wood, and was settling down to a night under a hedge, while all that was going on. I admit I soon got cold – it was October – and I was frightened by the sheer blackness of the night, and the strange, sudden sounds, but I was determined to see it through. At one stage, just before sunset, I was about to make myself a cup of tea to ward off the cold when I saw this shadow. I was terrified and jumped back behind the hedge. It turned out to be Dad looking for me – but I didn't know, I was just frightened, stubborn, because I'd been told by my mates, 'You'll never do that' and my parents had forbidden me to go out there. That was enough to fuel my fire and determination; I was going to prove them all wrong. Just me, in a sleeping bag, out in the open, braving the elements, proving something important to myself. At six o'clock next morning, with the ground white with frost, I got up, rolled up my sleeping bag and walked home. Mum hadn't slept all night, and I'm sorry now that I'd put her through all that anguish, but I had done something unusual. I wanted to be different from the others.

Even at the age of eight or nine, I had ideas to make money. I would go to Uplands Woods, near to our council estate and, wading through all the mud, I would dig the clay. I had this vision of claiming the land for myself, mining all the clay, gathering it in various wheelbarrows, then selling it to those in the pottery business. I also hit on a scheme to buy a lorry, turn a field into a tip, pick up people's rubbish and muck spread, getting rid of their waste in the mud. None of it came to anything, but even at that age I was determined to make something of myself. I was just looking to survive.

Predictably, I failed my eleven-plus and just counted the days until I could leave school at sixteen. I wanted to do something practical. My first ambition was to be a mechanical engineer, then a draughtsman. Dad was helpful in that direction. He was a welder who lived for his sport, his game of snooker and skittles down the club with the lads. He did me a big favour when I was nine, bringing home engineering drawings from his job, and I would sit at my little drawing board, copying them out. So I was interested in technical drawing at a very young age, and even though I'd landed an apprentice mechanical engineer's job at a local factory at sixteen, Dad talked me into staying on at school, to get my A-levels. He'd never given me such positive advice before on anything. Maybe he'd seen how ambitious and stubborn I could be when my mind was set on anything. Maybe he didn't want me to do the same job as him, because there didn't seem to be an exciting future in it, and he didn't want me to get sucked into dull conformity. I'll always be grateful to him for that piece of advice.

As a boy, the only time I was happy to shelve my solitary attitude to life was when I played sport, particularly cricket. I loved football – nippy left winger, Tottenham supporter – but cricket was my biggest passion. My brother David, who was two years younger, used to join me in games of cricket that would last all day if possible. Where we lived, at Uplands in Stroud, in a circular cul-de-sac, we played cricket on a patch of grass between the houses called the Circle. Around the corner, we would play football in the Square and the broken windows in both areas testified to our reckless enthusiasm. My earliest memory of an international cricket match was watching Ray Illingworth's England team win back the Ashes in Australia in 1971. We watched that on our black-and-white television at home, then David and I would rush out and simulate those games. All the other local lads used to join in, and it was a hive of activity. We even burnt a set of bails one day, and played for the Ashes, just like they did in Tests between England and Australia. In the summer, we'd only play at lunchtime and teatime, because we were too busy watching the Test matches on telly, glued to every ball; but at close of play we would spill out of our homes onto the Circle and battle was joined.

Dad played cricket for the village of Chalford, near Stroud, and David and I used to go there to watch him play. I didn't know it at the time, but Chalford weren't a bad side at all; they used to do well in the national village knockout cup regularly. We would play in the nets during the match, then at tea time we'd go out on the field and try to hit the ball as far as possible, taking it in turns to bowl and dive spectacularly for the ball, in an effort to impress the adults. We just hung around on matchday, hoping that one day the team would be short and we'd get a game. I would field twelfth man at first – I was ten when that happened – and when I scored 29, batting last man, the adults started to take some notice of me. I had already decided that I wouldn't give my wicket away (single-minded at an early age!), and I showed the same cussed determination at primary school, when we had a single forty-five minute session of cricket practice a week and I'd try to stay in batting all that time. Even then I saw no point in giving anyone a thing when they were all trying to get me out. I was the same in the school playground. Other cricketing avenues were opening for me at that time, but I didn't always appreciate them. At the age of ten, I went on a coaching course, organised by Gloucestershire CCC, at Charlton Kings School in Cheltenham. It was spread over four afternoons, and you would have thought this cricket-mad urchin would have loved it. But I hated those sessions, probably because again there were too many people.

Things perked up though when I failed my eleven-plus for grammar school and went to Archway Secondary Modern School in Stroud. My two sportsmasters, Graham Fryer and Rick Rutter, were fantastically supportive. They gave me every encouragement and opportunity to practise and play – so much so that they shielded me from the complaints of other teachers that I was neglecting my schoolwork. Nets at lunchtime, nets after school, being driven by one of the sportsmasters to county schools trials, then matches on Saturday mornings – it was a great time for me. I was captain of our side for four years, and in that time, we lost only twice. We were very proud of our record, and that strong desire for the team to win has never left me. Winning is one of my addictions, I make no bones about it. In that school side, I either opened the batting, or went in at number three and bowled a bit. I didn't keep wicket at any time for my school: I was busy enough as captain, batsman and bowler, and in any case another lad was keen to do it. I probably thought deep down that I should save the wicket-keeping for adult cricket, an arrogant attitude, probably, but that's the way you are when you're a kid and convinced you know best.

By now, I had joined the best club side in the region, Stroud Cricket Club, because I wanted to improve. As luck would have it, Stroud had decided to form a youth team, for the first time in their hundred-year history, so I dutifully turned up to enrol one damp April Sunday morning. We were so keen we played on a splintery clubhouse floor, with a stump for a bat and a matchbox for a ball. We had no equipment, but we didn't care. I was twelve and thrilled, especially when I discovered that wicket-keeping seemed to be great fun. At practice, I saw another lad keeping wicket and, as usual, I thought I could do it better than him. So I persuaded our coach, David Moore, to let me have a chance with the gloves. That was it – I was hooked after one session behind the stumps.

The winter nets for schoolboys at the county ground in Bristol saw a much more receptive young cricketer than at Cheltenham two years earlier. Some of the county professionals would come to those Monday nights, and we'd have our autograph books handy, but the most helpful was Andy Brassington, the county's first-choice keeper. He was so good to me in those early days, encouraging me all the time in such a kind, understanding way. A natural enthusiast in everything he has done, Andy Brassington continued to be a great help to me, even when I came on the staff and took his place in 1982, at the age of nineteen. Others would have moaned about the young oik from the sticks taking their first-team place after all those years of helping me, but not Andy. His supportive attitude is typical of almost all the wicket-keepers in the professional game. There is definitely an unofficial Keepers' Union, where it's second nature to help each other out.

I was thirteen when I played my first senior game for Stroud in the Western League at Newport. We were rained off halfway through our innings, so I didn't get on the field, but at least I was on my way. Years later, when we played Glamorgan in a Sunday League match at Newport, the memories came flooding back. It's always the same whenever I have returned to Stroud's ground. I'll sit outside the pavilion, look across the ground and the valley and think back to those great days. They were special, you can't buy them on a supermarket shelf. If I need my memory jogged at any stage Stroud's scorer, Graham Hogg has a record of all my performances, for the club, for my county and my country. I shall always be very touched by the pride they have shown in me at Stroud CC. It was also a thrill to play first-team cricket at the club with my brother, David, who was a very handy batsman and brilliant fielder. As we looked back to those intense games in the back garden, it was marvellous to share such happy times in senior cricket.

I'd broken into Stroud's first team at the age of fourteen, when something happened that made up my mind about the career that I was going to choose. I happened to be watching the Leeds Test in 1977, when England hammered Australia and Geoffrey Boycott scored his hundredth hundred. More important for me, I saw on television a superb diving catch by Alan Knott to dismiss Rick McCosker off Tony Greig's bowling. It was low to the keeper's right, it wouldn't have travelled to Mike Brearley at slip, and yet Alan dived full stretch and snaffled it up with such ease and athleticism. That catch still turns my knees to jelly whenever I see it on video. From that moment, I was hooked. I wanted to keep wicket for England and try to emulate Alan Knott, making fantastic catches like that one which leave everyone gasping in admiration. I was going to keep wicket for Gloucestershire as soon as I could, then for England, and no one would take my place for years and years. I'm not joking, I was *that* certain of my destiny. All my life up to that moment had been a preparation for realising a special ambition. It was as if some inner voice had been telling me all along that the conventional ways of getting a profession were not for me, that I had been right to go my own way, do my own thing and dig my heels in stubbornly whenever it looked as if I had to conform. Nothing was going to get in my way of keeping wicket for my county, then my country. I would put my heart and soul into it. At last, I had a purpose to my life!

It was to be another five years before I finally met Alan Knott, the start of a friendship that's seen him become the greatest influence on my career. From that day in 1977 though, he became an inspiration to me, not just in technical terms, or as a source of immense support, but also because he gave me the licence to be myself, to keep wicket in the way that was natural to me. 'Knotty' was a great individualist as a keeper, a genius who defied the textbooks, but still clocked up remarkable and consistent performances. He had the nerve, the guts and determination to do it as he saw, despite criticism. I would never have his huge natural talent, but following his career and marvelling at his methods gave me strength to do the job in the way that was best for me. In my teens, I was also a great admirer of Bob Taylor's stylish, unfussy wicket-keeping, and he too became a friend and mentor to me. England were so lucky to have two such marvellous keepers available at more or less the same time, and I just looked at them both and thought, 'I want to do that!'

By the age of fifteen, I was completely taken up by cricket. I had my first bat, a Slazenger, with red stripes which I had painted on. Every other Slazenger bat had the standard green stripes, but of course, I just had to be different. I'd practise three or four nights a week, play both days at the weekend, and again in midweek. I captained the Stroud Sunday XI at the age of fifteen, and even played for the masters at school; then there were games for England Schools, Gloucestershire Young Cricketers and finally Gloucestershire Seconds, when I was just fifteen. I remember coming up against Ken Higgs in one early Second XI match, and

3
HARSH
REALITIES

Before I reached my eighteenth birthday, I was lucky enough to be a record-holder in first-class cricket. At the age of seventeen years and three hundred and seven days I made my debut for Gloucestershire and took eight victims, a record for a keeper on first-class debut. I was thrilled, elated, proud and weak at the knees. I wondered what I looked like, a spotty kid from Stroud. My ambition to play for the county of my birth had been achieved and I had done well – all before I was eighteen. Many kind things were being said about me, and a golden future was forecast for me. The next few years, though, were to prove a major test of nerve and character for me before I established myself in my eyes as a worthwhile professional cricketer, never mind one with genuine prospects as an England player. Another six years were to pass before I finally made it on an England tour, a period in which I had to reassess my lifestyle, and come to terms with the reality that some of my Gloucestershire team-mates genuinely disliked me. It also dawned on me that I had a drink problem, and that unless I sorted that out, I would be an also-ran and would fade away from county cricket. Added to those self-inflicted problems, I lost my much-loved brother, David, after a freak accident. Dead at twenty-one, from a head injury, after falling outside a pub. His death and the divorce of my parents fuelled my desperate need to have a settled family life, and marriage to Aileen in 1985 and becoming a father so young helped me grow up quickly. My cricket career benefited from my change of lifestyle and new priorities – and not before time. When I see young professionals burning the candle at both ends, with their cricket suffering, I can honestly say, 'I've been there.'

Such realities weren't an issue for me in the summer of 1981, while I was still at school, waiting to take my A-levels, wondering if I would like Bath University, where I was heading that autumn if I managed to get good enough grades. Playing cricket was still my preference, though, and when a phone call came through to the school from Gloucestershire CCC, my wish was granted. Could I go straight to Bristol, to play for the county against the Sri Lankan tourists? Could I? Stroud was twenty miles away, and if they'd added the proviso that I had to walk all the way with my kitbag on my back, I'd have happily obliged. The school allowed me to postpone my Metalwork A-level exam until after the game, and I proceeded to make history. Don't ask me how I managed to take seven catches and a stumping in that game, I just floated in and out of it. I owed my sudden promotion to injuries to Andy Brassington and Andy Stovold, the usual Gloucestershire wicket-keepers, but I wasn't going to quibble. I was actually playing in the same team as Zaheer Abbas. He'd been one of the supreme stylists in world cricket for a decade, and I was a massive fan. He couldn't have been more charming to me that first day, nor Sadiq Mohammed, another famous Pakistani batsman, nor John Childs, one of county cricket's gentlemen. John provided me with my first stumping, a routine one to get Asantha De Mel and he went on to take six wickets. It was fascinating to keep wicket to a spinner with such control and flight.

Mind you, the day hadn't begun all that well for me. I was glad that we fielded first, so that my nerves wouldn't get the better of me while waiting until our innings was over, but the first ball of the match didn't calm me down all that easily. The Australian, Mike Whitney, who was also making his debut for us, fired it fast and wide down legside and it went for four byes. Now keepers absolutely hate giving away byes, even when it's not their fault, and I can still hear the thud of the ball as it hit the boundary board in front of the Jessop Tavern. Things could only get better after that! Thankfully they did, and I absolutely loved it. I didn't even mind that there was no room for me in any of the bed and breakfast places near the County Ground. No problem – I slept in our dressing-room on that first night. A distinct improvement from sleeping in a bush a few years earlier! I got more sleep than the night before, after I'd been told I was playing. Just to show how naive and excited I was, I went over to our local playing field at Uplands and played cricket with the lads! No gloves or pads, just for the sheer enjoyment of it all. I wanted to share my delight with people I knew. So in the space of twenty-four hours, I went from one scale to the other, playing on the village green with no equipment to speak of, then turning out for my county alongside Test players. All I had ever wished for had come true. When I was twelve, on Christmas Day I had pulled the wishbone of our chicken (we couldn't afford turkey), and my simple request was, 'Please let me play for Gloucestershire'. I was still a spotty kid, and it had happened. Unbelievable.

In the classroom things were going my way as well. I passed my Technical Drawing and Metalwork A-levels, but failed Maths. Perhaps the fact that the day before the exam, instead of revising, I played for Stroud CCC against Gloucestershire Gypsies might have had something to do with my failure. That proved a blessing in disguise. I couldn't now get into Bath University, so I enrolled at Bristol Polytechnic, studying accountancy. It wasn't a happy experience, and it lasted two months. I was quite interested in the accounts aspect of the course, but I couldn't handle economics and sociology on the course. All I could think of was playing cricket and after a time, I just walked out.

Typical Russell stubbornness. I left my tutor a note: 'I've decided that this course isn't for me. Decided to pursue a career on the cricket field. Thank you for your help.' I had to pay back my grant, but I've no regrets, much as I value education. If I'd stayed in further education, I would have lost out on four years of cricket education, and that was just too important for me. I knew I was gambling, but I really believed I could do it. I was so committed!

Soon after the inglorious end to my student career, I signed professional terms for Gloucestershire, but not before Worcestershire had come in with a very tempting offer. I was mulling it over, wondering why my home county had appeared to lose interest in me, when Gloucestershire's secretary, Tony Brown, turned up on my doorstep to talk to me and my parents. I went to Bristol next morning on the train, and signed for Gloucestershire without even looking at the terms of the contract. I had no idea what my wages would be, it was simply a case of realising an ambition that had burned fiercely inside of me. I hope my county coach, Graham Wiltshire, was as delighted as me, because Graham had spent so much time nurturing and helping me since the age of ten, and has continued to do so.

My first season on the staff was divided up between a handful of championship games, the occasional limited-overs outing, second-team cricket and playing for Young England against the West Indies in a three-match series. That was a real eye-opener for this youngster, playing against the likes of Roger Harper, Phil Simmons and Courtney Walsh, with players such as David Capel, Richard Illingworth, Paul Jarvis and Hugh Morris in our team. We lost the series 2-0, and there was a fair amount of acrimony on and off the field between the two sides, particularly at Hove, when our captain, Laurie Potter, made a threatening gesture on the field with his bat directed at an opposing fielder, and had to be persuaded by the rest of the team not to take his anger into the opposition's dressing-room. Heated stuff!

I got into Gloucestershire's first team in July that year, because Andy Brassington had been struggling with his form after an Achilles tendon injury. I'll never forget my first stumping in county cricket. It was in my first game at Northampton, and David Steele was the batsman. As he played forward defensively to a ball on middle and leg he overbalanced, ending up falling flat on his face in the dust as I took off the bails. The bowler was Barry Duddleston, who was winding down his career with us before going into coaching. Barry and I still reminisce about that wicket whenever we meet up. Wicket-keepers never forget their stumpings, and part-time bowlers like Barry never forget their wickets, as he's often reminded me! Anyway, after the heady delights of Northampton, it was off to Leicester, and an innings defeat on a fast, bouncy pitch. My first ball in county cricket, from Les Taylor, went straight past my nose, rearing up off a length. Welcome to the real world! Just a fortnight later, I was playing in a massive match for one so young – a NatWest Trophy quarter-final against Middlesex. It was at Bristol, in front of a packed house, against players like Mike Gatting, John Emburey, Phil Edmonds, Clive Radley and Mike Brearley. They were a very confident, hard side, used to winning trophies, but we gave them a fright, losing by just three runs. I was run out for ten, too excited, backing up too far, but not before I played a shot that some of the locals still remind me about. Somehow, I managed to pick up Norman Cowans over deep mid wicket and into the tennis courts. I can still see the ball sailing over Mike Gatting's head on the boundary, and yet it felt as if I'd hardly hit it. We lost, though, and that became a familiar story for Gloucestershire in the big games, but to this novice, a month shy of his nineteenth birthday, it was a fantastic experience. The end of that 1982 season came all too soon for me; I was relishing all those new experiences.

I was also drinking rather more potent brews. I had started to enjoy the social aspect of English cricket rather too much. Since getting into the first team at Stroud, I had taken rather too readily to the round of propping up the bar, talking cricket and getting sloshed. I had come out of my shell through club cricket. I still preferred my own company, but getting drunk seemed a pleasant way of passing the time when I was involved in my great passion, cricket. At college in Bristol, my short spell there was noted for hardly any academic work, and doing the usual daft student things, like walking around the city centre, with a bollard on my head, too drunk to care, and falling into nightclubs, just to get a few more down my throat. My first year on the staff at Gloucestershire didn't exactly wean me away from my self-indulgences, because drinking after the day's play was the convention. So I just went with the flow. In the winter of 1982–83, I was on unemployment benefit, but I supplemented that by playing pool – and winning money. I'd go to the Prince Albert pub in Stroud with my dole money, stick a fiver in the pot, clean up thirty quid by beating the others, and then spend it on booze. It wasn't as if I was a newcomer to drinking, and everything associated with it. When I was sixteen, I used to go for whiskey and lemonade down at Stroud Cricket Club, and one night I nearly fell down the stairs at home. Mum caught me just in time, as she stood behind me, otherwise I might have broken my neck. It was a bit of a lark, having beer-drinking contests at the club, doing daft things. One Sunday, I couldn't keep wicket for Stroud because I felt so ill after a big bender. I was only about sixteen then. Of course, teenagers do such silly things – better that than drugs, I suppose – but looking back on those years, I reckon I had a bit of a drink problem. I went for the booze too readily, too obsessionally. That's one of my traits, I do get obsessional about things, and it was to be some time before I snapped out of boozing and knuckled down to my cricket career.

In my second season, 1983, I had other things to battle against, other than hangovers. It slowly dawned on me that some of my Gloucestershire team-mates resented my presence in the first team. That was partly because of the deserved popularity of Andy Brassington, a great team man, a highly talented keeper and a guy who had grown up with most of the established first-team players. Andy was a terrific man on the field, in the dressing-room, and in the bar afterwards, and if you took a poll among players and members to name the most popular Gloucestershire player of the past twenty years, his name would be very high on the list. He was also marvellous to me, the ambitious teenager from the sticks, who was nine years his junior and very keen to make swift progress in county cricket. Not once did Andy ever show any animosity to me, or fail to give me sound, constructive advice. From the days when he first coached me on those Monday nights at Bristol, he was so kind and helpful. Yet I was now putting him under pressure for a place in the first team. Andy had never been a productive batsman, he was at best a stubborn, useful tail-ender, and the runs I had been scoring for Stroud and the Second XI had been noticed. On top of that, Andy's stylish keeping was losing a little bit of its edge because of various niggling injuries. So our captain, David Graveney, took the difficult decision to drop Andy and give me a run in the first team. I know it was hard for 'Grav', and I remember him saying, 'I've given you a big chance here. Don't let me down. Take it,' but I reckoned without the hostility of some of the senior players. I'll never forget one night in the bar, being told by Phil Bainbridge, 'You'll never be good enough to lace Andy Brassington's boots.' I was stung by that, and shattered by the lack of respect shown to me by a colleague. I know he'd had a few drinks by then, but all his bitterness towards me came out. I suppose I should thank Bainbridge because I've used those words of his to motivate me ever since. But there and then, in that bar, I made a conscious decision that I would never talk to a young player like that. You need encouragement and support when you're trying to learn your trade as a professional cricketer, not carping because you're taking the place of someone's mate.

It took me the whole of the 1983 and 1984 seasons to get anywhere near a level of consistency as a keeper, and that was partly my fault, but also because many of the senior players were on my back far too often. If I dropped a catch or didn't cleanly take a throw from the deep, I'd hear them tut-tut and say, 'Brassy would never have done that.' I felt they saw me as a young whippersnapper, far too keen and confident, trying to take the limelight away from them. I sensed resentment in some players that I was beginning to get noticed around the county circuit. I felt there had been a collective decision to cut me down to size. I now see that some of them knew they would get no better, that their best time had passed, and that they were just jogging along, waiting for the benefit. They lacked the guts to get out of the game, or go somewhere else, and give a younger player a chance. It was sad, though, that they failed to realise an ambitious youngster like me was crying out for guidance, rather than trying to show off.

In that 1983 season, I was second in the keepers' table for first-class dismissals, but I didn't fool myself that I'd cracked it. David Graveney stuck by me, despite my inconsistency, which was partly due to a lack of concentration. A young keeper coming into the county game has to get accustomed to the physical demands, but also the need to concentrate on every ball. I was falling down in that department, and I wasn't helping myself with my lifestyle. I was still propping up various bars around the country after a day in the field, and my work was suffering. Some of the senior players at that stage used to say to me, 'You're not a team man unless you stay in the bar till closing time,' and I didn't need much persuasion in that area. So I followed suit, staying up half the night, then turning up to keep wicket, the worse for wear. I thought it was the right thing to do, because my peers in the first team were more or less in favour of it. It hadn't dawned on me by then that perhaps those guys would have been better players if they had adopted a more professional approach. I think the worst time for me in those early years was the occasion when we stayed in Birmingham, during a match against Warwickshire. After the obligatory late session in the bar, I stayed up until six o'clock in the morning, sitting in the reception area, staring around me, glass-eyed, expecting something entertaining to happen, frightened that I'd miss out. Ridiculous. It was always a case of 'where are we going tonight then, boys?', especially when we were away from home. We'd get in a round, and I'd think, 'I've already stood my corner, I'm going to make sure they get them in for me.' It's never just one drink, is it? It always leads to others.

I now realise how worried David Graveney was about me, and how little I did to repay his faith in those first few seasons. He did blow his top at me at Northampton, though, in the 1983 season. I missed an easy stumping off his bowling to get rid of Tim Lamb, and when the innings was finally over, Grav rightly tore a strip off me as we walked off, and carried on the tirade in the dressing-room afterwards. 'You'd better get your life together quickly,' he said, 'or you're going to blow it. You're drinking too much.' I was too stubborn to take any notice of him, and I showed the same obstinacy in the following game, at Leicester, when John Shepherd had a go at me. Now 'Shep' was in his fortieth year, and he'd been a fine all-rounder for Kent, the West Indies and for Gloucestershire, despite the advancing years. I now realise what a dedicated professional he really was, but at the age of nineteen, I wasn't impressed at the way he kept ripping my head off, really giving me some stick in front of the other players. At the time, my work at diving one-handed for catches needed some practice, and for some reason I dropped a few of those off Shep's bowling. He never spared me. Once, playing at Bath, I dropped Jeremy Lloyds, diving in front of first slip. At lunch, Shep gave me such unmerciful abuse that David Lawrence had to stick up for me and say, 'That's enough.' When he said something like that, you tended to agree with a massive guy like dear old 'Syd', but I knew that his intervention had only postponed the stick I was getting accustomed to.

I used to travel to away games with Shep in those days, in which he would try to talk some sense into me, and I'd rebel because of the way it was done, without any thought or understanding. Once, coming out of Birmingham, I was so jaded after the usual social antics that I misread the map and we had to go several junctions in the opposite direction before getting onto the right section of the motorway. Shep climbed into me again so fiercely that I simply switched off, and let him get on with it. I knew I was at fault, being headstrong and young, but it was no way to get the best out of an impressionable teenager.

So when John Shepherd took me to task on the balcony at Leicester in the summer of 1983, he didn't find a receptive audience. He told me, 'If you think you're going to get anywhere in this game by carrying on this way, you're wrong. You won't last five minutes. Sort it out!' I reasoned that the captain, David Graveney, had put his senior professional up to give me the hard word and I just laughed off the advice. At that age, you think you know better, and I never said a word to Shep. That night, I went out and got legless – as usual. I thought I knew better. I respected Shep for his achievements, but I found him moody and bitter at times, so I categorised him as a jealous old lag. I simply didn't grasp the essential truth of his words. Although I now feel no bitterness towards Shep, there were times when I was nearly in tears, and I'll never forget the support and threatening presence of Syd Lawrence when he felt it had gone too far.

Looking back on those unsupportive times, I have to admit that I never thought of packing it in, in the face of so much hostility from some of the senior players. I seemed to be fighting my own team-mates, as well as the opposition. I did have confidence in my ability, and no other keeper on the staff was pushing me hard for a first-team place. I just couldn't understand why some of my team-mates were so against me. It was a really sad period, even though I still loved playing county cricket for Gloucestershire.

I suppose one of the wider problems was that the team wasn't doing well in any of the competitions, and with David Graveney under pressure as captain, there was a great deal of infighting and politics. We were basically a team of whingers, looking for excuses for our consistent under-achievement, trying to blame the various committee members for our failures on the field. Perhaps I was a convenient whipping boy for some of the senior players, because I represented the future, and they were only concerned with a contract for next season, and resented a colleague who might go further in the game than them. All this is with hindsight, of course. It may be that I was a complete pain in the backside to some in our dressing-room, and they looked for any chance to take me down a peg or two.

Amid all this infighting, I met Alan Knott for the first time. Our scorer, Bert Avery, knowing what a hero Knotty was to me, organised a meeting at our county ground during a Kent game, and he was so helpful and approachable. I told him about the amount of criticism I was getting from senior players, that I was concerned about my inconsistency, and he told me to keep going, to be strong-minded in the way I wanted to keep wicket, and never be afraid to be different. Wise words for me, and in the next few years, as I took steps to ensure I'd have a long career, I remembered the words of a genius who has been my greatest supporter and my inspiration.

Although I was still stubborn about the social side of professional cricket, I wasn't daft enough to content myself with a second successive winter of being on the dole in Stroud and playing pool for some extra cash. So I went to New Zealand in the winter of 1983–84, playing for Takapuna, near Auckland. It was a big call for someone of my background, at the age of twenty. Apart from going to Denmark with Young England in 1981, it was the first time I'd been abroad, and now I was on my own. At the airport in Auckland, I sat waiting to be picked up by a club official, and he was late. There I was, on the other side of the world, with not a soul knowing me, wondering if I was ever going to be picked up. I was close to tears, feeling sorry for myself, a refugee from a close-knit village community in Gloucestershire. It's all experience, though; the cricket was good, even though only at weekends, but the standard was fairly high and it did help my development as a cricketer. I even managed to watch England play a Test in Auckland that year, but I didn't go anywhere near their dressing-room. The likes of Bob Willis, Allan Lamb and Ian Botham were up in the stars for someone like me, so I stayed in the crowd.

Yet by the start of the 1984 English season, I was starting to get a few mentions as an England prospect. Bob Taylor was the man in possession, but this marvellous performer was nudging forty-three, in itself a tribute to his fantastic professionalism and fitness. His time was running out, and Paul Downton took over for the West Indies series, with his superior batting a plus. He was obviously going to be the number one contender for the tour that winter to India, but after almost twenty years of dominance by Knotty and Taylor, clearly the door was now open for a young contender. Now I knew as well as anyone that I was still inconsistent, that batting at number nine for Gloucestershire did me no favours, although at least I had started to open in some one-day games. Also, down at Bristol we all felt that a county like ours struggled to catch the attention of the England selectors. It was probably because we weren't winning anything. There were so many other England contenders around in 1984 to take over from Bob Taylor and their claims were superior to mine. Paul Downton was only 27, and yet he'd first toured for England in 1977. He was an accomplished batsman, and so was Jack Richards, who regularly batted in the middle order for Surrey, making handsome runs on those good Oval pitches. Bruce French was four years older than me, a fine technician, who was now getting a higher profile because he played in a successful county side, with Nottinghamshire, inspired under Clive Rice and Richard Hadlee. So there was no reason to suppose that someone of my inexperience and inconsistency would leapfrog those guys. Yet I still had my dreams.

The trouble was, I was still sloshing it down my neck in the 1984 season. Not yet twenty-one, and still convinced that I could get all the lads in the first team behind me if I stayed in the bar till all hours, then involve myself in the usual bragging in the dressing-room next day about how much we had drunk. Gloucestershire finished bottom of the Championship table that season, and with the knives out for our poor performances, team spirit was low, with too many senior players keeping their heads down, leaving David Graveney to take the flak. Little chance then for a young wicket-keeper to shine, even if my attitude had been sufficiently dedicated, which it was not. Well-intentioned people would remark on my talent, and I'd think that things would automatically come my way in a few years' time, which was incredibly stupid of me. Although my name was bandied around in the press for the India tour, I was never really a contender, and Paul Downton was selected as number one keeper, to be accompanied by Bruce French. So back I went to New Zealand for another good winter of learning my trade with Takapuna. It was to be one of the most significant periods of my career, because the time I spent out there that winter enabled me to crystallise my approach to life and my profession. I relaxed more with the gloves on. It dawned on me that I could play for England, so I decided to concentrate even harder.

One good thing had happened to Gloucestershire and myself before that disastrous 1984 season was the signing of Bill Athey from Yorkshire. Bill had come South with a few things to prove to himself, and he was highly committed to adding to his three England caps from a few years earlier. I soon noticed what a disciplined character he was, going to bed early, staying out of the bar, and giving himself every chance to maximise his undoubted talent. I roomed with Bill a few times on away trips that year, and I couldn't help but notice how his attention to detail and dedication were handsomely repaid when he batted. Some of the team thought he was set in his ways, a typical Yorkie, but his methods clearly worked for him. I thought long and hard about the Bill Athey approach when I went to New Zealand and I decided that was going to be my way, too. The others who had chivvied me into going to the bar were going nowhere in international terms, but I was young and had a chance of getting somewhere. I wanted it badly enough to make the necessary social sacrifices, but I would have been deluding myself if I thought I could wait until I was a little older, that you could have late nights as well as play to your best when you're in your early twenties. Motivation was crucial, the same steely resolve that was pushing Bill Athey to strive to get back into the England team.

Now I was going to stay the distance. It was simply a case of playing well every day to press my claims. I would catch every ball and score a lot of runs, and to do that I had to give myself every chance of being in the right physical condition. Sooner or later, people would have to take notice.

When I made it clear at the start of the 1985 season that I now had a new list of priorities, I had to steel myself for the inevitable jibes. The other players started saying I wasn't a team man, that I was only interested in my own performances – just because I wouldn't go in the bar! All this stuff about being 'one of the lads', and yet my most vocal detractors hadn't exactly made me feel all that welcome in the previous two years, when I was propping up the bar with them. Bill Athey's strength of character was very important to me that summer. We started to room together all the time and after play ended, we would go off for a quiet meal – including a lot of tomato ketchup for me! – and talk about the tactics from that day, and I would quiz him, tapping his cricket awareness and experience. Once play had ended, it was time for both of us to set out our stall for the next day. We would have an early night and we'd both be focused on what we had to do for the next day. It dawned on me that keeping wicket all day demands such a lot – concentrating on at least six hundred deliveries for a start, bending down, creating the right body movements, and reacting as swiftly as possible. You can't do that with a hangover, you must be at your physical best. Bill was very misunderstood because he could be a no-nonsense Yorkshireman at times, with a rather dour attitude on the surface, but I found him a tremendous help, an admirable professional. Some of the Gloucestershire guys said to me in the bar at Grace Road, Leicester: 'You don't want to be like him. Live your life, enjoy yourself. He's never going to play for England again.' He did, though, starting two years after he joined us, and he went on to play twenty-six times for England – that's twenty-six times more than the rest of those detractors put together. They didn't seem to understand that enjoying yourself for some is the satisfaction of doing things well. If you set yourself high standards, you want to get there as often as possible. From now on, that would be my gospel until I retired. I didn't want to run the risk of having a few one night, and kidding myself it was just an occasional bender and that I'd be fine with the gloves next day. That would be a delusion, it had to be all or nothing at all. Getting the sweater with three lions and walking out at Lord's for England was too important to jeopardise now.

The 1985 season was my best so far. I'd finally learned to keep wicket to a higher standard. I was finally getting there, slowly but surely. I averaged only thirteen with the bat, and that had to improve if ever I was to interest the selectors, but I reckon I dropped just three catches in all matches that season. I had got into a good rhythm in New Zealand, and it seemed just to carry on all that summer. It was a good feeling to be able to keep wicket without a sore head, and not suffer dehydration after too much booze the night before, and to feel confident that I was getting some consistency at last. I began to relax my arms and hands. John Jamieson, a former umpire, once said to me, 'If you relax your thumbs, your forearms relax'. That seems to work for me.

The 1985 edition of the *Cricketers' Who's Who* was the last time I listed one of my relaxations as 'Going to the Prince Albert pub.' I'd allowed that to stay in for previous editions, but that was a thing of the past now. My team-mates didn't seem to understand when I told them that getting drunk at night didn't constitute being a good team man, because that reduced their potential as players, and therefore the effectiveness of the team. I just seemed to get more unpopular with some of them. One day, Bob Taylor came to see me at Cheltenham, to discuss supplying me with some kit from Mitre, his new employers. Bob had just retired from the game, but as usual he was very supportive of me, asking how well was I doing behind the stumps, etc. The gloves that Bob recommended I used in New Zealand the previous winter had been terrific and definitely helped my keeping. We were chatting about the gloves when a couple of the senior players butted into our conversation and said, 'You don't want to waste your time with him, Bob, he's mad. No need to give him any gear, it'll be just a waste of time.' They made me look very small, and I just couldn't see why they felt they had to belittle me. At that stage, it appeared to me that I was hated by some of my team-mates. Just because I was different. They respected Bob Taylor, sure – but didn't it occur to them that Bob had still been able to keep for England in his forties because he had the same attitude to his profession that I was trying to attain?

I told myself it was just insecurity, Mr Average plodding along, worried about his own position in the side. I couldn't see what was wrong about wanting to play for England, because that indicated a certain degree of ability and consistency that you'd shown for your county. Therefore your performances must have helped your county side, surely? I told myself that I would never treat young players this way when I'd made some progress in the game, that the example set by great keepers like Alan Knott and Bob Taylor put these lesser players to shame. Anyway, it was too important for me to be swayed in my goal to play for England, and those who belittled me only made me even more determined to succeed.

I had another incentive at the start of that 1985 season. I was now a married man, and a father – well, in actual fact, a stepfather to five-year-old Marcus. I had met Aileen eighteen months earlier when I used to call into a newsagents near the ground to collect my *Daily Telegraph*. The owner of the shop was a keen Gloucestershire supporter and he'd save the *Telegraph* for me when I was on the circuit, so I'd be able to keep my personal scrapbook going when I came back to Bristol. Aileen then took over the safekeeping of the newspaper cuttings for me and we used to chat away happily. I knew she was married, but separated. In the end, Aileen asked me out. She's a down-to-earth Yorkshire lass, and she just got fed up of my absorption in cricket, and put the question to me. We got on really well, but there were obvious complications from her marital status, and then I went off to New

Zealand for the winter, which certainly tested the strength of our relationship. In March, 1985, when I came back, I said to Aileen, 'Can you get a day off work next Monday?' She asked why and I said, 'Because I've booked the registry office. We're getting married.' Just like that. I knew it was right. I wanted to be a father, and I was delighted to share Marcus with his Mum. Family life has always been an important thing to me, and I was sorry that my parents eventually split up. I wanted a stable home life, and Aileen, with her commonsense attitude, would provide it. Besides, it just felt right. Apart from my mum, she's the only lady on this planet who can put up with me. I know I'm difficult and take cricket home with me if it's been a bad day, but she knows how to switch me away from it and keep me sane. Besides, she doesn't understand cricket, which suits me, and she doesn't come to the cricket, which is even better, because I'm at work then and don't want to be distracted. Aileen's independent-minded, as stubborn as me, and just gets on with life. Nothing seems to throw her off course, not even the fact that on our wedding night I went off to Gloucestershire's nets! (After all, it was the start of my new disciplined period!) Since then, our extended family now comprises five children, with possibly more to come. (I don't fancy declaring yet!) The amount of kids we've had proves that I'm not away from home all the time – but they've given me stability and peace of mind. Aileen was crucial in helping me focus on that vital part of my early career, when I changed my social priorities. Somehow, standing at a bar seems less attractive when you've got a wife and son to go home to – anyway, I'd been there and done that.

Bill Athey was the only Gloucestershire player invited to my wedding, which suited me. I figured it had nothing to do with anyone else, and I've managed to keep my personal life separate from my job. Even now, with my relationship with my team-mates so much better than in the mid eighties, I don't invite any of them to my home. That's private, a part of me that I allow few to see. I need the mental space. I even get a bit ratty when some of my relatives just turn up on the doorstep, without telling me they're coming. That's just the way I am. Solitary, stubborn, wanting things done on my terms. Thankfully, Aileen and Mum understand me, or more importantly, indulge me.

Family life became even more important to me a year after my marriage when my brother David died tragically. It was one of those freak accidents that you just can't legislate for, and you think happens to others. Nobody's fault, but that didn't minimise the pain we all felt at the time. It was August 1986. I was playing at Old Trafford against Lancashire and Aileen phoned me to say that David had fallen backwards over a small wall, banging his head on a window sill outside a pub. A blood clot had developed, and although he had been transferred to Bristol's Frenchay Hospital, one of the finest neurosurgical units in the world, there was no hope for him. He was being kept alive on a machine for as long as the family wished. I took a train from Manchester – the longest journey of my life – and Aileen met me at Bristol Parkway Station. Somehow I had convinced myself that I would be the one who would drag him out of that dark world, and bring him back to consciousness. I'd talk to him about Manchester United, his favourite team, and how I'd get some of their players to come down to see him. I'd reminisce about the scrapes we used to get into on the Circle, about the times we batted together for Stroud. David was a good enough batsman to have played a Second XI game for Gloucestershire in 1985, so I'd jolly him along about two Russells on the staff, only one of whom looked like a batsman. It would work out fine. But then I saw David in the intensive care unit, with tubes everywhere. We were told the situation was hopeless. He was brain dead. He could be kept on the machine for as long as we wanted, but after a year or so, his body would deteriorate. As I tried to come to terms with the news, my family pieced together the incident for me. Apparently, he and a few mates had just a couple of drinks at a pub opposite Stroud's ground, when he slipped outside, falling over a small wall, banging the back of his head on a small ledge. He was taken to hospital in an ambulance, and he seemed fine. But then he collapsed next morning as he tried to get up to go to the toilet. A blood clot had lodged in the base of his skull overnight. We made the decision to switch off the life support machine. I went in to hold his hand, to say goodbye, and I remember my uncle Danny standing at the window, cursing and saying over and over again, 'Why?' Good question. I kissed David's hand, walked out of the door and the tears just burst out of me. I couldn't bear to see him like this, just a few weeks since we'd last been together, when he popped in for a cheery word at the Cheltenham Festival. It's amazing that it's always too late to tell someone you love them – and I thought the world of David. Always did. So full of beans, so active in all sports, much more popular than me. I can't ever repay him for all the support he gave me, all the fun we had together.

I don't remember much about the funeral, I was in a complete daze. One thing I do recall is the gesture by the local policeman, PC Haley who was directing traffic near Uplands Church. As we passed, he stood to attention and saluted, a brilliant, touching moment. At the service, one of the pieces of music played was 'Brothers in Arms' by Dire Straits. That song is now very special to me. That night, I went down to London, to get ready to play against Surrey at the Oval. I just had to immerse myself in my cricket to come to terms with my grief, and I know that David would have wanted that. Somehow I concentrated hard enough to make my highest first-class score up until then, 71 against the intimidating pace of Sylvester Clarke. I also took a hat-trick of catches, only the second time in history that had been done. None of that would bring my brother back, though.

I regret so much that David didn't see me play for England. I know how proud he would have been, and he and Mum would have had my complimentary tickets, no problem. When I finally ran onto the Lord's turf on my England debut in 1988, I did what I had promised myself two years earlier – I thought of my brother and dedicated the moment to him. I like to think he's watched all of my career since he left us on that dreadful day in 1986. I still can't get over a sense of guilt that he can't have any of the personal pleasure that I've got out of my life. I'm probably having his as well. He was cut off at the age of twenty-one. Maybe that's why I seem to do so much work now, and try to cram so much into my life. Perhaps I'm trying to do things for him, to compensate for his tragic early loss. I still think of him, the pain won't totally fade. I wear one of his jumpers around the house, and I've still got the last bat he used for Stroud. Treasured memories.

I still don't find it easy to mention him in the company of other people, but it seems to be a little easier than it used to be since I wrote notes for this particular chapter. I'd been putting it off for ages, knowing I had to face up to it at some stage. On a spare day with Gloucestershire while in Ireland, I forced myself to set down my thoughts. I sat next to our coach, Paul Romaines, on the flight home and he saw me making notes. Paul asked what they were for and I let him read them after telling him they were for this book. Within a couple of minutes, I turned to Paul and to my amazement, he was in floods of tears – Paul, who had played for Gloucestershire in my early days, knew David and was greatly moved. So was I at Paul's emotion.

David would have relished Gloucestershire's revival in the 1986 and 1987 seasons. In fact, at his death, we were pushing for the Championship, but it was not to be. We finished second to Essex in 1986, having been fifty-four points clear of the rest at one stage. In the final seven Championship matches, we picked up only twenty-eight points. We thought we'd cracked it after bowling out Hampshire for 98, when they only needed 116 to win, at Cheltenham. Champagne was brought into the dressing-room, and too many of our players behaved as if we'd won the title. I felt uneasy, not because I'd curtailed my consumption of alcohol, but because we hadn't won anything yet. The celebrations seemed premature to me that day, and so it proved. We didn't get the job done, and we settled subconsciously for just doing well. Our batting – with Athey, Stovold and Bainbridge the backbone – was fairly solid, and at the time we had the best bowling attack on the county circuit in Courtney Walsh, Kevin Curran, Syd Lawrence and David Graveney, but we blew it when it was there for the taking. Gloucestershire hadn't won the title since 1877, and we could have been all-time heroes, but we lacked the dedication and commitment when push came to shove. Too much internal politics, too much bickering among senior players, not enough backing for the captain. I could never understand why Bill Athey allowed himself to get sidetracked by Kevin Curran's upbeat attitude. Now I accept that Bill must have appeared a little set in his ways to some of the more extrovert characters in our dressing-room, but he was such a good cricketer and strong person that he had no need to get uptight at the way Kevin antagonised people. I was a big fan of 'KC' as a cricketer, and I'm proud to say I never dropped a catch once off his bowling, including one catch low to my right, one-handed with a broken thumb. We had some terrific partnerships as well, and he remains a very good, combative cricketer. But he was no respecter of authority, and he just wouldn't toe the line. He could be very disruptive, which did nothing for a team spirit that was never all that strong in the 1980s. If it had been better, we would surely have won at least one Championship. Teams like Essex, Middlesex, Worcestershire and Nottinghamshire had their fair share of difficult characters during this period, but they hung together out there on the field. Pride in performance was crucial to their success. We didn't have enough of that at Gloucestershire, and it still rankles with me. Not enough mental hardness, bottle, ruthlessness – call it what you like. Perhaps that's why I remained unpopular with some of my team-mates. I made it clear I would be ruthless enough in my own section, and that it was up to the others to do the same if they wanted worthwhile careers. Soon I'd be able to point to my progress into international cricket as a justification for my approach.

4
THREE LIONS
ON MY SHIRT

The summer of 1987 was the most significant one of my career so far, both on and off the field. I was picked to go on my first England tour and I made my first tentative steps to becoming a painter. One came about purely by chance, the other was the result of hard work and absolute determination that nothing would stop me realising my ambition. I'm sure you now understand which one falls into which category, but the beauty of my first tour with England was that I could further my cricket education, and also stretch my wings as a fledgling artist. It lead to some degree of financial security for my family, an important factor for someone who's been brought up on a council estate and never known what it's like to feel comfortable about his earning capacity. Apart from that, my art work has kept me sane during the bad times of my England career.

Selection for the England trip to Pakistan had followed another good summer's work for me with Gloucestershire. My ability to concentrate had improved so much, and I felt in control of my glovework. Alan Knott and Bob Taylor were always ready with a word of encouragement or a technical tip whenever we met up, and nice things were being said about me in the national press. There were a couple of good displays from me in televised matches as Gloucestershire advanced in the one-day competitions, and that sort of exposure never does you any harm. With the bat, I was definitely improving, cutting out the rash shots, learning how to build an innings, averaging almost 29 in Championship cricket. I was still down at number eight in the order, though, and I knew that I had to get more consistency with the bat, and more chances up the order, to make a serious push for the England position. I had seen how Bob Taylor had suffered over the years, losing the position at times to keepers like David Bairstow, Paul Downton and Roger Tolchard, all of whom lacked his class. Only Alan Knott had seemed to be able to satisfy the purists with his keeping and the realists with his weight of runs – but he was a genius. Lesser mortals like R C Russell had to keep working at the vulnerable areas of his game. Yet the wicket-keeper's position in the England side was definitely up for grabs at the start of a busy period for the players. Why else would the selectors nominate four keepers for three separate tours in the winter of 1987–88?

First up was to be Paul Downton for the World Cup in India and Pakistan in the autumn, followed by Bruce French and myself for the Tests and one-day internationals in Pakistan, then Bruce would be joined by Jack Richards for the tour to New Zealand in the New Year. Confused? Me too. I am still none the wiser why so many keepers were involved – it is, after all, a key position and you need continuity – but I realised that no outstanding candidate had been able to seal his place. Richards was the best batsman, good enough to score a Test hundred against Australia the year before; Downton had great experience standing up to the spinners at Middlesex, as well as scoring gutsy runs; while French was a naturally deft keeper, who didn't get as many runs as he would have liked, because he batted down the order with Nottinghamshire. Then there was me. At the time of my selection, all I felt was elation. I allowed myself a quiet moment or two of satisfaction that my detractors in the Gloucestershire dressing-room might have to eat their words, and the fact that Bill Athey, my major supporter, was also going on the England tour pleased me enormously.

Right from the start of that Pakistan tour, it was made clear to me by the captain Mike Gatting that I was going to be Bruce French's understudy. He said I would be one of the back-up players, that I was there to learn and that the tour would be hard work for me at times, and that I must try not to get dispirited. I was a bit shocked at the apparent brutality of the news that I was going to be a drinks waiter on a tour lasting eight weeks. It seemed an odd way to motivate someone on his first England tour. I thought I might have been tossed a bone, something along the lines of 'keep fighting for your place, work hard, nothing is set in stone, illness could easily get you in the side in place of Frenchie' – but no. No matter; I was determined to prove to Gatting that I had the required discipline for touring, that my support for the team wouldn't flag for a moment, and that if the call did come, I'd be ready. I kept telling myself, 'At least I'm on the tour, as one of England's sixteen best cricketers.' Bob Taylor had adopted a similar attitude when he was understudy so often to the brilliant Alan Knott. That situation never affected their close, supportive relationship, and Bob managed to keep going. If a great professional like him could behave that way on countless, frustrating England tours, what had I to complain about?

And yet I managed to get into the side in the very first game on tour, at Rawalpindi, against the President's XI, all due to a freak injury to Bruce French. During practice the day before, one of the locals threw a ball back into the nets and it hit Bruce above the eye. Later he complained of headaches and on the way to the ground on the first morning, I was told I was playing. It was the greatest moment of my career so far, but I had no time to take it all in because we were almost at the ground when I was told the news. Perhaps that was a blessing in disguise, because there was no time for me to get nervous. In the event, it was all a bit of an anti-climax, because Bruce recovered after a day and a half to keep wicket. We batted first, I scored just four runs as we batted for ages on a low, slow pitch, and after three days the game was left drawn without the opposition even completing their first innings. Their captain, Abdul Qadir, only bowled three overs, because he didn't want us to have a good look at him, with the Test series imminent.

A week later, I made my international debut, playing in the one-day international at Peshawar. We had won the first two games, so I was given an opportunity and I was thrilled. It was what I had worked hard for, and nothing will dim the memory of that day. The venue was memorable for a start. Peshawar, just nine miles from the Khyber Pass on the Northwest Frontier, is a town full of the old colonial atmosphere, reminiscent of the days of the Raj. You could almost feel the history. As for the cricket, we won the game, and I was very happy with my performance. I caught everything that came my way, three catches, and the first one is firmly lodged in the memory bank – Ijaz Ahmed, caught down the legside, standing up to the spinner, Nick Cook. I felt very fulfilled. I'd crossed that mental barrier, I could now say, 'Yes! I can do it!' Jack Russell, of Gloucestershire and England. All right, it wasn't a Test match, but I had represented my country at senior level. No one would ever be able to take that from me.

And that was it for me as an active cricketer on tour. The sum total of two and a half days on the field. Mike Gatting hadn't deceived me after all! Yet I wouldn't have missed that tour for the world. Having been brought up on slow, low Bristol wickets, I wasn't troubled on the same sort of surfaces in Pakistan. It proved to be the best possible training for future England trips abroad, because no other has been so hard mentally and physically. When I have been really down at times on subsequent England tours – especially this last one to Zimbabwe and New Zealand – I can draw strength from getting through that Pakistan one cheerfully enough. At times the facilities were poor, the comfort zone was non-existent and the long periods of inactivity were a test of morale. The team microwave was an absolute lifesaver for me. I'd heard all about the dangers of eating certain foods in Pakistan, and I was determined not to get caught out. I've always been an eccentric, faddy eater anyway, but the thought of missing out on a Test just because of an upset stomach was too much for me to bear, so I played safe. I decided to stick to cuppa soups, tinned stew, baked beans and well done steak – hardly the most balanced of diets, but I wasn't sick once. Most of the other lads decided just to eat normally, especially in the more classy hotels, and I suppose that, as usual, I went too far the other way, but the proof of the pudding is in the avoidance of the head down in the bucket! As a result, I did a lot of twelfth man duties, as some of the players turned various shades of green after being adventurous with the menu the night before.

Sahiwal proved to be the most amazing place we stayed at on that tour, and whenever someone talks to me about how pampered England cricketers are on tour, I'll mention Sahiwal. We got there in two mini-buses after a five-hour journey that was the hairiest I've ever experienced. Our coach drivers simply ignored oncoming traffic, right of way, gear changes and anything that was in the way. The other drivers were just as bad, overtaking oxen and carts, with traffic advancing pretty swiftly from the other side of the road. We passed through a checkpoint, where automatic machine-guns were brandished, just like a scene from a war film. When we finally got to Sahiwal, nerves shredded, one sight of our sleeping quarters didn't exactly make us feel that the journey had been worth it. We ended up in the Montgomery Biscuit Factory. There was only one phone to serve the entire town, so we were cut off from the outside world, having to make our own entertainment. That proved to be interminable games of charades, in the absence of television. We fancied ourselves as expert mime artists, and I shudder to think now about the poverty of entertainment we must have provided each other. But the real fun came at night-time, when the mosquitoes gathered, looking for vulnerable areas of pink English flesh. There were no mosquito nets, but the Englishman abroad doesn't lack flexibility and a cunning plan. I went to bed fully clothed, with socks and a tracksuit on, wearing my wicket-keeper's inner gloves, and my face and hair covered with repellent gel. I looked like Ken Dodd! The only thing missing was a tickling stick and the

Diddy Men! The mosquitoes seemed bigger than me, and they were persistent. They just kept coming at us in swarms. Finally, I managed to slip into an exhausted sleep, only to be woken up a minute later by the wailing of the faithful starting up their morning prayers. Adapting to hand-to-hand combat with mosquitoes was all part of the learning curve on my first England tour! Compared to those nights in the Montgomery Biscuit Factory, trying to unravel the complexities of Abdul Qadir's bowling was a breeze.

But that trip to Pakistan was memorable for something more than having to ward off persistent mozzies. The incident in the Faisalabad Test between Mike Gatting and Shakoor Rana made cricket history, and led to unprecedented scenes, with both governments getting involved as tempers frayed and heels were dug in. To me, on my first tour, it was an amazing few days, and I still have difficulty taking it all in. We ended up threatening strike action in support of our captain, and yet we were then handed a hardship bonus by Lord's! What was going on?! Well, what has to be said from the start is that the seeds for the flashpoint had been sown earlier. Relations between England and Pakistan hadn't been all that cordial on the field for some time, because of fundamental disagreements over umpiring standards, and what to do about them. English players had long fumed at the umpiring on Pakistan tours, while they thought ours were no better when they came over to us. They wanted a panel of independent umpires, to eradicate suggestions of home bias. England believed that all umpires were neutral, irrespective of their nationality, so the system should stay in place. Unfortunately, Pakistan had toured England in the summer of 1987, winning the series, and there had been several incidents on the field between the players, and dark comments from the Pakistanis about the integrity of our umpires. That didn't impress some of our players, who had suffered in their eyes on tours to Pakistan. So the hostile brew was bubbling under by the time our Test series started a few months later, and on top of that, many of our players were tired after touring India and Pakistan for the World Cup. They had been very disappointed to lose out to Australia in the final, especially as we genuinely believed we had been the best side in the competition. So several of our lads were jaded, and with that comes irritability when you have to come to terms with the unique challenges that are set by a tour of Pakistan. This is not an attempt to justify what England did wrong on that trip, merely an explanation of the state of mind of some of our players.

The first Test, at Lahore, did nothing to ease Gatting's fears about their umpires. We lost badly, to inspired bowling from Abdul Qadir, but the feeling in our camp was that we had been given the rough end of some dubious umpiring decisions, with close fielders around the bat appealing for everything and getting the nod too often. By the time our second innings started, some of our lads were mutinous. When Chris Broad was given out, caught behind, he simply refused to go. He stood his ground, and informed everyone around the bat, 'I didn't hit that. You can like it or lump it, I'm not going.' Now that was amazing, an England cricketer refusing to accept an umpire's decision. Eventually, his partner, Graham Gooch, persuaded Broad he had to go and he stalked off in a fury. He came into the dressing-room, and soon he was in tears. After we had lost, our tour manager, Peter Lush, issued a statement deploring the standard of umpiring, and confirming that Broad wouldn't be fined for his astonishing actions. So this was Test cricket? I could barely credit what was going on. It was to get even more incredible.

By the time we got to Faisalabad for the second Test, the siege mentality had descended on our dressing-room and Mike Gatting was particularly incensed. He'd had first-hand experience on his first tour of Pakistan in 1977, when he felt he'd been unlucky to be given out, lbw for nought, in his first Test, so Gatt wasn't exactly all that calm at the time. When the flashpoint came between our captain and the umpire, Shakoor Rana, Gatt simply boiled over and all his pent-up frustrations poured out. The actual incident that sparked off the row was very mundane.

Towards the end of the third day, Pakistan were 106 for five, in reply to our score of 292. We were on top, pressing for more wickets, trying to get in as many overs as we could before the close. Eddie Hemmings was running in to bowl, as Gatt, at short leg, motioned to David Capel – the fielder positioned on the legside for the sweep – to come in to save the single. 'Capes' didn't quite grasp what the captain wanted, and Eddie was still running up to bowl when this was going on. The batsman, Salim Malik, pulled away, quite rightly, as the confusion continued, but as he did so, Shakoor Rana came bustling in from square leg, wagging his finger at Gatt as if he was accusing the England captain of some misdemeanour. That was too much for Gatt, and he flipped. He responded in kind, and Bill Athey had to pull him away from all the finger-jabbing and swearing. As I watched the incident, I said to the other lads in the dressing-room, 'Look at these two!' It seemed a joke to me at the time, but I didn't realise the repercussions until later. It looked awful, and sadly Gatt had forgotten in the heat of the moment that the umpire is always right, no matter how wrong you think he is.

We knew it wasn't good for the game, but we honestly thought no more about it that evening. Just shows how wound up you can get in a Test match, doesn't it? Next morning, we soon realised that wider issues were involved. We did our usual warm-ups and net practice on the ground, and I had to nip back to the hotel to pick up Eddie Hemmings' chewing gum that he had forgotten and would need on a dusty, hot day out in the middle. I got back, ten minutes after the scheduled start of play, to find our lads standing around in the middle, waiting for the umpires to emerge. Shakoor Rana had been persuaded to stay in the changing-room, as he demanded an apology from our captain. If one wasn't forthcoming, he'd stay there all day if necessary, and there could be no play without the umpires. My first thought was that this would severely affect our chances of winning the Test as we were in a good position, and soon that was the general feeling expressed in our dressing-room. We heard rumours that Shakoor

Rana had been persuaded that the honour of himself and his country had been impugned by Gatting and that, at the very least, he was owed an apology. So it was stalemate, because Gatt wasn't having any of that, and the day just drifted away without any cricket.

Our team meeting that night was a very tense affair. We knew that the situation had escalated so rapidly that Gatt's job was on the line, and ours too if we backed him. There was talk of strike action, with some of the guys saying we shouldn't take the field under any circumstances. I think one or two of our boys secretly relished the chance of getting the next plane home, because by now many were thoroughly sick of Pakistan. In the end, we backed our captain one hundred per cent, and agreed on strike action if necessary. Now we had to tackle the tricky question of breaking our tour contracts if we refused to play, and what to do about making public comments that would no doubt be construed as being hostile to the Pakistanis, and bringing the game into disrepute? John Emburey came up with a good idea – make a statement to the press. 'Embers' felt it would be unfair on the new tourists to risk their Test futures by voting to strike, so he suggested a statement drafted with the help of Jack Bannister, Secretary of the Players' Union, who was covering that tour as a journalist. We knew this would possibly get us in hot water with Lord's, and lead to large fines, but we thought it was right to risk that in the interests of giving our side of the story. After issuing the statement, we would then walk onto the field, to ensure that no one would then say we had broken our tour playing contracts.

The incident had now become more than a cricketing issue. Rumours were flying around that Downing Street had got involved, and we heard that word had come down from on high that the matter must be sorted out and the match resumed at all costs. Trade considerations were now a factor, big contracts might be at stake. Our manager, Peter Lush, went on a wild goose chase, halfway round Pakistan, to see the head of the Pakistan Cricket Board, but he was nowhere to be found when Peter arrived for the appointment. After he had fixed another time for the crucial meeting, that appointment too was broken. It wasn't difficult to work out why; the next day was a scheduled rest day, and we had suggested we should play, to make up for the wasted fourth day, when Shakoor Rana had refused to stand. Their board refused to budge, but I wonder if they'd have viewed it differently had they been in with a shout of victory? By now, we were totally supportive of Gatt. We knew the row shouldn't have happened, that it was bad for cricket's image, and that Gatt was at fault, but it was a human reaction.

Eventually, peace broke out and Gatt handed over a handwritten note to the umpire, with a curt apology, and the word 'Faisalabad' spelt wrongly, an appropriately farcical epitaph. Shakoor Rana made a great show of brandishing the note to the cameras, and his honour seemed to have been satisfied. We got on with the game, but we had lost a crucial day, and it dwindled away to a draw. Then it was time to consider what penalties would be imposed on the England players and our captain by the Test and County Cricket Board. We had, after all, sailed very close to the wind by threatening strike action and it could be considered that Gatt had brought the game into disrepute. One or two of our lads were convinced that Gatt was for the high jump, even though we all had massive sympathy for him. Conduct not becoming an England captain, and all that. The television pictures of the row made for spectacular viewing, as they were beamed all around the world, and many jokes were made at our expense. Fair enough, it should never have happened, but it was hard to see the funny side of it when the odds are so heavily stacked against you.

There was a remarkable sequel to a remarkable incident, though. The chairman of the Test and County Cricket Board, Raman Subba Row, flew out to discuss the row and its ramifications, and he was very sympathetic. Before the meeting ended, he completely floored us by saying we would each be getting a hardship bonus of £1,000 at the end of the tour. It must have looked amazing from the outside that players representing their country should be given a handsome bonus after threatening strike action, and I was terrified by all the ramifications. Would it count against us for future tours? Did it mean that our England careers might be over? Mine had hardly started, and although another thousand pounds was very welcome at that period in my life, it all seemed rather odd.

I did have a more pleasant distraction in that tour, from my sketches. Something that began as just exploratory doodling a few months earlier had developed very rapidly. The spare time I had in Pakistan was a bonus to me, as I explored the remarkable sights of an astonishing country. To my amazement, I managed to complete forty sketches in Pakistan, and when I came back an exhibition was held in Bristol by a gallery owner. He had recognised me when I came into his gallery before the tour started, and although I told him I'd be far too busy on the tour to do much drawing, I ended up doing more of that than playing cricket. The exhibition of my work sold out within two days. I was absolutely staggered that people would think my drawings would be worth paying for. Two years later, I held my first exhibition of paintings, and all thirty sold out very quickly.

And yet it had all started so innocently. On the morning of Wednesday, 17 June 1987, we were due to start a Championship game at New Road, Worcester. It was pouring with rain, and we soon realised there would be no play that day. By now, I was fed up of the usual rituals when play was called off. I had lost too much money playing cards recently, and I was also tired of watching television. I was getting bored with inactivity, and on top of that, Worcester brought its own particular hazard when rain stopped play: Ian Botham. A great player, one of my all-time heroes, but not a man to get anywhere near when he has time on his hands and he's bored. His japes could home in on you if you weren't careful, so I resolved to keep out of his way. I don't know what possessed me to walk over the bridge and into town to buy a sketchbook and pencils, but I did. Anything to do something constructive and get away from the claustrophobia of the dressing-room. So I wandered up and down the river bank, alongside the ground, observing the various scenes, wondering if I could pluck up enough courage to do a sketch or two. Technical drawing was my best subject at school, but I couldn't see how that would qualify me to sketch. I suppose it was just in me, and I decided to have a go. Nothing ventured – no one else would see the finished product, I could always throw it away. I saw a man sitting by the New Road bridge, reading a newspaper, and I thought, 'Let's see what I can do here.' It was a simple subject, and done from a distance, but I was really pleased with the result. I spent the rest of the day walking up and down that river bank, making sure that nobody noticed what I was doing. I didn't want anyone to come up and say, 'Can I have a look?' because I would have been too embarrassed to show the results. Soon I was to become fascinated by boats and water. As far as I'm concerned, where there's a boat, there's a picture!

A couple of weeks after those first faltering efforts at Worcester, I found myself at Folkestone Harbour, profiting from two more days of county cricket being washed out. Gloucestershire's scorer, Bert Avery and the match umpire, Kenny Palmer, were sitting in a cafe with me alongside the harbour, and I kept sloping off to see what I could make of the seagulls, the boats, the fishermen and their nets. It was so therapeutic. They were the first sketches I did on A4 paper, the first proper drawings I'd attempted. I was hooked, and days off from the cricket away from home were no longer a bore. The sketching stretched me mentally and the possibilities of improving myself all the time were exciting. As I became a little more confident about my work in the summer of 1987, I tried a few sketches in our dressing-room. I was very taken with one of Bert Avery catching up on his scorer's duties at Trent Bridge, and when this lovely man retired that summer as our scorer, I was proud to frame the sketch and give it to him as a retirement present. The following game, at Headingley, I sketched Vibert Greene, our overseas player, relaxing before going into bat in typical West Indian fashion – listening to music on his Walkman. Suddenly, I was drawing portraits!

So when I took those early sketches into a Bristol gallery, I was really chuffed that the owner thought there was promise in my work, because I was surprised how well they turned out, and getting reassurance from a professional was a boost to me. I looked forward to getting out the sketchpad in Pakistan on one or two occasions, but I had reckoned without having such time available and the sheer variety of life that I could draw. If I had stayed another six months, I doubt if I would have been able to do justice to the things I saw.

Fort Lahore was remarkable. Bill Athey and I went there a few days before the Test, and it took a couple of hours to walk around, through the gardens, the mosque, past the sleeping beggars to the museum, which contained manuscripts that must have been a couple of thousand years old, and books beautifully bound, written in Urdu. The poverty was indescribable, you could not even begin to prepare yourself for it, coming from the West. At Fort Lahore I sketched a peasant boy eating a cob, sitting with his feet flat to the ground, knees to his shoulders, and a blind beggar, mumbling away in Urdu, on the cobbled road leading up to the fort's main gate. At Faisalabad, during the days off before – and during – that acrimonious Test, a few of us went for a walk around the market. It was an amazing experience. The first thing that hit me was the smell of the place, but you can't sketch that. Bruce French was horrified at the sight of hanging meat, coloured black with flies, and he became a vegetarian there and then. There were so many people that you had to keep dodging around, you could barely see ten yards ahead of you. Traders dealing in everything from boxes of matches, guns, to nuts and cereals, cobblers in back streets, a hot chestnut seller in what looked suspiciously to me like NHS glasses, women covering up their faces, with their male companions looking daggers at us – it was remarkable, God's gift to a trainee sketch artist who was just trying to catch something different. The carts, drawn by donkeys, mules and camels, were a major challenge to me, and so was the barber, who worked amazingly quickly with his razor and cream. I'll never forget the one-legged beggar in Faisalabad market, sitting in the market square by a crossroads of at least six streets. He was at the centre of a hive of activity, with human ants teeming all around him, but no one actually getting close to him. He sat there, with his bucket outstretched, as the mayhem revolved all over him, a man alone. I can't vouch for the quality of workmanship by the surgeon on his stump, but I felt for him. In Peshawar, I sketched two hotel guards off duty, camped in their tents near our hotel, chanting to Allah on their rugs at various intervals, rapt in reverence to their particular god. The rest of their time was spent having a joke together, sharing a cigarette, cleaning their guns, polishing their shoes, and then reporting for duty to the Pearl Continental Hotel, where a group of privileged England cricketers were staying, oblivious to the hardships so many endured in this country.

There was a simplicity about so many of those people that I found endearing. On my last day in Pakistan, I was wandering around the various souvenir shops at our hotel when I chanced upon an old man making handkerchiefs. I stood talking to him, sketched him and he persistently asked me to buy one of his colourful designs. I told him that if he could produce a special one for me, with a personal message for Aileen, I would buy it – but I was leaving in a few hours. Ten minutes before we were due to leave, I came back, and he had it ready for me. And it was lovely, a tribute to his craftsmanship.

The locals fascinated me so much in Pakistan, nothing was too much trouble for them if you would part with a few rupees. A humbling experience, and something I would recommend to any Westerner who believes time in Pakistan has to be endured, rather than enjoyed. I wouldn't have missed that first tour for anything, even though I barely played. It was an education in all areas, and an experience that I've been able to tap into when I want to get away on subsequent tours, to take time out from cricket. And, as I've been gratified to discover, my sketches and paintings from those tours have been appreciated in various quarters! I could still be there now, sketching away: the material is endless.

As for my cricket ambitions, it was frustrating to have to sit out the New Zealand tour at the start of 1988, as Bruce French and Jack Richards took over. It wasn't as if I had done anything wrong in Pakistan, but just two and a half days of active service hardly shouted my credentials from the rooftops. It was simply a case of biding my time, and earning a living while waiting for the English season to start. So Jack Russell the cricketer became Jack Russell the carpet fitter. For a couple of winters, I found a job working from eight in the morning until ten in the evening, most weekdays, fitting carpets, for the princely sum of ten pounds a day, reduced to a fiver in the second winter when business was bad. After two years of working for my brother-in-law, I decided to go it alone. Mike had trained me well. During the next cricket season, I did an interview with local television, with the proviso that they would give the carpet business a plug. At the end of the discussion, a caption appeared on the screen saying 'Catch a carpet with Jack Russell!' It was hard work, on your hands and knees for hours, banging in carpets, but it was more satisfying than playing pool for money – and I couldn't always rely on a thousand-pound hardship bonus every time I went on tour! As a second career, painting was much more enjoyable. Easier on the knees too!

When the 1988 season started, my immediate aims were obvious – to get into the England side by playing well for Gloucestershire. I believe I managed the latter, averaging more than 27 with the bat in county cricket, and keeping up my standards behind the stumps. I had now nailed down the number eight position in our batting order, but the England selectors were obviously still unconvinced about that aspect of my game. With the West Indies here, the need for runs from the lower middle order against their powerful bowling attack was clear, and I was ruled out of contention, as the 'can't bat' label continued to hang over me. Bruce French was set to miss out early on, because of a serious finger operation that he had postponed for a couple of years. So Paul Downton was picked for the one-day internationals and stayed in for the first three Tests. But Paul didn't get many runs against Ambrose and company (not many did in those days), and he was dropped in favour of Surrey's Jack Richards, who was averaging 50 in county cricket. For those last two Tests, Jack couldn't get a run and the bandwagon on my behalf really started to roll in the national press. My county captain, David Graveney, nagged the selectors at regular intervals, and Bob Taylor was often quoted, pressing my claims. Bob had suffered his fair share of disappointments in the past, being passed over by England because of supposed batting deficiencies, and he was conscious that West Indies were the only side he had never played against in a Test, and he didn't want the same thing to happen to me. By the Leeds Test, when Richards had replaced Downton, the hype really went into overdrive. I remember a piece in the *Daily Mirror* by a columnist called Michael Bowen in which he slated the chairman of selectors, Peter May for maintaining England's best eleven available cricketers had been selected for Headingley. He wrote, 'The chairman of selectors was being economical with the truth. When practically anyone sits down to choose a World X1 nowadays, the name of Gloucestershire wicket-keeper Jack Russell is the first to be inked in. Jack Russell has never played for England. That, Mr May, is a national disgrace.'

Now I appreciated the sentiments of the writer, but he did get carried away. You can't assess the real merits of a cricketer until he's been tested at the highest level, and to call me 'world class' at that stage of my career was over the top, but it was great to get a mention. It was open season on the selectors that summer, because the side wasn't doing very well against the West Indies and because Peter May had sacked Mike Gatting as captain for a curious reason. It seemed his birthday celebrations had got a little out of hand during the first Test – a tabloid newspaper alleged that Gatt had invited a barmaid into his hotel room after midnight, with the fourth day's play at Trent Bridge due to start later that morning – and although Peter May issued a statement, accepting the truth of Gatt's explanation, he was still sacked for conduct not befitting an England captain. The hangover from Faisalabad must surely have been relevant in all this, and Gatt had to go. I was sorry about this, because I respected him, as did all the other players, and he had worked well with Micky Stewart, the coach. They seemed to be on the right wavelength, with great pride in England's performances, and losing Gatt's drive and ability was a major blow that summer. It was also a great media story, and the sequels from Gatt's sacking rumbled on for the next few weeks. England ended up with four captains in six Tests – Gatting, John Emburey, Chris Cowdrey and Graham Gooch. What a total farce, looking back on it. No wonder we struggle at times! The opposition understandably laugh at us, use it to their advantage, then smash us. With all this mayhem going on, the claims of Jack Russell to be in the team were hardly high on many priority lists.

I got there, though. The last Test of the summer was a one-off against the Sri Lankans. Micky Stewart rang me at the weekend, to tell me to report to Lord's the following Wednesday lunchtime. My first Test – at Lord's! *Boys' Own* stuff! I was so overwhelmed that I thought of ringing Micky back, in case it had been a wind-up and someone in our ranks at Bristol had concealed hidden talents as a mimic. I decided against that, just in case it was a hoax, because I wouldn't have been able to cope with the disappointment. I soon learned it was true, and to make it an even better occasion, the selectors had also called up David Lawrence. We were to be the first Gloucestershire-born cricketers to represent England since David Allen in 1966, and I was almost as pleased for Syd as myself. We had first played together for Gloucestershire Under-13s and I'll never forget the sight of Syd charging in to bowl at terrified kids. He was so big and muscular even at that age that he had a huge advantage already against skinny opponents who would never have seen anything like him. Once, on a Gloucestershire Under-13s Federation tour to Sussex, he bowled the longest over I have ever kept wicket to. His six deliveries took up almost half an hour. His run-up, which started on the boundary rope, didn't exactly help the over rate, but the batsmen took an age to get out to the middle at the fall of each wicket. Syd took five wickets in that over, breaking the stumps twice. The batsmen were deathly pale as they dragged themselves to the crease, and as soon as they were out, they scarpered back to the pavilion, relieved they were still intact. When we got into the county side, and I kept wicket regularly to Syd, there were times when an occasional delivery that whistled past me almost went for six byes. Once at Hove, on a fast, bouncy wicket, Syd was in his element, roaring down the hill, breathing fire and fury, rushing in out of the sea mist, like a train suddenly shooting from a tunnel, bowling at the speed of light. One ball that he really let slip took off from short of a length, careered over my head at speed, and bounced just once more, a few inches inside the boundary rope. He was seriously fast, and a great trier, loved by the Gloucestershire supporters for his huge heart and support for the rest of the team when he wasn't bowling. We often used to daydream about playing together for England, and having so many dismissals in tandem that we'd have the English version of 'caught Marsh, bowled Lillee', but at least this scorecard for the 1988 Lord's Test would be precious to both of us. Tragically, because of that dreadful knee injury Syd suffered a few years later in the Wellington Test, we were only to play in four Tests together.

I didn't sleep very well in the days leading up to my Test debut. I was just too nervous and excited. When I arrived at Lord's the day before, there was a lot of media interest, because there were four new caps – Phil Newport and Kim Barnett, as well as the two Gloucestershire lads – so there were many photos to be taken and interviews to be done. Perhaps I wasn't psychologically settled, because it all seemed such a rush. Certainly the rule in later years that you assemble two days before the home Tests suits the players; you get time to soak in the atmosphere and attune your mind to the job in hand. I slept badly the night before that first day, and I woke to stacks of faxes and telegrams. There was one from my old school, Archway, from Stroud Cricket Club, from Aileen and my two children, and one from Alan Knott that said, 'Dear Jack, I am so delighted for you STOP have a wonderful match STOP very good luck STOP Knotty STOP'. It was a terrific boost that a legend had thought about me on my big day, and it was an even bigger thrill to meet up with Knotty during that Test and talk about my performance.

I certainly wasn't pleased about my first-day efforts. I was glad that we fielded first, so that I could get involved right away. Following my captain, Graham Gooch, out of the dressing-room, through the Long Room and out down the pavilion steps was one of the major experiences of my life, and as I ran onto the outfield, I thought of my brother, David, who'd been dead for two years. I dedicated the moment to him, knowing that he'd be looking down on me, willing me to do well. I didn't do well on that first day, dropping two catches. The first was a regulation effort off Syd Lawrence, that went through my hands for no apparent reason. The other was more difficult, trying to take one, diving in front of first slip, that I ought to have left alone. No excuses; I was probably tense from the occasion, and I don't think I had prepared properly the day before, but playing for your country presupposes you have the ability and character to surmount such obstacles. On that basis, I had failed at the first time of asking. We had done well to dismiss Sri Lanka for 194 just after tea, and perhaps Graham Gooch and Micky Stewart realised I needed something to distract me from my patchy start, because I was told to put my batting pads on. I was to be the nightwatchman.

Tim Robinson was out with sixteen balls left in the day, and I walked out to bat for England for the first time in a Test, at the home of cricket. I think you could say my heart was pumping! While waiting for the call, I had been very focused, watching the bowling, concentrating as if my life depended on it. I squirted one around on the legside for my first two runs, and felt very relieved that I wouldn't get nought. That really would have made my day after two dropped catches! Not out two overnight, I was just relieved to have survived – and shattered. All the tension and excitement of the previous few days caught up with me. Tension makes you tired, draining you of energy, but I was absolutely determined still to make that bad first day a thing of the past. Well, the second day of that Test was certainly special for me. I made 94, the highest score of my first-class career. It should have been 150. Not many England keepers have got Test hundreds, especially in recent years, least of all coming in as nightwatchman in your first Test. On the one hand, there was disappointment at missing out on the landmark, yet there was still huge satisfaction that I had more than surpassed expectations with the bat, especially as it had been suggested that my delayed introduction into Test cricket had been due to my batting frailties.

On that second morning, my initial task was to show enough determination to hang around, support Graham Gooch, and see off the shine of the new ball. Yet in the morning session, I outscored Gooch, 35–30. Batting with Goochy was a great experience, he was so calm and masterful, but that day he seemed to be a little in his shell. It was a good pitch, the bowling wasn't too demanding and I was absolutely keyed up to make the most of it, loving the situation.

After lunch, I got to my fifty, pulling a short ball to the fine leg boundary and Goochy shook my hand, telling me to keep going. I had one slice of luck in the morning, when I was dropped by the keeper, as I tried to drive to mid-on and got an outside edge. The keeper was going the wrong way, tried to get back and spilled it. I put on 131 with Gooch, and when he was out, I kept going until tea. With my century there for the taking, I played a dreadful shot, chasing a wide ball to be caught at cover. So, after four and a half hours, I finished six runs short, yet my initial reaction was one of pleasure as I walked off to a standing ovation. That was a magnificent moment for someone who had dreamed of playing for England. Yet exhilaration soon gave way to irritation at missing out on my hundred, especially when I saw how disappointed Syd Lawrence was for me. It was inexperience at that highest level that led to my dismissal, and I was left wondering if I'd ever get the chance to come near again to a Test hundred.

There were huge consolations, though, from that Lord's Test. We won, for the first time in eighteen Tests, I kept wicket much better in their second innings, with one of my better catches, low to my left off Phil Newport. It was a crucial catch, boosting my self-belief. I felt that I had made a good impression on Graham Gooch, not least of all in our long partnership together. I even managed to fit in a little sketching on the final day, as we cruised to victory. We didn't need many runs to win and I knew I wouldn't be called on to bat, and Robin Smith kept chivvying me to show him what I could do. Our physiotherapist, Lawrie Brown, persuaded me to sit on the balcony and sketch something. I decided to sketch the old scoreboard in the Lord's Grandstand, the one with Father Time on top, scythe at the ready. The television cameras picked up on it, talking about the 'artist at work'. That was the first time I'd had much national media exposure for my drawings, and it didn't do my reputation any harm at all! The resulting sketch wasn't too bad either, and it made a memorable souvenir of my first Test.

That 1988 season ended too soon for me. Having done well overall in my first Test, it was frustrating to realise that it had come at the end of a six-Test summer, and I now had to wait for the tour to India to try building on my debut. It was exciting to think about touring India, with the chance of standing up for long periods to our spinners, Eddie Hemmings, John Emburey and John Childs, that lovely man who had provided me with my first stumping for Gloucestershire in 1981. Syd Lawrence was also in the tour party, so there would be any amount of laughter and support if the going got hard.

Steve Rhodes was the other keeper picked after a good season with Worcestershire, but I felt I was now the man in possession, and would give everything to ensure I held on to the position. I assumed that I would get the same amount of support that Bruce French enjoyed on the Pakistan tour the previous year, and that Steve would be my understudy. With India so full of contrasts, it would also be a fascinating place to continue my education as an artist. I couldn't wait to go.

In October, though, the tour was called off. The Indian government refused visas to eight of our tour party, because of their links with cricket in South Africa. They were particularly concerned over our captain, Graham Gooch and vice-captain, John Emburey, both of whom had gone to South Africa in 1982 with the South African Breweries team, the so-called 'rebel' side. Yet no objection had been raised to the presence of Gooch and Emburey in the England party that played in the World Cup in India in 1987.

I know a year can be a long time politics, but there was no doubt in my mind that cricket was being used for political purposes in some quarters. Pakistan got involved as well, vetoing a proposed tour to New Zealand by England that would have involved themselves, the home country and ourselves. It was arranged hastily for the following February, scheduled to last seven weeks, and also involved two Tests against New Zealand, but our party's South African connections scuppered that idea. So we ended up kicking our international heels in the winter of 1988–89. The players were paid a proportion of our tour fee, which was generous of the TCCB, but nothing could compensate for missing out on playing for England on tour.

We were all terribly frustrated, and from my perspective it was doubly galling. I had been happy to serve my time as understudy the previous year in Pakistan, but now that the number one spot was there for the taking, I'd be kicking my heels. Would I get another chance? What would happen if I picked up the sort of finger injury that had put Bruce French out of action for a season?

Down the pecking order I would go. The Australians were due in England the following summer. The thought of missing out on that series was almost too much to contemplate. I was coming to realise that nothing comes easy in this world.

5
TOP OF THE CLASS

Between my first Test in 1988 and the 1990–91 tour to Australia, I was England's number one wicket-keeper, playing twenty Tests in a row. They were proud times for me, a vindication of the methods that I had adopted to become an England player. Every time I walked out to play for England I got a huge buzz, and I changed my diet and worked devotedly at my game to give myself the best possible chance to remain the top keeper. So it was ironic that, at the time I was keeping wicket better than at any stage in my career, I was dropped by England. That came in the Adelaide Test, early in 1991, when I was told the news just thirty five minutes before the start of play. The captain giving me the bad news was Graham Gooch, and he stressed it was through no fault of my own. That was to become a recurring theme in my England career, as I had to get used to being sacrificed, because we needed an extra bowler. 'It's no reflection on you, Jack,' they would say, but that was hardly a consolation for being left out. At the end of my first series, against the Australians in 1989, Graham Gooch had told me he thought I'd be England's keeper for the next ten years, yet less than eighteen months later he had dropped me. As I soon learnt, things change swiftly in English cricket.

I learned so much in that 1989 series against the Australians. It was the original boyhood dream to play for England against them, and the fact that I kept wicket well and finished second in

England's batting averages for that series was doubly satisfying. It was a remarkable summer of turmoil for England, with Australia thrashing us 4–0, and a lot of our players defecting to South Africa for another 'rebel' tour. With Mike Gatting among those signing up, there was a feeling at the end of the summer that radical changes were afoot to get us back to international prominence and I was excited that my performances seemed to have consolidated my place in the team. I wanted so much to be part of England's future, I was enjoying it so much.

And yet the summer didn't begin all that well for me. Steve Rhodes edged me out for the one-day internationals ahead of the Test series, which disappointed me, because I considered myself the man in possession after my good performance against Sri Lanka. In the intervening nine months, England hadn't played representative cricket, yet I missed out. We had a new captain now in David Gower, who had taken over from Graham Gooch, and a new chairman of selectors, Ted Dexter, who appeared a bigger fan of Gower than Gooch, so it was now a case of trying to impress the new regime. Justifying the selection of Rhodes, Dexter said, 'He just edged out the other contenders after we looked at all the possible batting combinations.' In other words, Steve was the better batsman, and that my 94 on England debut counted for nothing. So if Steve did well in the one-dayers, that might be curtains for me for the whole summer. Not for the first time, I cursed that aborted tour to India.

You can imagine how delighted and relieved I was to get the call for the first Test, at Headingley. Now I had to make myself indispensable, to perform so well that they couldn't drop me. Ted Dexter said some positive, supportive things about me before the first day, telling me, 'You're a good cricketer, you deserve to be here', and I felt good about my prospects. The night before, at the team dinner, David Gower said a few words about the game, led the toast to the Queen, and told us to enjoy it. No discussion about tactics, or the opposition, just go out there and do your best, because you've been picked for your country, therefore you're good enough. A bit of a contrast to the Graham Gooch method that I soon got to know, but I can't knock David for that, this was just his way. I was simply the new kid on the block, thrilled to be there, with no real views on the best way to prepare for a Test. Playing against Australia, years after watching us beat them on our telly back home in Stroud – that was enough to keep me on cloud nine, no matter who was captain.

That Leeds Test turned out to be a nightmare for us. Somehow we contrived to lose eight wickets between lunch and tea on the final day, when we ought to have batted it out easily for a draw. It started badly, and fell away from there. Dexter had persuaded Gower that the weather would be uncertain on the first couple of days, so the best strategy if we won the toss was to omit the spinner, John Emburey, play four seamers, stick the Aussies in and bowl them out in conditions that would favour our seamers. Well, we put them in and fielded till Saturday lunchtime, when they declared on 601 for seven. That was a new experience for me, and I was pleased that I didn't miss a chance or concede a bye, and stuck to the task. When we batted, on a good pitch, we saved the follow-on (I remember seeing us past the total by hitting a four off Alderman), and then it was surely just a case of keeping it tight in the field, to get a creditable draw. But the Aussies slogged us around, giving them enough time to have a dart at us in the second innings. They created enough pressure to get us wobbling and we folded badly, losing by 210 runs.

We deservedly took a lot of flak from the media for losing that Test, but I was surprised to be singled out for some vitriol. I didn't bat well, making 15 and 2, edging to gully, and the keeper in the second innings. It was clear I had to make a better contribution with the bat, it wasn't enough to have done my main job well as the keeper. For a day or two, though, I was really singled out for the treatment. I remember a particularly savage piece by the former England captain, Tony Greig, in which he laid into me. Sadly Jack Richards, once my rival for the England spot, also climbed into me in the press, which was disappointing, but on reflection not surprising because Richards had always been a difficult character, never a member of the Wicket-keepers' Union. Still, it felt like a case of kicking a man when he's down, but I was especially troubled by several negative comments about me on BBC TV's commentary of the Leeds Test. Now, as a cricket-mad youngster, I use to love the television coverage of England's Tests. That fantastic music from Booker T and the MGs at the start of each day's coverage will always be a *Desert Island Discs* choice for me, and I'd sit down and listen to the thoughts of Richie Benaud, Jim Laker and the others with due reverence. To me, they sounded as if they knew what they were on about, especially Benaud, who had always struck me as a very fair-minded commentator. Yet, during the Leeds Test, he was intimating on air that I didn't fancy Australia's fast bowlers, that I also didn't have the technique or the guts to cope with them. Now I've never been frightened of a cricket ball in my life, and nobody hit me at Leeds. I just didn't judge the line right, and played tentative shots – does that mean I'm scared? I was saddened at Richie Benaud's comments, because that didn't appear to be his style. I soon learned, however, that he didn't rate me. Benaud has never shown much appreciation of the way I play my cricket, compared to other figures in the media, who generally have been supportive of me. Years later, after I had scored a hundred in the Lord's Test against India, Benaud had to interview me and it was a fairly awkward situation for both of us – I hadn't forgotten what he had said about me at the Leeds Test of 1989.

So as I drove away from Headingley, I had a lot on my mind. I hadn't been physically bothered by the Aussie quicks, but now that such rumours were flying around in the media I knew that the opposition would be going for my jugular in the next Test, at Lord's. They would now be trying to bounce me out and Merv Hughes in particular would be testing my nerve with some choice verbals. There had been little of that at Leeds, but the Aussies were far better at the psychological warfare than we were. They had thought long and hard about the way they would approach this series, after losing the previous two to England, in 1985 and 1986–87. Ian Chappell, their former captain, had criticised captain Allan Border for being too friendly with the Poms on and off the field. Border had excellent relationships with Ian Botham, Allan Lamb and David Gower, sharing a beer or two with them after play, but with the Aussies losing to us their captain had been accused of being soft on us. Border made a conscious decision not to fraternise with us during the 1989 series. The method used at Leeds was silence. The Aussie players just stared at us out in the middle. There was simply no recognition; it was unnerving and unpleasant. Terry Alderman, who had played for Gloucestershire the season before, barely exchanged a word with me all series. 'Good morning' was all I'd get – and that was on one occasion!

So I knew I'd get the full works from the Aussies at Lord's and that I had to be ready to meet the psychological and technical pressure head on. For me, this Test was make or break, my career was on the line. Everything I had ever dreamed of could soon be taken away from me unless I came through this test of nerve and temperament. If they had a go at me on the field, I'd give it back, and I'd be as snarling and unpleasant as them. First, though, I had to get into a groove of playing comfortably the short-pitched bowling I knew would be coming my way from Hughes and his mates. The day before the Test started, I got to Lord's early and discussed the situation with Alan Knott, who was now the England wicket-keeping coach, to my great joy. Knotty understood right away what concerned me, and he organised for me a practice session that I honestly believe saved my England career. Typically inventive, he rounded up a few boys from the MCC ground staff and made them bowl at me from sixteen yards, with bouncy orange rubber balls. For thirty minutes, I didn't play a shot, I just ducked and swerved, getting used to the line and the lift. That helped me sharpen up my reflexes. Knotty and I worked so hard together that it was nearly six o'clock when we finished, and I was almost late for the team dinner. But I was happy at what I had learned from that session, and nothing had been left to chance. Another session next morning would just top up my knowledge. I told myself that if I failed after that, and was dropped, I could at least say that I'd given myself the best opportunity to make things go my way. And yet, I didn't sleep well that night; I kept thinking about the possibility of failure, the real prospect that everything I had dreamed about as a cricketer might come to an end over the next few days. The wrong shot to the wrong ball, and that would be it, nothing to do with my alleged reluctance to get behind the line and fight it out against their quicks. It wasn't enough to do my number one job well, that of keeping wicket. If I didn't get runs, I was out.

On the first morning, David Gower won the toss, we batted badly on a pitch that helped their seamers and I walked out at 185 for six, with our backs to the wall and my neck on the block. I felt like Gary Cooper in *High Noon*, with everyone craning their necks, watching me, waiting for me to fail. Showdown. Somebody was going to be disappointed. It was not going to be me. As expected, Merv Hughes let me have the short stuff, and the verbals. I was ready for both. Whenever I hit Merv for a four, I'd shout some choice Anglo-Saxon vocabulary. I couldn't hold back on it, I was almost out of control, shouting 'Come on Merv, say something!', and telling the bowlers that the ball had gone to the boundary. I was so wound up, I was spoiling for a fight and all the frustrations and resentment at the slurs about my physical courage came pouring out of me. As I grew in confidence, I could tell the Aussies were getting a bit cheesed off. The short stuff held no terrors for me, and most of my runs came from the pull, the steer over slips and gully, and one shot in particular which I laced over cover like a tracer bullet, the power coming from my anger. I was running on adrenalin, no doubt about it. I was like a man possessed, and disappointed when we were all out for 286, leaving me high and dry on 64 not out. It certainly quietened down the Aussies, and I was pleased that they all stood at the pavilion gate, waiting for me to lead everyone off the field at the end of our innings. They all applauded me, one or two even said

Left: Mum with her two boys, David and Jack.

Right: I suppose my hairstyle hasn't really changed that much over the years – I was always a trendsetter!

Left: Just fifteen … and the moustache is in place already!

Below: Making my way in local cricket. Here I am dozing off in the front row of the Gloucestershire Federation Under-15s.

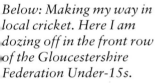

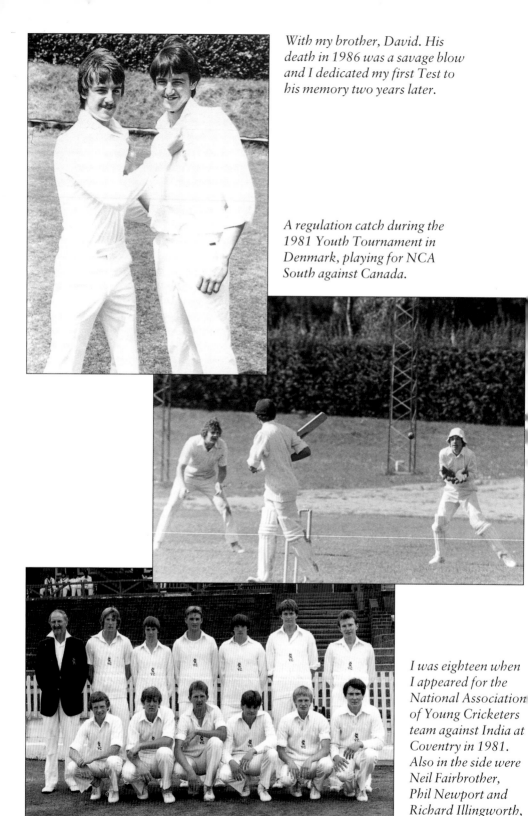

With my brother, David. His death in 1986 was a savage blow and I dedicated my first Test to his memory two years later.

A regulation catch during the 1981 Youth Tournament in Denmark, playing for NCA South against Canada.

I was eighteen when I appeared for the National Association of Young Cricketers team against India at Coventry in 1981. Also in the side were Neil Fairbrother, Phil Newport and Richard Illingworth, so four of us went on to play for England.

The moment that inspired me to take up wicket-keeping at the age of fourteen. Alan Knott takes a screamer to dismiss Rick McCosker off Tony Greig in the Leeds Test against Australia in 1977.

A few years later, at the start of my county career, I was trying to emulate my mentor, taking Lancashire's John Abrahams off the bowling of David Lawrence.

At the age of twenty, I almost lost a foot under a flymo blade, as I helped out on groundsman's duties while playing for Birkdale in Auckland.

On my first England tour, to Pakistan in 1987, everything was overshadowed by the dispute in Faisalabad between the umpire Shakoor Rana and our captain, Mike Gatting. Tour manager Peter Lush did his best to mediate.

A special time for me. On my way to 94 on my Test debut, against Sri Lanka at Lord's in 1988 – just six runs short of the magic figure. To this day, I'm still annoyed that I got myself out.

Edging towards my first hundred for England, at Old Trafford in 1989 (above). It was made all the sweeter because it was against the Australians. On reaching the milestone, it meant a lot to be congratulated by the Australian captain, Allan Border (right).

David Gower had a difficult time as captain against Australia in 1989. At least he is one left-hander with slightly more grace than me!

Micky Stewart was the England coach in my early days in the Test side. He was a players' man and a great patriot.

Below: Taking time off to make friends with one of the locals at St Lucia in 1990.

Right: The worst day of my career. The shattering knee injury sustained by David Lawrence, my county colleague, while playing for England at Wellington in 1992.

Below: I held Syd's hand as we carried him off the field.

In Portugal for pre-tour training before the England tour to the West Indies in 1993, with our coach Keith Fletcher. Sadly, 'Fletch' never inspired me or told me I was a good player.

Bob Taylor, another of my heroes as a wicket-keeper. Stylish and highly professional, he was still keeping for England in his forties.

Mike Atherton and Ray Illingworth – a captain/manager relationship that never really gelled.

Alongside Alec Stewart – rivals but great admirers of each other. His two Test hundreds in a row in 1990 didn't exactly help me!

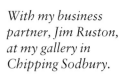

With my business partner, Jim Ruston, at my gallery in Chipping Sodbury.

My mentor, Alan Knott, has been a constant encouragement and inspiration – a legend and a hero to me in my England career.

'Well played', and by their standards, that's a rich compliment. They were the only civilised words I heard from them all that summer. They never said a thing to me out in the middle for the rest of the series, and I took that as a compliment.

I owed such a lot to Alan Knott for his support before that crucial innings. He came into our dressing-room on the first morning, with a bag full of his old bats, and asked me which one I would like. He was keen for me to try them out, because they were all super short handles, and he felt that with them I'd have better control against the short stuff. I chose one with a very short handle and it worked. What a man! My hero, now my mentor, and he gives me one of his bats to get me through the most vital innings of my career. That night, I watched the highlights of my innings on television and it was a pleasure to see David Gower, Mike Gatting and Micky Stewart standing on the dressing-room balcony, applauding my fifty. In the second innings, I was promoted to number seven. I thought to myself, 'Maybe I've arrived. Perhaps they do think I can play.' Without that innings at Lord's in 1989, there would have been no Test hundreds for Jack Russell, no rearguard action with Mike Atherton to save the 1995 Johannesburg Test. I'm certain of that. I crossed a mental bridge that day.

My rehabilitation didn't lead to the sight and sound of some of the former players in the media eating their words, because they had more pressing matters to examine. We lost by six wickets at Lord's, which meant we were now 2–0 down in the series, and getting close to praying for miracles. 'Send for Ian Botham' was the cry and I had no complaints about that. He had missed the first two Tests because of a fractured cheekbone, but now he was back for the Edgbaston Test, and I for one was absolutely delighted. To me, he was the greatest, you could do anything with him in your side. He's number one to me and always will be. I forgive him all his excesses. He's a legend in my book. I listened on the radio to his exploits against the 1981 Australians, when he wrote the script to end all scripts, and here I was, changing in the same England dressing-room as the great man, eight years later. I remember standing alongside him behind the wicket, with him a few yards in front of me at first slip, intimidating the batsman, and I'd be thinking, 'Beefy, get out of the way, for God's sake, I can't see the ball, you're in my eyeline!' To my delight, we shared a stand of 96 in that Edgbaston Test, as we fought to save the follow-on, and I was struck by his determination to go on for a big score on his comeback. He was furious when he got himself out, swishing at a wide one from Merv Hughes, and I was out next over to Trevor Hohn's leg-spin, but we managed to get past the follow-on target and save the game. And I'll be able to tell my grandchildren that I batted for England with Ian Botham. That Test also gave me the opportunity for more drawings. The thunderstorm at close of play on the first day was the most amazing I've seen in England, and the sight of a policeman up to his knees in water directing traffic outside the ground was too good to resist.

The rains at Edgbaston at least gave us an outside chance of still retaining the Ashes, with three Tests still to go. But we were ripe for plucking by the time we came to Old Trafford, and not just because the opposition were playing so well and we were demoralised by lack of form and injuries. South Africa lay on the horizon for some of our best players, and clearly some minds weren't on the job in hand. David Gower was under pressure, and he didn't have the full concentration of every one of his players, some of whom had decided to turn their backs on playing for England. There had been rumours of an unofficial tour to South Africa all summer, and the TCCB had been trying to smoke out the guys who were going, after numerous warnings to them of the consequences. The Board sent out a letter of intent in which the player concerned had to state that he was available for the winter tour to West Indies and I signed it like a shot. Maybe I was too naive, too wrapped up in my own game, but I had no inkling about the South Africa thing. It was a crazy situation, terrible for David Gower. How could he get the guys focused on getting back in the series? Three players from that Old Trafford Test – Tim Robinson, John Emburey and Neil Foster – signed up, plus Mike Gatting, and a few others whom I had toured with like Chris Broad, Bruce French and Bill Athey. I wasn't personally disappointed with Bill, a colleague who had done so much for me in my early years at Gloucestershire. In one way, I was sad that Bill and the others no longer wanted to play for England, but that was up to them. To me, playing for England was the ultimate and no amount of money would deflect me from that, even though, understandably, I wasn't asked. Of course, some of the guys had a beef with the Board about various things, but they were basically saying they didn't want to play any more for England, and at the time I didn't understand that. The Aussies must have thought it was Christmas. They had come over, aware that they would have to play really well to regain the Ashes, only to find the England team in disarray right from the off. And it got worse. By the time we got to Old Trafford, with the ghost of a chance that we would start to fight back, some of our players decided they didn't want to remain any longer in Test cricket. How can you stage a comeback in those circumstances? I know it's easy for me to say all this now, because as a newcomer to the England scene, I just kept quiet and concentrated on getting my own game right. If I had been a regular for a few years, I might have spoken up in the dressing-room, to try to get the guys fully behind the captain and forget their own futures, but here I was, too young to notice! Anyway, there was more than enough to occupy my thoughts during that Old Trafford Test.

We were on the end of another hiding on the fourth afternoon when I came in to bat at 38 for five, still a long way behind, with an innings defeat looming. David Gower soon departed, and John Emburey and I lingered to the close. I was 47 not out, and determined to sell my wicket dearly the next day. As I walked out to bat the following morning, the news had broken about the England players going to South Africa. One of them was my batting partner, Emburey. I was angry at the match situation, that the Aussies were laughing at us, and that some of the English guys were abandoning ship. I decided to block everything out and concentrate on saving the match, and winning back some pride for us. I felt I was fighting for my life, ball by ball. Embers and I saw it through until after lunch, and I got nearer and nearer to my first hundred in first-class cricket, never mind Tests. The wicket was very flat, and although Merv Hughes and Steve Waugh peppered me with bouncers, I had already shown them at Lord's that I wasn't fazed by those tactics. Waugh called me a 'smart arse' while fielding at silly mid-off, which was music to my ears – I was getting them ratty!

I remember running a sharp single that took me into the nineties, and suddenly doubts swirled into my head. My innings against Sri Lanka in my debut Test came back to me and I started to worry that I'd blow the chance of a hundred again. I got to 96 and hit a screamer that looked a certain boundary, only for Allan Border to dive full-stretch, at wide mid-off, get a finger to the ball and deflect it away for three. I wondered again if I was fated to fall short. Then Terry Alderman bowled one well up to me, and I squirted it down to fine leg. I was there. I ran down the wicket, bawling my head off, absolutely elated. After all the criticism about my batting and supposed lack of bottle, I had been vindicated. I had also proved to myself that I could do it, in only my fifth Test. A nice touch then from Border. He came forward to shake my hand. Considering the lack of communication from the Aussies during that series, I considered that gesture a huge compliment from a very tough competitor.

Sadly, we couldn't hold out for the draw, and I was left, unbeaten on 128. I was desperate to pass the score of 135 by Alan Knott against the Aussies in 1977, the year his catching had inspired me, but perhaps there would be other opportunities. We lost by nine wickets, and as that hammering started to sink in afterwards, I felt little satisfaction in what I had achieved in nearly six hours of defiance. The announcement of the 'rebel' tour took precedence over England losing the Ashes. The column inches wouldn't feature much of me over the next few days, but I was more concerned at how easy we had capitulated to the Aussies all summer. We went into their dressing-room for the usual platitudes, but after a few minutes of champagne swilling from their lot, I didn't have the stomach for any more of that. It took me two hours to shower, get changed and unwind, and by then, all our lads had gone. I sat alone, sipping a cup of tea, feeling gutted. The Ashes – to me the greatest prize of all since my childhood – had disappeared Down Under. It wasn't until a couple of days later, after I'd watched my innings on the video, that I felt any sense of pride in my performance. I had felt empty inside, on what was the greatest day of my career so far.

The Aussies weren't finished with us, and we experienced another thrashing by an innings in the Trent Bridge Test. There were significant new faces in the England side. A fresh-faced lad just down from Cambridge University called Michael Atherton came in to bat at number three, beginning his Test career with nought. I gave him a bit of sophisticated advice on the eve of the game: 'If they have a go at you, mate, just tell them to "F*** off",' which didn't impress David Gower, who told me to keep those thoughts to myself. As I got to know Athers, I realise now he didn't need any advice on how to look after himself against the Aussie verbals, even at the age of 21. Devon Malcolm played in a Test for the first time, a little raw and loose, but blessed with genuine pace. He also swung the ball as well, and that, plus his speed, meant you really had to concentrate when Dev roared in. But he had a big heart, and I always loved to see Dev on the field for England. He's someone to rough up the opposition a bit. With Angus Fraser making an impressive start that series, and Robin Smith batting staunchly in only his second series, the new England team was starting to take shape. I hoped I'd be part of it, and some reassuring words during the drawn Oval Test made me feel ten feet tall. By that sixth Test of the summer, I was starting to feel the physical strain, and as Goochy walked up to me at the end of one over, I mentioned that to him. He said, 'Don't worry about it, Jack. You've had a great summer, and you'll be England's keeper for the next ten years.' It was great to have a compliment like that from such a great professional, especially when he became England's next captain a few days later, and I filed that remark away in the memory bank. The new skipper rated me, and that's always a big plus when the new regime comes in.

David Gower and I were the only ones to play all six Tests in that traumatic summer, and I was voted England's Man of the Series. I was very pleased with my wicket-keeping. By my reckoning, I'd missed just one chance, a difficult inside edge off Neil Foster that I just got a finger to. I could live with that. My batting had passed a few stern examinations as well, especially in terms of my temperament. But I needed to work on my fitness, to enable me to sustain my concentration through the long days and not get tired. With the West Indies tour coming up early in 1990, it was vital that I became stronger for what is the toughest tour for any international cricketer. This is where Graham Gooch's philosophy on training was so good for me at that stage in my development. Gooch had replaced David Gower as captain after the disastrous Ashes series, and he made it clear that the old days of turning on the tap just at the start of a Test had gone. Goochy's motto was 'If you fail to prepare, prepare to fail,' and I had no problem with that. Micky Stewart was of the same mind, and we assembled at the National Sports Centre in Lilleshall for some very hard work and specialist coaching. It couldn't do us any harm to get super-fit against the best team in the world, in conditions that really sap your energy. Fatigue causes mistakes to occur more often and we couldn't afford to be found wanting physically against the West Indies. Those sessions at Lilleshall opened up new horizons for me, and I'm certain that I've got fitter and fitter as my career has progressed. As I acquired more knowledge of fitness. that undoubtedly helped me to maintain my standards. I wouldn't be playing for England all these years later if it hadn't been for the Lilleshall experience. If you're physically fit and mentally strong, you've got a chance. We had to move with the times, we were being lapped by fit sides like Australia and the West Indies. On previous tours, England players would simply turn up at the airport overweight, with the management taking them on trust that they had prepared properly. Important time was then lost on tour, getting those players fit, when that time ought to have been spent on cricket skills.

We also received valuable advice on diet at Lilleshall, particularly useful for someone like me who's never been a disciplined eater. I had found that a cheese roll and a cup of tea at lunchtime wasn't helping my stamina by mid-afternoon, and definitely not in the final session. So I was advised to alter my intake of food when playing. I started to eat snacks that contained lots of carbohydrate, and cereal and bananas for breakfast. I'd have another banana before start of play, more cereal at lunchtime, bread and strawberry jam at the tea intervals, and more bananas. A spoonful of honey in my tea seemed to help, and at times I'd just have a spoonful of honey on its own. I'd have only one main meal, in the evening, and get by on small snacks during the day, burning them off while playing. I found that gave me extra energy. People say I have odd eating habits, but it depends on what you're trying to do. All I'm looking for is the fuel to keep me going. I'm not a gourmet, I'm not the slightest bit interested in food as a source of enjoyment, just as something that will improve my chances of getting through the day's play without being fatigued. I have to confess to liking baked beans though! I'm the same weight – just over nine and a half stone – as throughout my career, and for my height, 5ft 8¼ inches, that's an acceptable weight for a keeper. So I must be doing something right.

So by the time we flew to the Caribbean at the start of 1990 we were the best-prepared England party ever. Not only were we fit and fresh, we had even managed to get in a few weeks' serious cricket, in October, when we joined the other Test countries in India for the Nehru Cup, a series of one-dayers. We played well, getting to the semi-finals, but more importantly, those long nights in hotels gave us the chance to forge an excellent team spirit that nearly helped us bring off a remarkable series win in the West Indies. I was in great spirits when we landed in the Caribbean, after a chat I'd had on the plane with our new captain. I initiated the conversation with Goochy, asking if he saw a place for me in the one-day games, as well as the Tests. I was well aware that Alec Stewart, on his first major tour, was capable of donning the gloves and doing a competent job, as indeed he had done in the semi-final of the Nehru Cup, against Pakistan. He was also a superior batsman to me, and the balance of the side might mean I would be sacrificed at times. Gooch reassured me, saying that taking catches behind the wicket in the keeper and slips cordon was a key area in winning cricket matches, and that I was central to that policy. He also said, 'I need you to help me, to give me confidence as captain. I want you to get involved, to point out things on the field I might have missed.' That was music to my ears. I was going as the number one keeper, the captain had made it clear he rated me, and that my input was important. 'You'll be England's wicket-keeper for the next ten years' he had told me at the Oval Test, and that was before he had been made captain. My morale couldn't have been higher.

We surprised a lot of sceptics on that Caribbean tour and I know we caught the opposition cold. They had reckoned without our fitness and focus early in the series. We had hammered home to our bowlers the need to concentrate on an off-stump line, to bore out their strokemakers, and it worked a treat in the first Test in Jamaica. The West Indies were complacent, and we were dedicated, bowling them out cheaply on the first day, and then putting them under pressure. We batted them out of the game, with a superb hundred from Allan Lamb and then winkled them out, with Devon Malcolm giving them a taste of their own medicine. Victory by nine wickets led to a fair amount of booze being consumed in our dressing-room, and even I found myself up on the table, dancing a victory jig, having a swig at a can of

Tetley's beer. I also managed to turn the moment of victory into one of my favourite and now famous paintings. As Wayne Larkins hit the winning run, courtesy of a misfield by Patrick Patterson, I snapped away with my camera. So, working with these, and my colour notes, I managed to re-create that moment. It was my first colour limited edition print called 'Moment of Victory', which I published myself. All 405 were signed by those England players involved in that match. I'm pleased to say the whole edition sold out rapidly and each one is a collector's item. The original hangs in my art gallery in Chipping Sodbury, and I don't think I would ever part with it. I've refused a lot of money for it, but it's too precious, too magical a moment in my life, and technically it's a very satisfying picture.

One-up in the series, and we really fancied our chances of ramming home the advantage against a West Indies side not used to being in that situation, especially at home, and resenting the accusations of complacency and lack of planning. Then the fates took a hand, giving them breathing space. The next Test, in Guyana, was rained off completely and rain took a crucial hand in the Trinidad Test, when we had the game in our grasp. We only needed 151 to win, and the atmosphere in our dressing-room before our second innings was amazingly euphoric. Just a case of batting properly and we've won here, and they won't come back in the series, they'll be too demoralised. The atmosphere was getting out of hand, though, and I called for a bit of quiet, so that our batsmen could concentrate on the job in hand. Sometimes there's a fatal tendency to relax when you've rolled over a side cheaply, and all you then have to do is your job in a competent fashion. I was worried about that. I never thought about rain getting in the way, or Graham Gooch getting a broken hand. Ezra Moseley was the bowler, a dangerous customer, because while the other guys would be pinging you around the head and chest, he'd be skidding it in at your hands and lower rib cage at deceptive speed. He hit Goochy twice on the knuckle and the second time was crucial. There was no way Gooch would bat again in the match, but we kept news of his broken hand from the press, because we knew how important Gooch's absence was to the opposition, he was the player they really rated. Yet, at lunchtime, it didn't seem as if Gooch's injury was going to rob us of a win. We only needed another eighty-odd, with nine wickets in hand and Alec Stewart was going very well. Suddenly, the rain pelted down from nowhere and it absolutely hosed it down for about an hour. When we resumed at 4.30, the playing area was very muddy and clearly the West Indies didn't want to be out there. They were taking an eternity to bowl their overs – forty minutes for three overs at one stage – but to be fair, I didn't blame them. They were calling for sawdust, having false starts with their run-ups, and taking an age to set the field, but I'm sure we would have done the same in similar circumstances. There was so much sawdust out there it looked like a sawmill, and we did well to get on.

Suddenly, after a quick clatter of wickets, I found myself out in the middle with David Capel, needing another forty, with five wickets left, but one of them was Gooch, so in effect we were six down. By now it was so dark that we couldn't see as far as our dressing-room for instructions. It's bad enough to locate their fast bowlers in normal light, but not when you can't even see your captain, who's waving at you. David and I were so frustrated at getting so close, but it was the sensible thing to come off. Graham Gooch was right to wave us in; it was very dangerous to stay out there in that light, and understandably, West Indies would have kept on their fast bowlers and made it as hard as possible for us to get the runs. So we were thwarted and I was left to reflect on missing a chance that might have seen us wrap up the Test before the rains came. On the first day, we had them 29 for five, and one more wicket would have finished them off. That's when I dropped Gus Logie. It was a difficult chance. Devon Malcolm was the bowler, and with his tendency to fire it in to the right-hander, I was going slightly legside when Logie slashed at the ball and although I dived to the offside, I couldn't quite hold it. I was annoyed at myself because Alan Knott had been on at me about improving my diving. I'd dug my heels in on this one, feeling that I didn't want to get too technical about that aspect of my keeping, and that it was best to keep it simple and natural. If I'd taken Logie, West Indies would have been 40 for six, but he ended up making 98 and they recovered to 199. Our lead on first innings was only 89 when it would have been far more if I'd caught Logie. One consolation, though; in the same innings, I took one of my best catches for England, taking Ezra Moseley, high to my right off Devon Malcolm; that was almost a carbon copy of the one I'd earlier dropped. Knotty had said to me in the past, 'If you miss one, it's how you come back that counts. You've got to concentrate on the next ball, because you might need to take a brilliant catch straight away after your mistake.' Quite right – but I wished I'd listened to Knotty about how to improve my diving.

I think that last day of the Trinidad Test was the crucial one of the series, the turning point. If we had won, there would have been no way back for them, but they drew strength from getting out of jail. Viv Richards, who had missed Trinidad because of injury, would be back for the Barbados Test, while we would be missing for the rest of the series our captain and best player, Graham Gooch.

The Barbados Test looms large in my list of disappointing matches, because of the last day, when we came so close to saving it. Another fifteen minutes would have been enough, with the light closing in, but we just couldn't do it. I was lucky enough to bat for five-and-a-half hours for a score of 55, after coming in as nightwatchman on the fourth evening, and it would have been the greatest innings of my life if we'd managed to hang on for a draw. They'd had the better of the game, no question, but as we had seen in Trinidad, that didn't mean a thing if you managed to get out of jail. Their declaration set us a target of 356 to win, which was never on, especially after we had been reduced to 15 for three on that fourth evening. I went in to bat, absolutely furious at a decision that saw Rob Bailey given out caught behind. To me, and the rest of the England players, the ball seemed to have come off his hip. Jeff Dujon, their wicket-keeper, had made a half-hearted appeal, but Viv Richards ran down the pitch, flapping his fingers, and made an impassioned appeal to the umpire. When the umpire raised his finger, we couldn't believe it. I had to be held back by Goochy as I raged at the decision; he was trying to get me to take my time going out to the middle, but I was too keen to get out there and tell them what I thought of them. As I stormed down the steps, I saw a television cameraman pointing his lens at me, and I looked straight at the camera and made some very uncomplimentary observations. It was a case of 'over my dead body' that evening, and I'd be giving everything to block it out on the final day.

By lunchtime, Alec Stewart and Allan Lamb were out, and with Nasser Hussain playing with a broken wrist, realistic hopes of a draw rested with me and Robin Smith. Robin, one of the gutsiest of players, would sell his wicket dearly and we set out to play no shots, and just grind out the overs, batting for time. I kept shouting at myself every ball, just to gee myself up. Richie Richardson and Desmond Haynes, who were fielding close in, thought it very funny. Every time I shouted, 'Come on!' Richie would echo me, and at one stage he and I burst out laughing. There was Ian Bishop, running in to bowl, trying to knock my block off, and I was trying hard to stop laughing! Bishop came round the wicket, firing the ball in short at my body, but I wouldn't budge. Malcolm Marshall was tearing his hair out at the way I was squirting him around into strange areas of the field. He never liked bowling at me, because I didn't play him in orthodox fashion, and the more he stared at me, the more I was certain we'd get to safety. Viv Richards tried a spell, to accelerate the second new ball. They bowled fifteen overs in forty-eight minutes, a sharp contrast to the final day at Trinidad, and Viv was getting very frustrated as I kept playing forward to him, trying all the tricks of the trade to slow down the over rate. Robin and I were encouraging each other constantly, and Viv was very ratty now. Viv Richards was the hardest, most intimidating cricketer I ever encountered on the field. His physical presence was awesome and disconcerting and he made you feel he wanted your neck so badly. I saw it as a compliment that we were rattling Viv so much. We made it to tea, still intact, and we felt that if we got through the blast with the second new ball, we would survive.

An hour after tea, Robin and I are still together. They take the new ball. Just weather a few more overs and we'll get there, I say to myself. Curtley Ambrose is to bowl and I've worked out that with his extra height, the new ball will bounce more, so I decide to play a little higher. With that, he surprises me with one that shoots along the ground. That was the only way they'd have got me, I promise you. I was so pumped and motivated that they would never have got me out under normal conditions. A fluke was my undoing. I dragged myself off the pitch, thinking that we still had an excellent chance of saving the game, as long as the rest of the guys rallied round Robin. But Ambrose was now irresistible, and he blew the England batting apart. He took five wickets in five overs, and we went from 166 for five to 191 all out. Poor Robin Smith, so heroic, was left 40 not out, after withstanding that barrage for almost the entire day. It was so painful. That taught me a lesson that stayed with me for the rest of my career. Never leave responsibility to others, even subconsciously. You have to take on the responsibility yourself, don't delude yourself into thinking that the task can be easily accomplished by your team-mates. I don't blame any of our lads for being brushed aside by Ambrose that day in Barbados, in fading light, and against the new ball – but if I hadn't got out, we would have saved the game. Yet I thought we'd still do it, even in the depths of my despair at being undone by a grubber. Never again. Without the experience of Barbados 1990, I would never have been mentally strong enough to help Mike Atherton save the Johannesburg Test five years later. I wasn't going to fail again when blocking out for a draw.

We flew out of Barbados that night, mentally shattered and in no state to play the decisive Test of the series two days later, in

Antigua. We tried to have some fielding practice next day, but we were too knackered. Robin Smith and I were like zombies after our efforts the day before, and with the West Indies now on a roll, we feared the worst. It seemed crazy to play such an important Test so soon after Barbados, but the crowded itinerary had to take into account the thousands of British holidaymakers who wanted to see two Tests, and the fact that we had to report back soon to our counties for the start of a new season. Predictably, we were hammered by an innings in the final Test. We had given our valiant best, giving blood right to the end, with Robin Smith breaking a finger, and Nasser still troubled with his broken wrist. So we lost the series 2–1, but 2–2 would have been a fairer reward. You had to respect and admire the West Indies for coming back to win the series after starting so badly, but we had shown guts, spirit and skill. I was so proud to be part of such a determined outfit, and under Gooch's leadership, we would have gone through the proverbial brick wall for him at that stage. The omens looked good to regain the Ashes later in the year; we would certainly be better prepared than we were in 1989.

We warmed up for Australia by winning our two home series, against New Zealand, then India. In a summer when the bat dominated, I was disappointed in a top score of 43 in six Tests, especially as I averaged 43 for Gloucestershire in county cricket, including my first two hundreds for them in the Championship. Graham Gooch showed faith in me with the bat all summer, batting me at number six in the one-day internationals and at number seven in the Tests, but I never really got going, apart from a couple of good knocks in the one-dayers. With Gooch in such amazing form all summer, there wasn't much call for major contributions down the order. Only a year earlier, he looked to be on the slide as a Test batsman, with Terry Alderman troubling him in the Ashes series, exposing some faulty footwork. But the England captaincy seemed to inspire him. He worked so hard at his game that he deserved all the plaudits going for his batting success in 1990. He became a batting legend over the next few years, and that says everything about his character and attitude to his profession. At this stage, I found him a good captain, very positive and receptive to ideas. As time went on, though, he went into his shell and he found it hard to communicate with us. If you were playing well, it was easier to deal on a satisfactory level with him, but he tended to shut you out if you weren't performing. Goochy couldn't understand why some players didn't give their all, like he did, and this was the root of his communication problems, the longer he stayed as captain.

That 1990–91 tour of Australia took a lot out of Graham Gooch as captain, and I don't think his standing was ever the same again. We played badly, losing the series 3–0. We just weren't fit enough, going to Australia a couple of weeks after the English season ended, and don't forget that we had gone straight from a draining West Indies tour into the English season. We just didn't have time to train properly before going to Australia, but we caught up when we got there. Our main problem in that area was that we got the balance wrong, having only five days off on the whole tour. I believe there was a subconscious feeling that Australia couldn't possibly be harder than the Caribbean, where we'd done so well. One or two individuals didn't put in as much as the captain expected or deserved, and when that happens, you can lose the team direction too easily, especially in a place like Australia where there are so many social distractions. Our fielding was poor, compared to the Aussies, who seemed so far ahead in their approach and attitude.

On that tour, the relationship between Gooch and David Gower deteriorated, and that didn't help team morale at all. There were faults on both sides. I don't think David gave enough to the captain. He also had a few other things on his mind, like catering for a group of punters who had come out on a tour of the wineries, and who were expecting to have David as their guide at various times. Unfortunately, we were playing so badly that Goochy insisted on extra nets – 'naughty boy nets' we called them – and David wasn't impressed. He was such a brilliant player that he felt he could be trusted in his judgement in how best to prepare for a big game, and when you consider the two lovely hundreds he made in this Test series, it's hard to argue with that. But you couldn't expect him to be allowed time away when the rest of us were practising. David felt we were too involved in cricket throughout the tour, and said so rather caustically at times, and that led to a difficult atmosphere between him and the captain and coach, Micky Stewart. On our previous tour of Australia four years earlier, Micky was on his first trip as the new coach, and the captain Mike Gatting made it clear that things would be done his way. So big-occasion players like David, like Ian Botham and Allan Lamb were given a long leash and plenty of time off, along with the rest of the squad. It worked, we played well after a bad start and retained the Ashes. Now it seemed that Micky had found a kindred spirit in Graham Gooch and he was determined to work us hard if we didn't perform well. The result was that we had just five clear days on a tour that lasted more than four months. That was crazy. We needed a break at various stages on that tour, if only to stave off the inevitable boredom that stems from netting day after day, but the management couldn't see that. Graham wrongly felt that what suited him should be the same for everyone else.

You can't expect someone like David Gower to have the same attitude to training as someone like Alec Stewart, myself or Graham Gooch. You need to be flexible, knowing that a genius like Gower can win you games if he doesn't have to go on five-mile runs and bat for two hours in the nets. David was a complex character, he needed handling with flexibility and sensitivity, but Goochy just couldn't do that, so he also lost the full support of David's great friends, Robin Smith and Allan Lamb, on that tour. Gower had been playing the game long enough to know what suited him in terms of preparation, and he should have been asked for help by the captain. Something along the lines of, 'David, I need a lot of these guys to work harder, because they'll be better players as a result. Now I know that doesn't apply to you, but if you could support me, and I'll see if I can keep you away from some of the training stuff, we could all be happy.' David got his back up because he was being treated like a junior player, rather than a recent England captain, who could still bat as well as anyone around. If Goochy's man management had been better, David would have come around, and been visibly supportive. As it was, they drew up unspoken battle lines. So it led to a negative reaction from Gower, culminating in that flypast in the Tiger Moth during a game that so angered the England management. I understand that there was talk of sending David home for that prank, but that would have been daft. It was just a laugh, and heaven knows we needed one at that stage of the tour, when we were 2–0 down in the Test series, with two to play and getting very tired. It was even funnier when we later learned that David had borrowed the money for the flight from our tour manager, Peter Lush – now that was a bit of style!

I'd been surprised that Gower hadn't been picked for the previous tour to West Indies, because he was still a marvellous player of fast bowling. It may not have worked for him in 1989 as England captain, but surely his successor must have wanted him in the Caribbean as a batsman? He was far too good a player to leave at home. It was significant that Goochy didn't take him; did he feel it was more trouble than it was worth? Would he have pushed through the Lilleshall Revolution so successfully if David had been part of it, hinting that all this training and emphasis on physical excellence was over the top? I'm not sure that Graham was ever entirely happy with David on tour once he became captain himself. David made it clear that a couple of laps of the ground and a relaxed hit for a few minutes was all the preparation he needed, and he could point to his figures as the justification. The difference between them was exemplified when we had a team meeting halfway through the tour, when it was obvious morale wasn't right and we weren't as together as we had been in the Caribbean. The captain said, 'Look, I'm a toolmaker by trade and I don't want to go back to that. I want to do my best in cricket.

To me, cricket is what I do best and I give it my total commitment. I expect that off you all.' I had great sympathy with that viewpoint, because that's the way I saw my career, but you can't expect everyone else to have exactly the same passionate desire on the surface. You have to search for the key that unlocks the personal motivation of each cricketer. In any case, team meetings only go so far. You need to deal on an individual basis. I got the impression Goochy thought every player should be handled in the same way, but that could never be right.

At the end of the tour, after we had lost ignominiously in the Perth Test, Gooch said to the press that every player on that trip had to take a long hard look at himself and ask if he could have done better, or tried harder. He questioned the motivation of some of the players, and that he ought to have had greater support. I think this was the time when the cracks started to show in his captaincy strategy. He couldn't allow himself to be proved wrong, because that's where he based his game, and it was right for him. Therefore he believed it was right for everyone else. Instead of blaming himself for not getting the best out of his team, the captain blamed his squad that he had picked. He was looking for scapegoats, instead of wondering if perhaps his strategy had been too rigid and dogmatic.

That Australian tour was a disaster in so many ways. Losing Gooch for the first Test due to a hand infection was a massive blow, because we needed a good start and he was our most reliable batsman, and our captain. At that stage, I had total respect for him, and with him in the side, I felt we could beat anyone. We were never the same unit after losing him at Trinidad, and I was worried it would be the same in Australia. But we were still poor when he came back and scored runs in the Tests. Allan Lamb replaced him as captain for the Brisbane Test, and he got himself involved in a rather needless episode when he stayed out late one night, playing the tables at a casino with Kerry Packer and Tony Greig. Unfortunately, Lamby was not out overnight, and after he was out in the first over the following morning, the news leaked out about his late night. More bad publicity, more divisions in the camp. At Melbourne, we lost by eight wickets, after going from 147 for four to 150 all out. Then at Sydney, as we failed to bowl out Australia swiftly enough on the final day, tempers frayed badly on our side. We fielded very badly, and I got very angry as we let them off the hook. Phil Tufnell, Alec Stewart and Eddie Hemmings all got narked about various things, and I can't remember in my time an England performance in the field that was so disjointed and ragged. We were bad-tempered and frustrated and I was no different. The draw meant we couldn't regain the Ashes, so now it was a case of playing for our self-respect.

I wasn't prepared for the bombshell of being dropped at Adelaide. I was keeping better than at any stage in my career. It's a great place to keep wicket because the bounce is usually reliable and I was relishing the conditions. In the previous Test, in Sydney, I had managed a legside stumping, standing up to a quick bowler, that remains one of the great moments of my career. Dean Jones was the batsman, a player who loved to move around in his crease, trying to disrupt the bowler's line, so I gambled by standing up to Gladstone Small, in the hope that Dean would be curbed. Gladstone accidentally slipped one down the legside, Dean pushed forward, missed it and I had the bails off smartly. When I saw the umpire's finger go up, I went berserk, leaping high into the air and jumping into Alec Stewart's arms at square leg. Not even Knotty had done that in a Test; at last I'd got one up on him. It was a magical moment, one that a wicket-keeper dreams about.

So when we came to Adelaide, I was concerned about my lack of runs but I had no worries about my wicket-keeping. I hadn't missed a stumping or a catch all tour. Angus Fraser's fitness complicated matters, though. He was starting to become troubled by the hip ailment that gave him so much grief for the next couple of years, and I read in the local press that if he was still struggling next day, they would bring in Phil DeFreitas as cover in case Fraser broke down. So Alec Stewart might keep wicket to accommodate the extra bowler, and ensure the tail wasn't too long. It was horrible, having to wait for the verdict next morning. As I went through my routines on the outfield, I caught sight of Gus Fraser bowling a few deliveries, and I prayed that he'd be fully fit and we wouldn't need to risk another bowler. I then went into the viewing area for a cup of tea, just waiting for the verdict. With thirty-five minutes to go before the start, and the TV cameras waiting for the captains to come out and toss the coin, Gooch came over, patted me on the knee and said, 'Sorry, mate, speak to you later.' Honestly, it was a bombshell. You can say that I must have had an inkling, but you try to think positively. I was in great form, I didn't deserve to be dropped. It was the first time I had ever been dropped from any cricket team in my life. It really hurt that the mould had been broken by England. I was numb, and sat there in a daze. It wasn't as if Alec Stewart had been pressing me hard for the gloves, because he hadn't been keeping wicket all that much, due to my fitness and excellent form. Whenever I've played subsequently at the Adelaide Oval, and I sit in the away team's dressing-room, that awful moment comes back to haunt me, when I was dropped for the first time in my life from a cricket team.

I soon snapped out of my misery and decided I'd show them what I was made of. I would be the best twelfth man any of them had ever seen. I'd do the most menial tasks for the next five days and show them nothing would break my resolve. Inside I was shattered. They'd preferred a half-fit Gus Fraser to me – didn't they rate me any more? Gooch had told me how important it was to have the best keeper alongside top-class slips, to ensure that every nick was taken. Everything in my career from 1984 onwards had been geared to being the best keeper in the world, never mind England, and now the guy who had forecast such a long career for me as England's number one had left me out. When I was on top of my game. What would happen if my form took a little dip? What guarantees would I have that they would stick by me, because they thought I was the best? As I mulled over the significance of my omission, I met up with the great Australian keeper, Rod Marsh and he was tremendously uplifting. He couldn't believe that I'd been dropped and rubbished our management in the press and on television. It was reassuring to have such enthusiastic support from such a distinguished quarter, but I had no answer to Rod when he said, 'What are they doing to our craft, Jack? Don't they understand wicket-keepers?'

At least one good thing came out of missing the Adelaide Test – I got to meet Sir Donald Bradman. I had heard that the great man was coming to the game and asked if I'd be able to thank him personally for signing a collection of limited edition prints that I had done of him a year earlier. The officials were very reluctant to grant me an audience with him, but I persisted. I was taken to an office on the ground that appeared to be locked up. Into a tiny room via a dimly lit corridor and there he was, sitting behind a huge pile of books, bats, photos – a diminutive figure in glasses. He gave me a very warm welcome – 'Ah, g'day, Jack, how are you enjoying Australia?' – and we talked for about ten minutes. He signed a few items that the lads had persuaded me to take along and it was hard to imagine that this man was over eighty years of age, because he was so switched on about the game, so shrewd in his assessments. And generous – not once did he give it 'well in my day', that you hear from so many old players. A truly great gentleman who gave me one of the most precious ten minutes of my life. And it wouldn't have happened if I'd been picked for the Test.

By the end of the Adelaide Test, I'd managed to persuade myself it was a one-off, that I would be reinstated for Perth. At the team meeting on the eve of the Test, it was announced that Alec Stewart was staying in as the keeper. Gooch took me aside later and tried, a bit unconvincingly, to explain the reasoning behind the decision. What he had to say didn't really sink in, because I was more concerned with the reality that I was out again. The next few weeks were hard for me as we went on to New Zealand for a series of one-dayers. We were all physically and mentally shot away. It was a shambolic tour, a sad contrast to the previous one in the Caribbean, where we seemed to have a common purpose and a collective desire to come out on top.

That Australian tour started a trend for me. The priorities had changed. No longer was it enough for me to focus on being the best wicket-keeper available, I had to make runs as well to challenge for a place in the side. I realised that I'd have stayed in the side even if I'd missed a few chances, but managed to score a couple of centuries. Legside stumpings off seam bowlers don't count in the equation. It was a shock to become aware that I wouldn't play that much more for England unless I started making runs. Another challenge had to be met, even though I was at the peak of my powers as a specialist.

6
BATTLING ON

Over the next few years, I had to get used to being no longer an automatic choice for England, to being on trial. From the Adelaide Test of 1991 to the end of the next Ashes series in the summer of 1993, I played in just eleven of England's twenty-four Tests, as well as missing out entirely on the 1992 World Cup. My lack of runs was the main reason for my omission, even though at times I didn't keep wicket to the standards that I demanded of myself. The vibes I picked up from being dropped at Adelaide and Perth weren't good for those who maintain that England should pick a specialist wicket-keeper. It now appeared that the keeper would get away with the odd missed chance, so long as he was scoring a lot of runs – but if he didn't bat well, mistakes behind the stumps were magnified, and his head was on the block. That view seemed to contradict the old convention that you picked your best players for the specialist positions in a Test side. A fast bowler doesn't miss out on selection because he averages eight with the bat, and an opening batsman who can do his job gets picked, even though he never bowls. Quite right, too. Yet the England wicket-keeper's role seemed to be one of shoring up the batting, and hoping he would take every chance that came his way. I'm sure that Ian Botham's decline as a great all-rounder didn't help me during this period. In his pomp, his fantastic matchwinning efforts with bat and ball meant that England could usually play a specialist keeper in Bob Taylor, who would come in at number eight, and try to nurdle a few runs with the help of the tail. Now, with England lacking an all-rounder of Botham's class, I was vulnerable.

I was very down when I came back from Australia in February 1991, because I knew that my batting had to be more consistent for England. I just couldn't get a run in Australia. When I got into the nets at Bristol, I was hopeless, I couldn't play a shot of any sort. I was in a mental hole and I asked for extra nets, enlisting the help of Gloucestershire's coach, Eddie Barlow. He stripped my batting down to its essentials, telling me just to smash the ball around. During my first net with him and the bowling machine, I was in complete disarray, getting hit everywhere, and nearly getting a broken foot. But Eddie said, 'Just get your arms moving, throw the bat at the ball, it doesn't matter if it goes in the air.' I enjoyed the feeling of release from just hitting the ball, and for the second session I was told to carry on doing that, but now the ball must be kept on the ground. That worked, and for the third session, I played properly, defending tightly and playing proper attacking shots when necessary. It worked, in just three net sessions. Eddie realised I was bottled up, frightened to play naturally, and I needed to free the spirit before reverting to basics. I started the season in great nick, scoring a hundred in a Championship match against Hampshire, when I played very fluently. I remember coming through a big staring contest with Robin Smith, as he fielded at silly point, and that really got me fired up. When I got to my century, Robin was typically sporting, the first to congratulate me, but the edge he had brought to the early part of my innings had helped me.

That innings helped get me into the one-day internationals against West Indies, but I only batted once. I was at number eight, then nine in the batting order, in contrast to six the previous summer in the one-dayers, and it seemed to me that Gooch and Micky Stewart had made up their minds about my batting potential. I didn't feel they had a great deal of confidence in me, and in all honesty, I didn't acquit myself well in the Test series, averaging just ten, going in at number seven. Not good enough. The only time I did myself justice was at Lord's, when my 46 in partnership with Robin Smith helped save the follow-on, but I should have gone to a big score, getting myself out to a daft shot off Carl Hooper. So, after four Tests, I was dropped for the Oval, and although many kind words about me were spoken and written in the media, I could see what the selectors were getting at. With Alec Stewart, the wicket-keeper, batting at number six, Ian Botham at seven and Chris Lewis at eight, the batting looked stronger than in previous Tests that summer – and that was always a key issue against any West Indies side of that period. The fact that I had almost helped save the Barbados Test just over a year ago didn't cut any ice, nor that Alec hadn't been keeping regularly for Surrey in the Championship that season. On behalf of specialist keepers, that latter point rankled – you can take being dropped in favour of another who does the job, day in, day out – but Alec kept for his county only on the rare occasion. That said, he did well at the Oval. He took some good catches, batted well in each innings, and with England winning by five wickets, you couldn't really fault the reasoning of the selectors. But now things started to get illogical. They brought me back for the final Test of the summer, at Lord's against Sri Lanka, with Alec playing as a specialist batsman. That didn't make sense to me. England desperately needed to win the Oval Test, so they gambled on Alec and dropped me. But don't we want to win all the time? So shouldn't the successful Oval formula be repeated at Lord's a fortnight later? By reinstating me, were they not so desperate to win as they were against the West Indies? Was it just a consolation prize to me, or were they tacitly admitting that Sri Lanka weren't going to be a major problem? It didn't make sense. I was confused, but there was little communication at that stage between Goochy and myself, so I just set out to do my best. We won easily enough, and I looked forward to nailing down a regular place on the winter tour to New Zealand.

It had been an ambition of mine to go back to New Zealand as

England's number one keeper, after I'd played club cricket out there between 1983–85. I had sat in the stand at Auckland, watching Bob Taylor keep with such artistry at the age of forty-two, and I vowed that I would do all I could to follow in his footsteps. So it was a great moment to play at Eden Park, and to win well. Graham Gooch played a superb knock in the circumstances, using all his experience and skill on a poor pitch, but the most significant innings for me was Allan Lamb's sixty. In his early days in the England side, 'Lamby' hadn't played with his natural freedom, letting the situation of the game and the conservative, safety-first attitude of the selectors inhibit him. He soon realised that he had to go for it, start playing his shots, otherwise he would lose his place. At Auckland, I was exhilarated by his innings, as he smashed fifty off just thirty-three balls, and just changed the complexion of the game. It takes a lot of nerve to bat that way for England, to play with freedom. I learned a lot from that innings. I thought back to my innings at Brisbane on the previous tour, when I blocked it for two hours for just sixteen in both innings. It was a difficult pitch, the ball was seaming around and swinging, but I got into a rut and bottled up all my aggression. I should have taken the bull by the horns and played my shots. That passive knock set the tone for my batting on the rest of tour, and I was still playing without confidence, more than a year later, in New Zealand. I should have looked at it in Lamby's way, and come out of my shell.

My work behind the stumps was still up to standard, though, and I like to think a smart stumping went some way to securing our victory in the first Test, at Christchurch. At tea on the final day, we still needed seven more wickets to win, and with John Wright in control, the odds were against us. But we persisted, and after the interval, Wright got stuck on 99. For five overs, he just blocked it, waiting for the single and using up valuable time. Suddenly, he had a rush of blood against Phil Tufnell and went down the pitch to him. Tuffers yorked him, in effect, and with the batsman so stranded, it must have looked like a routine stumping for me. But the ball went under his bat, I lost it for a split second, and then I had to adjust as the ball bounced up. I caught the ball up against my chest, didn't panic, and took off the bails. The floodgates were open, and we won in the most dramatic circumstances. Martin Crowe was in with the last man, and we needed a wicket in the remaining couple of minutes, otherwise the game was drawn. Crowe knew that four more runs would put New Zealand ahead, and even if they were then dismissed, the time lost for the change of innings would mean we couldn't bat again. So he gambled on hitting the four against Tufnell, but skied it and Derek Pringle took an excellent, running catch. It was a great win in the circumstances, when you consider the position we were in at tea. Without being egotistical, I do believe an alert stumping by a specialist wicket-keeper contributed to that collapse. Such moments are often forgotten when sides are picked, and the keeper's role is gauged by how many runs he can score, rather than batsmen he can dismiss through his particular skills.

I knew that moments like the stumping of Wright wouldn't be enough to get me a place in the World Cup party that was due to be announced at the end of this series. The lucky ones would be staying on for the tournament, to be held in Australia and New Zealand over the next month. I was sure I'd be flying home and I sought out Graham Gooch for confirmation of that during the Wellington Test, the night before the party was due to be announced. I couldn't be bothered waiting any longer, and Goochy was honest with me, saying that there was room for only one keeper, and it had to be Alec Stewart, because he was a better batsman. They would take a chance on the fact that Alec lacked my ability behind the stumps, but in one-day cricket, Alec's quality with the bat was decisive. The format of five bowlers, and six batters, one of whom would keep wicket, appealed to Gooch and Stewart, especially with so many in the side who could bowl capably as well. I was very disappointed, of course, and started to wonder if I would ever get to play in a World Cup. I had missed out in 1987 to Paul Downton, so now it would be India and Pakistan in 1996 if I was lucky.

I didn't have much time to mope about my exclusion, because more important matters took place on the field on the final day of that Wellington Test. With the game meandering to a draw, Syd Lawrence fractured his right kneecap just as he started to deliver the ball. It was the most horrific moment I've ever witnessed in cricket, and to this day I can still hear the sound of his kneecap cracking and his screams of agony. The noise of the fracture was just like someone banging together two cricket bats with immense force.

My first reaction when Syd went down was that he had snapped a hamstring or an Achilles tendon. In all our time together, I had never seen him show pain. Our physio, Lawrie Brown, ran on to the field, cut away the trouser leg and the sight was ghastly. His kneecap had disappeared from its normal place and had shattered in two: a small part was at the base of his thigh and the larger part had moved down to the top of his shin bone. Getting Syd off the field was the next problem, as he lay there in agony. It was left to the strongest players (Ian Botham, Graeme Hick, Robin Smith and Graham Gooch) to lift the big fellow up onto the stretcher, while the rest of us stood around in stunned silence, horrified at Syd's screaming. I went to sit at the side of the square, distraught. We had played cricket from the days of the Gloucestershire Federation Under-11s, and he had been a marvellous team-mate and companion. Syd had stuck up for me many times during my days of unpopularity at the County Ground, and no day was ever too long for him, he was hugely admired for his stout heart and support for the team. Now I could do nothing for him. He wouldn't be able to come back after this. Alec Stewart snapped me out of my misery and shouted over, 'Jack, you know him best, stay with him!' I held his hand and arm as we carried him off the field. That's when things started to get naughty. By the time we got to the gate, the media were out in force, cameras pointing. One cameraman, from New Zealand

Television, became particularly intrusive. He kept pushing the camera in Syd's face, recording all his agony, and he wouldn't go away. He parked himself in the small gateway, on the boundary edge, so he could film us as we carried the stretcher off the field. Micky Stewart pushed him out of the way, as we finally managed to get through the crowd, but he then tore up the steps, and carried on filming as we carried the stretcher to the dressing-room. That was too much for Micky, who started shouting at him, pulling at the cameraman, trying to drag him off his perch. I lost my rag as well. I was shattered at Syd's agony, frustrated at the delay in getting him through the throng, and disgusted at the insensitivity of that cameraman. So I chased him up the stand, shouting abuse at him. I felt Syd deserved some dignity during his trauma, and the resulting scenes didn't look too good on the television news that night. They showed me chasing the guy up the steps, then the camera turned away, with a shaking motion. That wasn't an accurate record of what happened. They edited the film to give the impression that I was tussling with the guy, when in fact I never got within five yards of him. They had inserted the moment when Micky had jostled him earlier. So I was accused of attacking the cameraman which wasn't true. I was all for suing the television station, but Micky had, after all, made physical contact with the cameraman, so we let it go. I was then called before our tour manager, Bob Bennett, who informed me that TVNZ wanted an apology from Micky and I. Bob said that sometimes you do things in the heat of the moment without realising, but was I sure I'd never touched him. I refused to apologise, because I had done nothing wrong in my eyes, my reaction was surely understandable. It's true the whole episode didn't look good; that wasn't our fault, the cameraman had been very provocative. I stood my ground, and Bob wasn't best pleased.

Syd's condition was far more important than a television cameraman's ego and wounded pride. When he was laid down in the dining area, he was still trying to get up, unaware how much damage had been done to his kneecap. Derek Pringle was doing his best to hold him down, and Syd just hurled him across the floor – and Derek was never the smallest of men. I can only imagine the agony Syd must have gone through before the medical staff finally gave him an anaesthetic and got to work on him. The operation that night went well, and they wired his kneecap back into place, but his career was wrenched from him, just as he was starting to make a name for himself as a genuinely fast bowler with the biggest of hearts. I have never felt so sad and anguished about anything else on a cricket field. The mental scars remain for all of us who were in that England tour party.

I knew what was expected of me when I started the 1992 season with Gloucestershire, if I wanted to get back in to the England team. Runs – and plenty of them. Well, I averaged 47 in Championship cricket, ending just short of a thousand first-class runs for the season, but I didn't hang on to my England place for the whole series against Pakistan. They were a brilliant bowling side, with Waqar Younis, Wasim Akram and Mushtaq Ahmed capable of bowling out any team cheaply, and the selectors were understandably jumpy about the need for solidity in our batting. Alec Stewart played ahead of me in the one-dayers early on, then made 190 in the first Test and a couple of fine half-centuries in the second, at Lord's. Meanwhile I couldn't get going, despite my good form for Gloucestershire. My top score in three Tests was 29 not out, and when I was off the field with a stomach upset and Stewie kept wicket on the last day at Old Trafford, the next move wasn't difficult to forecast.

With the Leeds Test due the following week, I was told on the previous Saturday morning by Graham Gooch that I'd been dropped. Of course, I was hurt but I wasn't going to crawl into a corner, feeling sorry for myself, licking my wounds. It was the weekend of the Cheltenham Festival, and with Yorkshire the opposition there was bound to be a big crowd for the Sunday League game. I wanted to make a public statement, to show I was going to fight to get my England place back – 'I'm still here', I was going to say. I talked it over with my agent, Jim Ruston, and he suggested chartering a helicopter from Bristol Airport, so I could arrive at the ground in style, making a grand entrance. Now this definitely wasn't my usual style, but I felt the need to show I wasn't going to have my tail between my legs. I knew I'd be putting myself under pressure to perform well in the game after making such a spectacular entrance. I told the lads the day before, 'Keep your eyes peeled for something special at midday tomorrow'. When I landed, my captain Tony Wright wasn't too happy, asking what I was playing at. So I had to get it right on the pitch after deliberately putting myself in the limelight. In a tight finish, we needed fourteen to win off the last over, bowled by Paul Jarvis. We won with three balls to spare, and I hit Paul for a six and two fours to see us home by three wickets. Before the final ball hit the boundary boards, I had stalked off. It was a hugely enjoyable day for me, because I'd done something uncharacteristic, while helping my team to win a tight match. I hoped the news would filter through to Goochy that I meant to be around still for a long time.

But for the time being, I was out. Alec would combine the two duties again – even though he was still an intermittent keeper for Surrey in the Championship – and that meant we could stiffen the batting for Leeds, with Graeme Hick batting at number seven. That's something I'm not sure about, it feels negative. If six batsmen couldn't do it, seven wouldn't. When we won at Leeds, mainly due to Graham Gooch's mastery, the series was squared, and there was no way the selectors would bring me back for the decider, at the Oval. Alec opened with Gooch, failed twice, and we were blown away by brilliant swing bowling, getting thrashed by ten wickets.

This was the summer when ball-tampering allegations and the intricacies of swing bowling occupied a lot of column inches in the British press, much to the disgust of the Pakistani team and their supporters, who felt the finger was being pointed unfairly at them. There was talk that their players were experts at picking the seam and altering the surface of the ball so that it would swing dramatically late, and the counter-allegation was that the English couldn't stomach being outbowled by some brilliant performers. I was too naive then to be aware of any possible ball-tampering. At no stage did I think that the ball had been tampered with, and although I played in three Tests for England during that summer, I don't recall any talk about it in our dressing-room. We were well aware that Waqar Younis and Wasim Akram were wonderful fast bowlers, and I think you've got to give them credit, rather than dealing in allegations of ball-tampering. Wasim, in particular, is the hardest bowler I've faced. In the Lord's Test of 1992, he bowled me in the second innings with an amazing delivery. It swung both ways before hitting my stumps, starting off as an outswinger, then coming in to take the leg stump. It was what we call 'the snake ball', snaking in at the last moment towards your legs. The leg stump hit their keeper on the chest, standing back. A remarkable delivery. Wasim comes in off a short run, and he's on you so quickly. You're gearing yourself to get into position early, but he still beats you for pace. A great bowler, so unusual and deceptive.

It couldn't yet be said that asking Alec Stewart to combine the task of opening the batting and keeping wicket was a success in 1992, because his classy batting appeared to be affected by the extra responsibility. For my part, I couldn't quibble at being dropped, because I knew the score about my batting – but I did feel that, on behalf of all wicket-keeping purists, the blow would have been easier to absorb had Alec been keeping regularly for his county. It just felt that the keeper's job was being undervalued, now that Gooch had decided on five bowlers and six batsmen, with the keeper in the top six. So his ideas about the need to have high standards behind the wicket that he had outlined to me two years earlier seemed to have been jettisoned.

By now, I was fully aware that I had a fight on my hands to get back as England's first-choice keeper, and I was soon to realise how big a task when I wasn't picked for the tour to India and Sri

Lanka. A month or so earlier, I had been sent a contract by the TCCB that guaranteed me payment for the winter months, as a member of the England elite, if you like. To me, that was a rather large hint that I would be going on the senior tour. Instead, I was sent on the England 'A' trip to Australia, as vice-captain. Graham Gooch phoned me to give his reasons: 'We didn't think you would want to be sat on the sidelines in India for all those weeks,' the implication being that Alec was now the first choice.

I was stunned. It hadn't occurred to me that the selectors wouldn't take the two keepers who had alternated since 1989 (especially to India) and when Goochy told me who was going as the second keeper, I was even more surprised to hear that Richard Blakey of Yorkshire was going to India instead of me. As for Goochy worrying about me sitting around on tour, that was nonsense. I couldn't stomach that. I had shown no anger or remorse when dropped in Australia, nor on my first tour to Pakistan, when I played so little cricket. If there's a chance of playing for England, you want to be on that tour, and the selectors had no right to assume I'd have a problem being second string. In the end, Blakey played in two Tests, where you need your best keeper on turning pitches. That would have been my job if Gooch had used some foresight, realising that illness could strike at any time over there, and that your first choice as wicket-keeper could easily miss out. That's exactly what happened, with Alec taking over the captaincy when Gooch became ill in Madras, and Blakey coming in as keeper. He was retained for the next Test, when Alec was no longer captain, and therefore available to take the gloves again. Confused? Me too. Poor Blakey scored just seven runs in his four Test innings, and wasn't particularly impressive behind the stumps. I felt for him, but I felt angry at being fobbed off. I would have loved to have been in India, even if it meant waiting in line behind Alec Stewart.

The media had a field day over the selection of that tour party, mainly because David Gower was also not selected. I was sorry about that, because he had proved in the home series against

Pakistan that he was still good enough. The omissions of Gower and Russell certainly stirred up some passions among English cricket supporters, even among MCC members. A group of them forced a Special General Meeting of the club, and they debated a motion of no confidence in England's selectors, with particular reference to the non-selection of David and myself. Postal votes made sure that although the motion was carried on the night, it was eventually defeated, but the strength of feeling about the issue was very surprising, and gratifying to me. I couldn't get involved at all, but it was good to know that so many supporters of English cricket were backing us. Not much of a consolation, it's true, but the resulting publicity certainly gave me some amusement and satisfaction, because I was angry at the reasons given for my omission. I still am. As for David Gower, the writing was on the wall after that. If he couldn't get in the party for a tour that was ideally suited for him, when would he? A year later, one of the great entertainers of our age had retired, frustrated at not winning back his England place. Along with many other professional cricketers, I was also frustrated at the way he had been mishandled in recent years. It was a scandal.

So I took myself off to Australia with the A-team, for a two-month tour that proved surprisingly fruitful for me. It was my first experience of management, and I found it enlightening. When the captain, Martyn Moxon broke a finger, I skippered the side in the last four games and really enjoyed the challenge, as we won three of them. My tactics weren't really up to scratch, especially when I gambled in the Northern Territory match at Alice Springs, by asking Mark Ilott to bowl six overs at the end of their innings, in the fiercest heat I ever remember for a cricket match. He did me proud, too, and we won the game. My concentration behind the stumps held up well enough under the extra demands of captaincy, and it made me less introverted about my cricket. That was a significant development for me. I had always shied away from taking on this extra responsibility, being so wrapped up in my own performances and preparation, convinced that a keeper just doesn't have the extra mental aptitude to cope with his own specialist role, as well as looking after the others in the team. To me, the wicket-keeper was the ideal player to gee up the others in the field, to keep them up to the mark, setting a high standard of keenness himself – but he was not there to take on the tactical responsibility, or demonstrate sound man-management skills.

I took on extra responsibility with Gloucestershire when I came back from that tour, agreeing to be the vice-captain. I had made it clear that my priority was to do as well as possible as a player for my county, then try to regain my Test place, so that thoughts of leadership were way down the list. But with Courtney Walsh willing to take over as captain, during a busy spell for him as an international cricketer, he deserved my support. We worked well together, trying to instil a more competitive edge to Gloucestershire's cricket and to get the guys thinking more about roles within the team unit. I was impressed by the way Courtney managed to keep up his own standards, and enjoyed talking tactical options and permutations with him. That season gave me a greater awareness of how everyone else in the side sees a match, and how they need to be encouraged to give their views, and dare to be different. My form held up as well, averaging almost 36 in the Championship and with the greatest number of dismissals among keepers in the season.

It was not enough to impress the selectors, though. Alec Stewart remained in possession throughout the summer. I had wondered if the disastrous tour to India and Sri Lanka might have led to a revamp, but although Graham Gooch resigned after four Tests, the new captain, Mike Atherton didn't disturb the strategy, and I stayed out in the cold. It really hit me on the first morning of the Lord's Test, as I sat watching England go out to field. For me, there's no greater sporting contest than England versus Australia at Lord's, and it hurt not to be part of it. Four years earlier, I had saved my England career by batting with guts on that first day, but now I was an onlooker. If hard work and pride in performance counted for anything, I'd be pressing hard for a recall. With England again having a shocking series against Australia, the knives were out in the media, and although I was often given the chance to air my views on the current set-up, I stayed out of it. I hated us losing so often to Australia, especially when I honestly believed they weren't that superior to us individually. They're so hard-nosed and macho out on the field that they make you really want to stuff them, and I was rooting for England as much as anyone throughout that 1993 series, saddened that so many cynics were having a laugh at our expense. The rehabilitation of the national side under a new young captain was far more important than the revival of Jack Russell's international career, but at least my selection for the winter tour to the West Indies gave me hope that the two would run in tandem. At least I hadn't been forgotten, and there were none of the daft assumptions made on my behalf a year earlier.

During this difficult, frustrating period, my painting was a great consolation to me. I could lose myself on days off and switch off from cricket. On the day when Graham Gooch phoned me to say I wasn't going to India, I immediately took my canvas and brushes into the Gloucestershire countryside, and immersed myself in the challenge of reproducing nature's glorious treasures. It was the best way I knew to work things out of my system. My painting also brought me into contact with a group of legends that truly helped me get things into perspective. I painted a picture that commemorated the attack on the French port of St Nazaire that helped change the course of the Second World War in our favour. In researching the story of the daring attack, I was moved by the extraordinary bravery and idealism of these men, who fully expected to lay down their lives for our country. Lord Mountbatten had said the reason the raid was impossible made it possible, so he managed, as Head of Combined Operations, to carry the argument about the need for a raid. What they did, and the way they dedicated themselves to the task, helped me get my own cricket career into some sort of perspective. As a boy, I had always been fascinated by military history, and I used to paint soldiers, make tanks and planes, imagining I was a soldier as I played at home. When I met with the St Nazaire Society to discuss painting something that would do justice to the operation, I asked my agent, Jim Ruston if he could help me with the research. It was Jim's idea to do the painting, because his brother was one of the commandos involved in the raid. Roy Ruston had been an inspiration in the raid and Jim had a book, detailing just what went on. I'm not a big reader normally, but I read this book in one sitting, and I was deeply affected by the heroism involved. I had waited a long time to paint a military scene, and it was music to my ears when a delegation from the St Nazaire Society met me in London and told me that my colour sketch was accurate, apart from a couple of minor amendments. Jim and I had already gone down to Falmouth to see some of the survivors and the memorial to the raid. They had left for St Nazaire from Falmouth, and this was my first Remembrance Day Parade. It was very moving for me to walk with them to the memorial and I was determined to do justice to their heroism.

'Operation Chariot' was designed to scupper the only dry dock on the Atlantic seaboard that was capable of holding the German battleship *Tirpitz*. It was learned through intelligence sources that the battleship was preparing to leave her secure dock in Norwegian waters for the Atlantic. If that dry dock in Normandy could be put out of action, the *Tirpitz* would not risk entering the Atlantic to threaten allied supply ships from the States, for fear of having no safe dock in the vicinity. Leading the attack was HMS *Campbeltown*, a British destroyer carrying five tons of high explosive in her bow, which would be detonated by delayed action fuse after ramming the dock gates. Fourteen light-service craft would follow in, carrying commandos, who would then inflict as much damage on the dock and the U-boats as they could.

The mission was a success, with the dock gate at the Bassin St Nazaire wrecked and the dock installations destroyed. At that time, it was one of the most heavily defended places in Europe, but it was damaged so badly that the *Tirpitz* never came out of hiding for the rest of the War, and consequently a greater number of allied supplies got through. 'Operation Chariot' has since been hailed as the greatest allied raid of the Second World War. It was made by just 622 soldiers and sailors; of that number, 169 were killed and 200 taken prisoner, many of them wounded. Of the 70 commandos who went ashore, only a dozen made it back. For all those who took part in the St Nazaire raid it was basically a suicide mission, but they understood how vital it was and that the likely loss of life was less important than the success of the operation. During my research, I met Captain Micky Burn MC, who still had in his possession a letter from his unit. It was from Lance Sergeant Bill Gibson to his father:

My dearest Dad,

By the time you get this, I shall be one of the many who have sacrificed their unimportant lives for what little ideals we may have. My own ideals I can thank you for. It is unnecessary for me to say how sorry I am, at not being able to do a lot of things I've longed to do in order to pay you back for the chance you gave me. At a time like this, I turn to you, Dad, and God – I hope there will be peace for everyone soon.

Bill Gibson was killed in the raid. It was a humbling experience reading that letter, and my limited vocabulary cannot for a moment express how much I admire those brave men. St Nazaire produced more awards for a single action by British servicemen than any other this century, including five VCs and many other bravery awards. Meeting some of the survivors of that raid remains one of the greatest experiences of my life. As I showed them my exploratory sketches, and asked naive questions about their involvement in the raid, I was struck by their humility. Whenever I pressed any of them on just what they had to do, they would wave it away. They would never say, 'I did this' or 'I did that'. They always gave the credit to someone else. None of them would take any credit for their part in the St Nazaire raid, but they didn't fool me. It was an honour to meet them, to marvel at their selflessness. After weeks of research, I finally decided on the moment I wanted to capture on canvas. It's when the flotilla was caught for the first time by enemy searchlights. I thought that must have been a very dramatic moment. After I'd finished the work I was very proud when one of the veterans said to me, 'You can feel the heartbeat.' That meant an enormous amount to me. These brave men had made me realise how futile it was to be obsessional about dropping a cricket ball, or missing out on an England tour. I used to get too uptight about my cricket, too absorbed in my pursuit for perfection. For the rest of my career, I'd try to get my head around my game, still hurting if I kept wicket badly, or if my team lost, but all the time telling myself it was no longer the end of the world.

Each year, the St Nazaire Society meets for a reunion dinner and service of remembrance and sadly the list of survivors is dwindling. I'll never forget the honour of meeting them, and marvelling at their integrity and understated heroism. Whenever I play in a home Test, I wear my St Nazaire tie with pride to the pre-match dinner. Lest we forget. I certainly won't. It was a milestone in my painting career when the Imperial War Museum's officials agreed to host the launch of my painting there, and when they asked if I would hang it in the museum for a year or two, I was ecstatic, deeply honoured. We printed a limited edition and I got six of the veterans to sign all 850 copies. I had another highly emotional day in the company of the St Nazaire veterans when I travelled with them to France to present the framed print to the Mayor of St Nazaire. We got to the ceremony by the skin of our teeth, just before the Society's patron, the Duke of Edinburgh, was due on stage to present the print. We had been held up by red tape outside the building, but Jim and I bluffed our way through and we made it by just thirty seconds. The night before, standing on the deck of the present-day HMS *Campbeltown* at a reception, I felt a tingle similar to when I first walked out at Lord's in an England sweater. The band of the Royal Marines played 'Land of Hope and Glory', and it made the hairs stand up on the back of my neck. It was a privilege to be among such men, and the reception they received next day from the locals made me very proud to be associated with them.

At a later St Nazaire reunion, I listened to a speech by the current captain of HMS *Campbeltown,* in which one particular phrase stood out: 'After the daring achievements of our brave soldiers and sailors at St Nazaire in 1942, anything in life is possible.' Those words will stay with me forever.

In fact, my involvement with the St Nazaire Society was beneficial in all areas. At the launch of the painting in London, I met the director of the Lord's Taverners, Patrick Shervington and Leo Cooper, husband of the writer, Jilly and a military publisher himself. Patrick was still commanding officer of the London regiment of the Royal Fusiliers, whose headquarters are in the Tower of London. He asked me to paint the Remembrance Sunday scene at the memorial in Holborn, which honours the Fusiliers killed in the two World Wars. When he told me that it would hang in the Fusiliers' Museum in the Tower of London, I nearly fainted. Leo Cooper then chipped in with an exciting suggestion – why not paint a tribute to the Cockleshell Heroes, with the fiftieth anniversary due in a few months? Leo said he could put me in touch with the sole survivor, Bill Sparks DSM, whose story he was about to publish. What luck! Meeting Bill and hearing the details of another remarkable day of bravery was just overwhelming, and when I was told the painting would hang in the Imperial War Museum, I was bowled over. Encounters like that made me realise my good fortune as embryo artist as well as England cricketer.

I lost confidence early in the Caribbean tour and never regained my touch behind the stumps. The wickets out there were up and down – I could never be sure whether the ball was going to rear up and hit me on the chest, or scuttle along the ground. I thought about wearing a chest pad, because I needed to stand so close to the stumps in case a nick didn't carry. I was uncertain a lot of the time. The timing of movements stood up to the stumps have to be precise to give a keeper the best chance on these difficult wickets – the kind of technical things a wicket-keeper does without thinking when everything's going well, but sometimes hard to regain when you're out of form. I wasn't happy about my form in the Guyana Test, and I struggled to regain it for the rest of the trip. We lost by an innings and plenty to go two down in the series, and that was bad enough. From my personal standpoint, it was the lowest point of my career. I missed stumping both Jimmy Adams and Brian Lara. With a total of twenty runs in my two innings, I didn't exactly redeem myself with the bat either. Neither of those two stumping chances were easy, but I don't think I was being hard on myself by being so depressed at my mistakes. The foundation of my argument in favour of picking a specialist keeper is that he's the one who can get out the best opposition batsman with a flash of class, rather than the batsman who keeps adequately enough but would get nowhere near the half chance. So here was I, giving lives to Lara and Adams, the main reasons for the West Indies first innings lead of 234, and then they could pressurise us when we batted again. Which is exactly what happened. I've played those two chances over and over in my mind, and I should have got them. The Adams one would have been a huge boost for my morale – he ran down the pitch when on 96 to Graeme Hick, played over the ball, and the off-break didn't turn, it went straight on, I was slightly out of position and the ball hit me on the shin. It wasn't easy, but at my best I would have taken it. I missed Lara because I hadn't realised how much of a rip Mark Ramprakash gave his off-breaks. I hadn't kept all that much to him on tour; in fact, he got through just twenty overs in the series. On this occasion he bowled one around middle and leg, and Lara shaped to play it through midwicket, with me moving a shade towards legside. But it turned a lot, ripped across the batsman, and with Lara's back foot in the air for an instant, I ought to have had him. But I got caught slightly. going legside, and I was in a bad position. So I only got a glove on the ball and the chance was lost. Lara scored another eighty runs after that escape.

They were the first chances I had missed standing up in 33 Tests. What really annoyed me was that I had confided that information to Nasser Hussain over a chat during the one-day internationals. I wasn't bragging about it, just exchanging methods of self-motivation with a batsman, how I strive to keep up my standards by recalling ways in which I had performed well. Nasser was impressed and took to calling me 'genius', which was all very well if you had seen Alan Knott, rather than Jack Russell, but still gratifying. Lesson number one in sport – keep your trap shut, if you're at all inclined to tempt fate. During that Guyana Test, I didn't go out of my room on the rest day, I just didn't want to see anybody. Geoffrey Boycott was in our hotel and he had been taking the mickey out of me the night before, telling me to get some bigger gloves and subtle advice like that. I get on well with Geoffrey usually, he talks a lot of sense, but I couldn't take his style of humour at that time. We all know how down Geoffrey used to get when he wasn't doing himself justice as an England batsman and he could have been a little more sympathetic towards me, I suppose. But it was my fault, there was no point in looking for excuses, even though Alan Knott did his best for me in a very supportive phone call. I was inconsolable, I felt I'd let the team down badly. I was so depressed I didn't even think about painting. I missed Aileen and the kids, felt homesick for the Gloucestershire countryside, and tried telling myself that at least I was on an England tour as the number one keeper, compared to a year earlier. I thought of one of my heroes, Winston Churchill, and the fact that he couldn't have a hotel room high up, because that used to bring on bouts of depression. So was I turning into some sort of depressive? Perhaps I'd always been that way inclined. I remembered Tony Hancock's suicide note that contained the desperate phrase – 'Things seemed to go wrong too many times' – and I wondered if that could apply to someone's cricket career. It occurred to me that a recent book had been published, dealing with cricket suicides, and just for a split second I wondered if I might be another candidate. My balcony at the Pegasus Hotel was five storeys up, and it would have been dead easy just to slip over the side. That's how low I was – I was thinking the unthinkable. I couldn't have done it even if I wanted to, because my wife, family and Mum were far too important to me, but I was so down that I entertained for an instant the thought of what it would be like. It would certainly end my misery. My errors had obviously been magnified via the television cameras and press photographs, and the various experts would have chewed the cud over my cock-ups and come to the conclusion that I was past it. At thirty years of age. Perhaps that was so. I'd never been through such a painful time of self-examination. I'd had to take a hard look at my batting on occasions, but never my wicket-keeping. It had always just been there, something I had managed more or less naturally. I sat looking at the four walls of my room on that rest day, convinced that my reputation had disappeared through the floor in the eyes of all cricket-lovers. It was as if someone was sticking a commando knife in my ribs, twisting the knife, while whispering 'Lara! Lara!'

I appreciate all this must sound ridiculously melodramatic and reading it now, it certainly does to me. It's not as if I hadn't started to get more relaxed about my cricket over the previous year, particularly after meeting those great men from the St Nazaire Society who had been such an inspiration to me. Their example had helped reduce my obsessiveness about my cricket, and I no longer took the game home with me after a difficult day. The vice-captaincy of England 'A' out in Australia had also helped me look at cricket and life in a more rounded perspective. But I still felt pain if I let myself and my team down by errors that I normally wouldn't have made. If I hadn't felt distraught at missing those two stumpings, I shouldn't have been an England player; you owe it to your team-mates and your country to give everything to the cause. After losing by an innings at Georgetown, I sat in the dressing-room with the rest of the lads, and felt all their eyes were on me. It wasn't enough for some of them to say kindly, 'We never expect you to miss one', and for Mike Atherton to tell me not to worry, because a keeper is bound to miss a chance now and again – the fact is that I'd contributed a great deal to our defeat by not doing my job.

A few days later, the rest of the team joined me at rock bottom, when we lost the Trinidad Test after being bowled out for 46 in our second innings. Ambrose was our destroyer again – eleven wickets in the match. It always seemed to be Ambrose. We should have won this one. We had chiselled out a lead of 76, and I was pleased to have been partly responsible for that, adding 82 with Graham Thorpe. With half their side out cheaply in the second innings, we were one dismissal away from having a small total to chase, but then Graeme Hick dropped Chanderpaul twice when he was on 4 and 29. He went on to make fifty, anchoring the tail-enders' recovery and we were set 193 to win, very attainable, but seventy more than it should have been. Poor 'Hicky', after my mistakes in Guyana I knew exactly how he must have been feeling. By his standards, those two chances at slip ought to have been snaffled, yet they went straight in and out. The longer that Chanderpaul stayed in, the more frustrated we became. On that fourth evening, we needed to get through the fifteen overs to be bowled relatively unscathed, so that we could set out our stall on the final day, with a target of only 193 making us slight favourites, on a pitch that had eased after the first day. At the close we were 40 for eight, and Ambrose had taken six wickets.

Losing Mike Atherton first ball was a huge blow and we never recovered. Ambrose was simply awesome, roaring in, with perfect rhythm. I went in at 27 for six, telling myself that whatever happened, I would be there at the close. It would be Barbados 1990 all over again. Subconsciously I was relishing the situation – it was do or die, in the trenches, the chance to be a hero. Well, I wasn't. A ball from Ambrose was fended off my nose and I feigned injury to my hand to waste time. As the spray was used by our physio, I saw some of the West Indian fielders grinning at me; they knew I'd give everything I had to survive, but they seemed so relaxed. Can't say I blame them: next ball I was out, caught at slip. I tried to get out of the way of another lifter, decided to play it at the last moment, and then just nibbled at it. That must have looked an abject dismissal, in keeping with our batting that night, and I was very annoyed at myself.

We were all out for 46 next morning, humiliated in a match we should have won. I can see those pictures now – as we stood outside the pavilion, during the awards ceremonies, with our heads bowed, like captured prisoners being paraded in the streets. Now we couldn't even level the series, and yet we really thought we had a good chance a few weeks earlier. West Indies with no Malcolm Marshall, no Viv Richards, Gordon Greenidge or Jeffrey Dujon – all retired – and their team in transition. It was such a blow to be 3–0 down, with only self-respect to play for, and the memory of that second innings in Trinidad there to haunt us for the rest of the tour. We were sure we would be crucified by the media, and by our supporters back home, and the dressing-room was very sombre. Keith Fletcher, our coach, looked completely shot away that morning. I don't think he ever recovered from that humiliation for the next year in the job before he was sacked. I was as shattered as the rest of the guys, but in a strange way, it was less galling for me than in Georgetown, because I'd felt responsible there for missing those two stumpings. Here, we were collectively responsible, and I didn't feel isolated.

I have to say I felt for Mike Atherton. This was the touring party he had wanted, trusting in young players, expecting them to fight the West Indies on the field until they dropped. He had stuck out for us, and we had let him down humiliatingly. He must have been in total mental agony, but he didn't buckle and set to work lifting us.

Things got worse before they got better. In our next match, in Grenada, we were hammered by the Board X1, containing a collection of young hopefuls. In the second innings, we were 140 for one, then all out for 165. Rock bottom. I felt the writing was on the wall for me as well. Keith Fletcher told me I needed a rest, that I should go away and do some painting for a few days as relaxation, but I wanted to play in Grenada. I told him I needed to work on my wicket-keeping, that I still didn't feel at my best, but he said that they wanted to try another bowler, so Alec Stewart would keep wicket. Here we go again. The team's not playing well, so I get sacrificed. What about the others? Fletcher was no use at all to me during this dreadful period of the tour. I tried to talk to him about my worries, but eye contact was in short supply, and I felt he was preparing me for being dropped for the next Test, in Barbados. At a time when, along with the others, I needed encouragement, Fletcher was found wanting. He seemed more concerned about me doing some painting than getting in some vital rehabilitation on the cricket field. Sadly, that summed up my relationship with Keith Fletcher. We were never on the same wavelength.

On the eve of the Barbados Test, I was on tenterhooks, wondering if I was to be sacrificed, after the ignominy of Trinidad. At the team meeting, Atherton read out the squad and I was mightily relieved when I heard my name. With so many English supporters flooding into Barbados, we owed them a gutsy performance, as well as needing to bolster our own professional self-respect. The captain got us in exactly the right frame of mind in our team meeting. I was watching him very carefully, to see if his private anger and disappointment would be on show publicly, but he did very well. He said we had to go out and enjoy it, give our supporters something to cheer about. Forget Trinidad – nothing could be done about that now, this was a new beginning. We had nothing to lose now, because we had been rubbished by many, so why not just prove them wrong? He didn't flounder at all, he was very articulate, and went on just long enough. I could see in the eyes of the lads that Athers had struck exactly the right note, and the enthusiastic vocal support when he finished was a great tribute to the positive approach he had brought into that meeting. I left it, convinced we would do well.

Atherton led from the front on the first day, putting on 171 for the first wicket with Alec Stewart, in his best 'over my dead body' fashion. That was a tremendous partnership, because West Indies had put us in, hoping we would still be demoralised and that we'd be whistled out on a fast, bouncy wicket. After that first day, we pressurised them, with Stewie's two centuries an absolutely brilliant effort. The situation was made for him, and his positive attitude inspired the team. West Indies batsmen lacked patience against the persistence of Gus Fraser and they kept getting themselves out. I missed another stumping chance to get Brian Lara, with the ball from Phil Tufnell going between bat and pad, hitting a crack and skidding through, and as long as he was there, we couldn't relax. But Tufnell got him with a fine, running catch on the final morning and soon we were home. It was a fantastic effort to come back so strongly after Trinidad to win by 208 runs, and the presence of all those swirling, waving Union Jacks only added further to the occasion. I always get very emotional when I hear 'God Save the Queen' and the flags and the enthusiasm from our noisy supporters made it an unforgettable experience. Our players had at last shown our true capabilities, and performed superbly under pressure, with the prospect looming of yet another 5–0 series defeat by the West Indies, the third in a decade. That we stopped the rot was a major tribute to Mike Atherton's motivational powers and his ability to lead by example in the toughest of circumstances.

At the start of the Caribbean tour, Athers had given every one of the touring party a watch, containing the inscription 'Don't let the buggers get you down. Michael', and his mental toughness was never better than during those difficult weeks out there. He showed his steel again in the final Test in Antigua. when we could have folded after fielding for two and a half days at the end of a gruelling tour. Brian Lara broke the world record with his 375 and we were pretty tired after conceding a score of 593 for five declared. At 70 for two, our innings was in the balance, but the captain wouldn't give in, and both he and Robin Smith went on to get hundreds to steer us towards respectability and an honourable draw. I thought it was a staunch effort to hang on in there after being put to the sword by Lara, and Atherton's personal example was fantastic. Only Lara scored more runs than him in the series, and he was now a batsman of great authority, ideally suited to the toughness of Test cricket. The way the West Indies fast bowlers tried to work him over in the first Test, and didn't try again, just demonstrated his mettle. They recognised a tough cookie. I had great admiration for the way Athers led from the front, instilling extra determination into us by toughing it out at the crease. Whatever the subsequent reservations expressed about Mike Atherton as a tactical captain, no player on that tour of the West Indies will forget the lead he gave us. He made you want to go through barbed wire and brick walls for him.

In that Antigua innings, there was little that Atherton or any of his bowlers could do about Lara, who never played a false shot in his entire knock. That guy has so much time to spare he could be sipping a cup of tea between delivery of the ball and the stroke. He has a magnificent eye, an amazingly high backlift and remarkable speed in bringing down the bat. I haven't stood behind a better batsman. What sticks in my mind about his 375 was that he was nearly out when playing the shot that took him past Sir Gary Sobers' record of 365 not out. I had the best view in the house as he swivelled and pulled Chris Lewis to the boundary. He touched the bail at the moment of playing the shot, and I stared at the bail, willing it to fall off. It was tantalisingly close, but it stayed on. I wonder what would have happened if that bail had fallen off? Dominic Cork got away with it in the Old Trafford

Test of 1995 against the West Indies, and would the umpires have had the bottle to deny Lara the world record and rightly give him out? I would have left them in no doubt what had happened. By then, I was sick of the sight of him and wanted him out. There was also some bad feeling between us after an incident in the previous Test in Barbados. I had appealed for a bat-pad catch, and he turned round and stared at me. I shouted, 'What are you looking at?' and he didn't take kindly to that. Throughout his innings in Antigua, we didn't say a word to each other, and although I clapped him when he got the record, I didn't shake his hand. I was asked why when I got home, by my Gloucestershire team-mate Paul Romaines, and I said it was because he'd made our lives a misery by staying in so long. That sounds churlish now, I agree, and it was a privilege to be so close to a genius at work, but at the time I was hot, frustrated and fed up and he was the opposition, who I don't care much about when I'm on the field. I know there was an air of inevitability about it all once he got past three hundred, but we were still trying our hardest to get him out, until the moment I caught him off Andy Caddick. At least Brian Lara can content himself with the fact that there were no cheap runs on offer in that historic innings, even if the wicket was flat. I admired what he did, but I wish it hadn't been against England.

Perhaps my churlish mood had something to do with my conviction that I was playing my last Test. For me the writing had been on the wall for a week or so, since Raymond Illingworth had been chosen as the new chairman of selectors, with wider powers than previous chairmen. So when Raymond started to make it clear in a series of interviews that he wasn't too impressed with our performances on this tour, and that changes would need to be made, it didn't take a genius to grasp that the captain would not have the decisive say in future in team selection. I knew that Raymond was a big fan of Steve Rhodes, a fellow Yorkshireman, who grew up in the same tough Bradford League as the new chairman. So when I walked out to bat in Antigua, I set myself to get a hundred, because it might have been the last time I batted for my country. I mentioned this to Alec Stewart and he told me I was daft, but I felt the skids were under me. I hadn't kept well on this tour, and I knew that I needed to score fifty in every Test to survive, if my keeping was below par. So when I was out for 62 in Antigua, I was disappointed. I wanted a hundred, it was there for the taking on a flat pitch and I wondered if an England career that had begun with 94 at Lord's had ended with me missing the boat on a century again.

I didn't have to wait too long to know my fate. Within a couple of weeks of getting back home, Raymond Illingworth gave an interview to BBC television's *Grandstand* which sealed my fate. He talked about the areas of our game that needed improvement, and up on the screen came a couple of my missed chances in the West Indies, and he discussed me in terms that were less than glowing. I knew I would be out in the cold. Mike Atherton rang up a few weeks later, and told me the chairman had chosen Steve Rhodes for the Tests, as well as the one-dayers. I could tell Athers was down about having to break the news to me, especially as it appeared that Illingworth was now getting his way in selection matters, so the captain had his own worries. I appreciated his call, and told him so, wishing him all the best, and that I would be rooting for him and the lads. That was true, and heartfelt, and has been the case every time I've been dropped by England. When I played for Gloucestershire that season, I put a brave face on it, but inside it was killing me. Everyone at Bristol was very kind and supportive, but I only had myself to blame.

Steve Rhodes did very well for England that summer. He batted well, helping to save the Lord's Test, and ended the season with Atherton hailing him as England's player of the summer. So he was going to Australia as England's number one keeper, with Alec Stewart as number two, and me not in the party. Of course, I was very down about it, but good luck to Steve. He had served his time, having been on four 'A' tours, as well as missing out on the aborted tour to India, as my deputy, in 1988. He had timed his bid for the senior side well, getting a hundred against the New

Zealanders early in May, with Illingworth looking on. I've always got on well with Steve (by and large we keepers are like that), and there was no animosity at all on my part towards him. As for me, I just had to knuckle down. I needed distractions, and they came in the form of my benefit year, which was marvellously supported by Gloucestershire folk, master-minded by my car sponsor and benefit chairman, Steve Patch. A year earlier I'd opened the Jack Russell Art Gallery in Chipping Sodbury, not far from Bristol, and was negotiating for larger premises with a view to expanding. The mental demands of getting that up and running helped to take my mind off my international disappointments to an extent. I was building professionally for the future, and getting pleasure out of those new challenges, rather than moping around. Cricket was still the number one priority, but there had to be more to life than bending up and down, catching cricket balls. At times during that period in the England wilderness, I'd make myself snap out of my gloomy mood by putting on a video of the First World War, and look at what those guys had to do in the trenches. After a while, I stopped feeling sorry for myself.

By August, with Steve Rhodes doing so well, I knew I'd miss out on the tour to Australia, because Alec Stewart would fill in for Steve out there if necessary. So what would I do in the winter? If someone had told that I'd be flown out to Australia just after Christmas, and then spend the next 42 days trying to get a net, never mind a game, I would have suggested they lay down in a darkened room. But that's what happened. I managed to get three nets in all that period, but, apart from fielding as a substitute, never got on the field. This despite Steve Rhodes struggling for form on the tour, both with the bat and with the gloves on. I ended up very disillusioned with the inflexibility of the England management in their refusal to give me a chance to stake my claim for the last couple of Tests. It wasn't as if we were doing all that impressively as a unit, yet they seemed reluctant to change their minds about Steve, when his confidence was clearly draining away from him. I got the impression that Illingworth was still flexing his muscles over that one. He had pushed for Steve, and he was staying in. So I kicked my heels for six weeks.

I had been asked if I wanted to go with the A-team to India, but I honestly didn't see the point in that, at this stage of my career. Far better to take two young specialist keepers to gain experience in a country where keeping wicket to the spinners is such an important factor. They made the right decision eventually, taking Keith Piper and Paul Nixon. I was placed on standby for the Australian tour instead, which meant I did all the training work at Lilleshall, and then wished the boys luck. I was contracted to keep fit, and that was no problem, but I didn't want to wish my time away, hoping for the call to come from Australia. I threw myself into the gallery, enjoyed being at home with my family, yet kept wondering if I would get the gloves out at any stage that winter. Just after Christmas, I got the call. Alec Stewart picked up a hand injury in the Melbourne Test, and so the standby was on his way. There was one slight problem, though. I had no visa. With all the appropriate offices closed over Christmas, the TCCB had been unable to get the necessary paperwork organised, so I flew out without a visa. I was told there wouldn't be a problem about it when I arrived at Sydney Airport – but there was. Customs officials interrogated me in an office for an hour, and all the time my kit was going around the luggage carousel, and with no one there to claim it for me and cut through the red tape. Eventually, they gave me a six-week holiday visa to get me through, with instructions to get a proper working visa pronto, otherwise I wouldn't have been allowed on the field. I was met at the hotel by our manager, M J K Smith, who told me there was nothing to worry about. Oh yes there was. I love Mike Smith to bits, he's a great guy to talk to about cricket, but his strong point isn't sorting out the adminstration, and I was led a merry dance for the next few days about this visa. I spent two days down at the visa office, trying to get a work permit, baffled why Mike Smith and his Aussie counterparts couldn't make things happen for me. If Steve Rhodes had broken a finger during that time, I would not have been allowed to represent England because I didn't have the proper documentation. Instead of being at the ground, getting acclimatised to the conditions, I was sitting in the visa office, waiting to hear my name being called.

That particular shambles was mirrored in our cricket on that tour. We were a joke to the Aussies. They couldn't believe how badly some of our guys fielded, they loved it when we were blown away twice by the young kids from the Australian Academy, and the selection of Graham Gooch and Mike Gatting backfired, as they struggled in the field and failed to get many runs. It's good having older, senior players in any team, but to warrant a place they must play well all the time. John Crawley, a batsman for the future, was sacrificed for them, and that wasn't a good idea. There were so many illogicalities. Angus Fraser hadn't been originally selected, much to Mike Atherton's displeasure, and yet when he was drafted into the team because he was in Sydney, playing grade cricket, that meant Joey Benjamin, an original selection for the tour, was passed over. Players were coming and going on the tour like ships passing in the night, and I could never get near a net. As soon as I met up with the squad in Sydney, they looked shot away. They were already 2–0 down in the Test series, with three to play, and Atherton was having trouble rallying the troops. Graham Gooch, who had to be persuaded by Atherton to make the trip, had withdrawn into his shell because he wasn't making enough runs. Sadly, Keith Fletcher, the coach, didn't inspire me at team meetings and at times I felt for him because he didn't always get the message across. Although I know he has an extensive cricket brain with lots of experience, it didn't have the desired effect. Meanwhile Illingworth had flown over from his Spanish holiday home for a couple of weeks, gave the press a few quotes, underlining that he was in charge, but it was Atherton's fault if we failed – and then flew back. The management showed great tact by rooming me with Steve Rhodes as soon as I arrived, which must have made Steve feel really chuffed! There he was, having a rough tour, with his confidence seeping away, and I turn up, full of beans and bounce, dying to get involved. Steve wouldn't have been human if he hadn't wondered whether I had been flown out to replace him as well as Stewie. It was very unfair on Steve to have to share a room with me.

We were wandering around like zombies when I joined the squad, as the injuries piled up and form proved elusive. By the time we got to Bendigo, on the eve of the fourth Test at Adelaide, it was time for me to find out where I stood. Did I have any prospect of getting a game at any stage on this tour? I asked Mike Atherton about the position, and he was ill at ease with me, not his usual strong-minded self. He said the priority was to get Steve Rhodes back on track, and he had to play at Bendigo. I just had the feeling that Athers was following the dictates laid down by Illingworth before he left a week or so earlier, and that perhaps explained why he was uncharacteristically diffident with me when I broached the subject of getting a game. He had been very pleased to see me when I flew out to Sydney, leaving me a note in my hotel room as a welcome, and making it clear when we first met that I was very much part of the squad. Yet here, in Bendigo, he was struggling to justify his position, as if he was aware that what I was requesting was perfectly reasonable. I asked to see him again after the Perth Test, which was another shambles, leaving us 3–1 losers in the series. I hadn't missed a chance on the previous trip to Australian nor on the 'A' tour, and one of the reasons is that it's a terrific place to keep wicket, with the clear light and even bounce. Poor Steve Rhodes had dropped quite a few catches on this trip, hadn't made any runs and yet had played in all five Tests. I told Athers that I had deserved to be dropped after the West Indies tour, but where was the consistency now? I wasn't having a go at Steve Rhodes at all, there was no aim to kick a man when he's down – I simply wanted to know the ground rules for next summer, against the West Indies.

Athers told me what he wanted from his wicket-keeper. He said he wanted him to be aggressive, bouncy and noisy, to be a general pain in the backside of the opposition batsmen, and be the focal point in the field, dictating attitude and aggression. Getting runs in whatever style suited was also desirable, and on that basis Steve Rhodes had done all he had wanted when first picked. I never got to the bottom of why I didn't get a single game on that Australian tour, but Atherton had given me a valuable signpost to the way I could get back into contention. From now on, I would bat in my own unorthodox fashion, to hell with the purists, and I would impose myself on the opposition batsmen. If Athers wanted noise, he'd get noise – starting with the county game involving the England captain, the first time he played against me, the following summer. That's how I got back into the England team.

8
UP FROM THE CANVAS

I had started 1995 kicking my heels in Sydney, wondering if I'd ever get a game again for England, or even some batting practice in the nets. That year ended with me in Cape Town, back as England's number one keeper, a world record holder, and with an excellent chance of going to the World Cup for the first time. Funny old game, isn't it? In between those months, there was a lot of soul-searching, a change in attitude from me, and a spot of luck. Without Alec Stewart's broken finger in the Edgbaston Test, I might never have had the chance to re-establish my international credentials, but I had learned enough by now about myself and cricket to realise that you grab your chance with both hands, and make the most of the smallest opportunity.

The first important decision I made was to accept the offer of the Gloucestershire captaincy. It was one of the best things to happen in my career, because it made me tougher mentally and also brought a fresh insight into the way the other players see the game. Before, I had been very wrapped up in my own game, sitting in a corner of the dressing-room, offering my thoughts when asked, a committed team man, but dedicated to maintaining my own standards. I got the impression other players thought I was selfish. They're entitled to their opinion, but they couldn't have understood the mental process needed to focus on my game. I thought at the time that if everybody else did the same and put their life and soul into it, we'd have a better chance of being successful. Now I had to change my approach to cricket, while keeping up the quality that had brought me England recognition. Could I look after my wicket-keeping, while worrying about the rest of the players and their standards? I wasn't sure I could do it, even though Courtney Walsh kept nagging me. Courtney had done the job in 1994, with me as his vice-captain, and we had worked well together. Now he was due to tour England with West Indies, so we needed a new skipper. He said that Jeff Dujon had managed the task of keeping wicket and captaining Jamaica, so what was my problem? When I had captained the side on a couple of occasions, I had been very concerned about dropping the ball, and that was no good for the team because the keeper is the focal point and the fielding standard emanates from him. I wasn't bothered about the tactical demands, because that is basically a matter for commonsense. Getting the best out of the individual players was a major concern for me. How do you maximise each players' contribution so effectively that it benefits the team as a unit? How do you ward off selfishness, while at the same time wanting the individual to have pride in performance and higher standards?

The club was also anxious about my image as a rather intense character, someone who didn't socialise in the bar afterwards, who basically did his job to the best of his ability and then went home. My bloody-mindedness could be a stumbling block, as the members had discovered the year before, when we played the South Africans at Bristol. I was captain, with Courtney having a rest. With a Test match due the following week, the South Africans were keen to get some batting practice on the final day, but I wouldn't play ball and killed the match off, by batting on. They hadn't bothered to approach me, suggesting we set up a finish. Because of rain, they were still in their first innings on the final day and it was clear to me they wanted batting practice. They batted on, and that backfired because they lost wickets and nearly followed on. They saved it, declared, expecting us to score runs quickly, to give them another bat. We were expected to make things easier for the tourists, and I wouldn't have that. I'd been on enough tours abroad to have experienced the way England gets treated, with poor net facilities, indifferent groundsmanship and everything stacked against us – so why should I help South Africa in their preparation to beat England? So we batted on because our chances of bowling them out in thirty-odd overs were slim. I made six runs in twenty-nine overs, and, when I was out, my home crowd cheered for a moment. Then I walked off to total silence, apart from one guy who stood clapping me – I wasn't sure if he was backing my decision or taking the mickey. At one stage, I thought we were going to have a bad incident in front of the pavilion, because some of our members were now very angry, blaming me for giving them no entertainment on that final day. Some were demanding their money back, throwing their membership cards away, and my name was mud. I decided I'd better get out there and try to explain my reasoning. I tried to point out that I too wanted to play entertaining cricket, but the South Africans wouldn't come halfway and gave us nothing. Why should Gloucestershire provide South Africa with valuable time out in the middle, making sure we had no chance of winning the game? I said, 'It would have just been Mickey Mouse cricket', which was a mistake. That led to howls of abuse, and they just shouted me down. I responded, 'Right, if you don't want to listen to me, I'm off' and closed the door. I was very shaken by the experience, and I was aware that my image as a local hero had been tarnished in the eyes of many Gloucestershire supporters that day. That saddened me, because I was only doing what I thought was best for English cricket, while the South Africans reacted with injured innocence – as if they had no part at all in the stalemate. County cricket members seem to want their cake and eat it at times. They want England to be a top side again, yet they're not prepared to go through the pain that helps you get there. Why make things easier for the tourists, so they've got a better chance of beating England the following week?

The club took a dim view of my stubbornness in that South

African game. They were worried by the hostile letters, by some supporters returning their memberships, and threatening not to renew them for the following season. Perhaps I should have used the media more cleverly that day to get my message across, rather than get into a shouting match with irate supporters, which I was never going to win. I had to brush up my public relations skills if I was to become Gloucestershire captain, and our chairman, Dickie Rossiter, made that point forcibly when we talked about the job. I could see his general drift, but I wasn't going to compromise on my desire to compete for every ball, in the process doing my bit to help English cricket get tougher. I was fed up of being on England tours, where we folded up and ended up chastened and pilloried by all. It was time that county captains started to stand up for what they saw was right for the national side, as well as their parochial interests. To me, the two aims could merge, if I could have the power to make our players mentally tougher, giving no concessions to the opposition. That's how they play it in Australia, South Africa and in the West Indies, so why should we keep lagging behind?

So I agreed to captain Gloucestershire for the 1995 season, despite my misgivings. Courtney Walsh had insisted that my wicket-keeping wouldn't suffer, because I'd be concentrating on that part of the job so naturally because of my experience. He said I was no longer a young kid who needed to learn how to concentrate all day behind the stumps, I could do it without thinking. I still wasn't sure about that, I was still worried about catching the ball, but I decided to give it a go. The first thing I wanted was some organisation, a sense that we were all going in the same direction. So I wrote to every player on the staff, asking them to set out for me their capabilities as professional cricketers, their defects, and what they were prepared to offer the team, and what they thought the team could achieve. After I'd gathered in their replies, I wrote back, telling them what I expected of them as individuals, and then as part of the whole unit. I was adamant that you can't treat professional cricketers all the same way, there has to be room for manoeuvre when you're dealing with human beings, who have different fallibilities as well as plus points. It's the easy option to treat everyone the same way, and I'd seen its deficiencies too often before. Of course, you can lay down general policy and have sound team goals, but you need to get the best out of each individual for the team to be stronger as a unit. We were all cogs in a large mechanism, and it was my job to ensure that those cogs of varying sizes had to slip easily enough into the appropriate slots. In my England career, I had seen the pitfalls of trying to treat all players exactly the same way, with the same disciplines. Graham Gooch didn't understand that you didn't get the best out of David Gower by asking him to run ten laps of the ground, or telling Ian Botham to get in the nets morning and afternoon. Great players are individualists, and they need handling differently. Then you have to make sure that the rest of the team accept, and understand why certain players are preparing in their own way. If those gifted individualists respond in the appropriate way, by utilising their talents productively, then the team has a far better chance of winning games. Then, everybody's happy.

That's why I agreed to let Javagal Srinath go home to India at the start of September, 1995. He had bowled brilliantly for the team in his first season in county cricket, winning us a lot of games. But he started to tire towards the end, and he became troubled with a virus as well. Early on, I'd agreed to give him Sundays off, because we weren't going to win the league. In return, he would bowl his heart out in the Championship, which we had a chance of winning, with four games left. We agreed that if we couldn't win it towards the end, we would let him go home to recharge his batteries and get ready for a heavy international schedule with India. I had no qualms about doing that, because he had been magnificent for us, and I think the other players realised that he had to be treated differently. We kept all this between us but I believe it was justified. Management is about maximising the assets of players.

My experiences with England also helped me in terms of communicating with the Gloucestershire players. That hadn't been one of my strong points, but I was determined not to make the mistakes that other captains made when things weren't going their way. You need to talk more to those who are struggling than to those who aren't. When it's going well for you, you don't lack self-confidence, all you want is the next day to roll up fine and dry, so you can get out there and perform again. Gooch didn't talk enough to those on the periphery of the side, the ones who would possibly have improved if the captain's arm had been around their shoulder more often. I hadn't forgotten the way some of Gloucestershire's players had treated me in my early years on the staff, and although I may have been a bit bolshie and slapdash, I lost respect for a few of them. As captain, I was committed to earning the support of the younger players by treating them with respect. I had learned that timing is crucial in building up respect for the captain. He must be firm and dominant at the right times, lighten up when the atmosphere needs it, and don't hammer the players too often. I was looking forward to those particular challenges.

First, though, we had to get fit. Fitter than ever before. I asked the club to put up a bit of money as an incentive to the players to report back a month early. I wanted as many as possible to get themselves fit in the early part of spring, rather than just before the season proper began. Eight of the players came in a month early, and all the others had valid excuses for not making it, like being abroad or having jobs that couldn't be left early. Those who couldn't get back early were told that they were expected to be as fit as the early birds at the official return day of April the first. After that, I wanted to concentrate on cricket skills, rather than worrying if the guys were fit enough. Those who made it on the first of March did me proud, especially in one endurance test we set them. There's a hill called Stoney Lane, which we nicknamed 'Heartbreak Ridge', just around the corner from the County Ground, that is very steep indeed. Most people who simply walk up that hill are out of breath when they get to the top, it's incredibly steep. I wanted us to be able to run up that hill without pausing for a rest. By the end of March, all the guys were managing it every day, and we'd learned a lot more about each other's character in the process. Every day, we'd be talking about that hill, about the necessity to conquer it, and it was great to see such determination. One day, we managed it five times, with me crawling the last few yards on hands and knees during the last attempt. It was important to be able to set the appropriate standard while maintaining my own fitness levels. Our team attitude definitely improved during that month, and it stood us in good stead throughout that summer. When the others returned to duty on 1 April, I was pleased to see they had reached the required levels of fitness. Even old-timer Kevin Cooper was putting everything in – and that, for an older player, is all you can ask. This was a good omen; we were on the way to showing extra toughness.

One new player set a great example of mental and physical toughness. Andrew Symonds had come over from Australia to take advantage of the registration rules which appeared rather lax. They certainly worked in our favour, so much so that some of the lads in the England dressing-room used to pull my leg about Gloucestershire having two overseas players. As far as I could see, we never did anything wrong technically, we just used the system, and pushed it to the limit. I know Andrew has become even more unpopular with many in the English game. Whatever the rights and wrongs of the situation, there was a loophole and we took advantage of it. He was also tremendous for Gloucestershire in his two years with us. In 1995, he opened the eyes of all of us, particularly the young batsmen. He was excellent on the right attitude to adopt and how to get the best out of yourself. He was very happy to share his thoughts with the others, and he was very instrumental in our team having a lot more guts and drive than previously. I had him down the order at number six early in the season, but after a couple of brilliant knocks there was a move to get him in earlier. I wasn't keen on that, because I thought he was ideal at number six – either turning the game round if we had started badly, or coming in to dominate if the earlier batsmen had done their job. He would sometimes get himself out by trying to get after the bowling, but that's what happens with believers, who think anything is possible. They need to be encouraged, to be able to feel they can go with their instincts. Monte Lynch, another one of our attacking batsmen, was the same; let him play in a certain way, knowing it looks bad if it doesn't come off, but that it's brilliant entertainment and valuable when it's his day. That's what happened at Canterbury, when Monte and Andrew came together at 42 for four, added 114 at five an over and set up our victory. That was the best way for those two to play, and I didn't want them shackled.

As Andrew Symonds gets older, he'll refine his game and get even better. I'd like to think he'll recognise that we gave him the opportunity to play naturally in his two seasons with Gloucestershire. In England, we stifle some players by getting them to play a certain way all the time. Andrew was different and it was right to handle him differently. He was disliked on the county circuit because he came through the back door, but I believe other counties would have been looking to sign him if we hadn't got in there first. I thought he handled his award as Young Cricketer of the Year brilliantly. At the dinner where he got the award, he stood up and said he was aware that he wasn't the most popular player around, but that he was honoured to have been voted in top place by his fellow professionals. He was also generous enough to say how much it meant to him to play against the likes of Graham Gooch and Mike Gatting in county cricket. He was a confused young man around that time, with England claiming him, and Australia still at the forefront of his mind, and at Gloucestershire we felt that he received an unfair amount of stick. It wasn't Andrew's fault that the registration rules were a little woolly.

Gloucestershire finished sixth in the Championship in 1995,

winning eight matches, and one of those victories helped restore me to the England side. That was at Cheltenham in late July, where I batted and kept wicket well, and we had a great win against Lancashire. In their team was the England captain, Mike Atherton and the chairman of selectors, Ray Illingworth also came down to watch. With Alec Stewart sidelined with a broken finger after the Edgbaston Test, the England wicket-keeper's job was up for grabs again, and I was determined to state my case in front of the England captain as firmly as I could. It looked as if Steve Rhodes had faded from contention after the second Test at Lord's, when Illingworth had underlined his power by passing over the keeper who had been originally chosen – Rhodes – and going for Stewart. Steve had had a poor tour in Australia, and therefore shouldn't have been in the frame again. It was right to drop me after I had kept under par in the West Indies in 1994, and yet Steve had fared even worse than me – yet here he was, getting the vote of confidence from Illy for the Lord's Test. Then Illy changes his mind, overturns the decision taken with his fellow selectors, and turfs Steve out the day before the match! It all seemed very strange, and Steve must have been as confused as the rest of us. Why had Illy moved the goalposts? It didn't seem logical to me and I was a little aggrieved. So with Alec keeping wicket very well at Lord's, the door seemed closed to me for the rest of the summer. Until Alec's finger injury. So I had another chance to force my way back in.

I hadn't forgotten what Mike Atherton had said to me in Perth about the need to impose myself on the opposition. Well, he was going to get the full treatment from me at Cheltenham. It was a fast, bouncy wicket and with Lancashire all out for 231, I walked in at 44 for six, with Wasim Akram really up for the contest. I was determined to take the game to them sensibly, and let them know I wouldn't be pushed around, so when Atherton and Neil Fairbrother both said a cheery 'good morning' to me, I gave them the stoniest of stares. Peter Martin, a genial guy, shouted, 'Let's get Robert out', and I rapped back 'Call me that again, and I'll deck you' – all the repartee of the playground! My new tough image was dented a little when I stared back at Graham Lloyd, and then spat on the ground. Unfortunately some of the spittle didn't reach the ground, and it was left dangling there from the grill of my helmet. That started the Lancashire boys off, they were wetting themselves at this, and I had to control myself and not join in. I bent down to tie up my shoelace, to cover up my laughter and when Neil Fairbrother came alongside me, I nearly collapsed. But Atherton was my number one target. When he batted in this match, I would hurl the ball down at his end as he ambled into the crease, say various things directed at him, and do my best to unsettle him. It was the biggest mental conflict I've ever had with another player, and although I'm sure it was water off a duck's back to a tough character like Mike, he must have noticed how much harder I was now on the field. When I batted, I'd stare at him every time I hit a boundary, and hold the gaze. Even when he caught me at slip for 83, I didn't walk and waited to be given out. Was that tough enough for him?

We recovered superbly, bowled them out cheaply second innings, and won by ten wickets by mid-afternoon on the third day. A great win for us. Ray Illingworth was there on that Saturday, and he and the other selectors would be meeting that night with Atherton to pick the squad for the Old Trafford Test. Illingworth asked me how the wicket had played and I said that if you played properly, you could stay in, but if you weren't tight enough, you would get out. 'Well, you made it look easy enough,' he told me, and I thought, 'Hang on, this is Illy talking here, he's never gone out of his way to praise me before. I might have a chance here.' I was thrilled with that comment. Next day, I was back in the England fold. I'm certain that seeing me at close quarters in this Cheltenham game had forced Atherton and Illingworth to the same conclusion. It would be my first Test since April the previous year and I told myself I was going to approach it as if it's my last. From now on, I would have the same philosophy, that I no longer had anything to lose. I'd be aggressive and positive in the mould of the current Gloucestershire team, and wouldn't let anyone dictate to me out on the pitch. If Athers wanted a noisy, bubbly keeper, that would be me. He'd get sick of hearing me out in the middle.

I was totally fired up when I went up to Manchester. I was absolutely determined to prove the selectors wrong for leaving me out for such a long time. Athers came into my room on the eve of the Test, and caught me writing out our eleven. He wasn't sure who he would play, and after making himself a cup of coffee, sat down. I could tell he wanted to talk about my role in the game and before he could utter a word, I said, 'Look, Athers, I'm going to play exactly the same as last week at Cheltenham, against your lot. Nasty and aggressive. Okay?' He was happy with that. End of conversation. That night, at the team dinner, I felt I had to make a bit of an impact. I felt I also wanted to impress Illingworth, so after he and Athers had said their pieces, I stood up and said mine. I gave it the full works – about believing we can win this game, that we have to be up for it, they've got more weaknesses than we can list on a toilet roll, that they'll buckle under pressure, etc. etc. We've just got to believe it. I ended up with a warning: 'If any of you are fielding at mid-on or mid-off, keep an eye out for the ball whizzing at you from my end. Get your backside into gear, because they're going to know I'm around.' That brought a big laugh, and yet I felt it struck a chord. I really felt we would win after that positive atmosphere from our dinner.

We did win the game, by six wickets – but it was so close for a time! I played one of my most important innings for England to help seal the win, and I was delighted that I did it by playing positively and refusing to get tied down by the West Indies fast bowlers and the fear of failure. I made just 31 not out, but when I came in, we were looking down the barrel at the sort of defeat we suffered in Trinidad the previous year. This time, the target was just 94, but already we'd been reduced to 48 for four and Robin Smith had smashed a cheekbone, edging a lifter into his face. He wouldn't bat again, so we only had five wickets left as I walked out to join John Crawley. With Ian Bishop and Kenny Benjamin bowling fast and tight, we were up against it. Trinidad revisited? I couldn't have faced another one of those days. I felt very positive when I got out in the middle. I knew the main thing was to regain the initiative, because we had only scored ten in the previous eleven overs. I told John, 'Just stay in. I'll take the chances', and he seemed reassured by that. I got off the mark straight away, blocking a quick single to cover and there was a massive roar from the crowd. Well, they were on our side anyway! Then a ball hit me on the left shoulder joint, missing all the padding, as I dropped my hands and squared up to to a nasty bouncer. That certainly woke me up! So now I was in pain as well as determined. I was really flying now, chattering away to myself.

I got another enormous cheer when I square cut a ball to the third man boundary. That forced Richie Richardson to bring back Curtley Ambrose. Why is it always him? In my mind, I could see the grubber that bowled me in Barbados, 1990, then his devastating spell that cleaned us up in Trinidad four years later. This was the crucial phase. I had bitter experience from Barbados about the way the tail subsides once they get the breakthrough. We just couldn't afford to lose another wicket, but if we just decided to hang around, they would only bowl better. When you're concentrating on survival, you get in a rut and don't score any runs, and along comes the unplayable delivery. So I decided to carry on taking the fight to them, to stand up and play my shots. Ambrose bowled me one that stood up in front of my nose, and I hooked it safely to the boundary. The crowd erupted. They knew as well as I did that this had been the decisive delivery. Ambrose was soon removed from the attack, John Crawley hit the winning run, and we scampered off in delight, pursued by some ecstatic England supporters. I grabbed two stumps and bails as souvenirs, and then realised I hadn't shaken hands with my pal, Courtney Walsh. So I went back to find him, and that proved to be a mistake, because the crowd caught up with me. They pulled and grabbed at me, I almost lost my helmet and bat, and in the end had to concede one of the two stumps. The bails were safe, I'd stuffed them down my trousers.

Mike Atherton was there to greet and embrace us at the top of the dressing-room stairs and I was very proud that we had kept our nerve. As the adrenalin wore off, and fatigue set in, I came to realise that I had treated the job like a commando raid – taking the attack to the enemy and returning home with the booty against all the odds. A St Nazaire job in cricketing terms. Huge satisfaction. I was back. Surely I'd proved a few points here?

And yet something I'm sure I overheard from Ray Illingworth during the next Test made me wonder just how secure I was in the current England side. I missed stumping Sherwin Campbell off spinner Richard Illingworth, for the elementary reason that I had snatched at the ball, rather than waiting for it to come to me. That was something that I had thought I'd mastered ten years ago, but there was one significant reason for the mistake this time. This 1995 series had seen the use for the first time of the third umpire to adjudicate on line decisions, for example stumpings. I got it into my head that I then needed to be a little quicker in my movements, because the replays would allow the third umpire to give decisions that umpires on the field would never have given with the naked eye. So I was rushing things, hoping to take advantage of television replays if I completed the stumpings quickly enough. That's what happened with the routine stumping chance at Trent Bridge. Sherwin Campbell was able to get back in to his crease as I lost the ball in my haste, rather than doing what came naturally. But, in my new positive frame of mind, I was determined to put that error to the back of my mind, even though I knew it looked untidy. When I came off the field at tea, I happened to overhear a conversation between Ray Illingworth and England's batting coach, John Edrich. I heard Illy say, 'Did you see Jack miss that stumping? How did he miss that? Stewart would have taken that.' It became apparent to me that he considered Alec Stewart a more than adequate keeper, with his batting an extra bonus. That intimidated me, so I wasn't exactly feeling secure after hearing that. Suddenly, my place on the tour to South Africa was no longer a probability. I put it no higher than a possibility.

So when we came to the Oval, I had no doubts that I was still on trial and playing for my place on tour. For all I knew, it was my last Test, so I decided to give it my all, and keep playing positively. I made 91 and should have got a hundred. I came in to join Graeme Hick with an hour left on the first day, and had to hang on as Ambrose really worked us over in a fabulous spell of hostile bowling on a wicket that did him no favours at all. He peppered me all over my body with the short stuff, and I was pleased to have survived the onslaught. Next day, I played well, going for my shots, until I made a mistake through fatigue. Ambrose bowled me with a good one just before tea, but I honestly believe that if I hadn't felt so fatigued, I would have kept it out. It's difficult to know why I suddenly got so tired, because that hasn't been a problem for me generally in my England career. Perhaps the tension involved in wanting to seal my place on the tour in this match took its toll. At least my wicket-keeping was tidy enough – I conceded just five byes in a West Indies total of 692 for eight declared. So ended an exciting series, with honours even at 2–2 and me back in the team. It was strange to think that I might also have captained England in one of those Tests. When Mike Atherton suffered a back spasm on the eve of the Trent Bridge Test, Ray Illingworth nominated me as the skipper if Athers was ruled out. That would have been some comeback – in the wilderness for over a year, then the captain for the first time in my second game back! There were no other candidates in the England squad for that match, with Alec Stewart unfit, but Atherton's recovery scotched that prospect.

My main mission had been accomplished, though. I was back in the team, and batted well enough to suggest that any further omissions wouldn't be because I wasn't scoring runs. I felt positive about staying in the England set-up. When I was picked for the South African trip, I set to work on my batting. I rang

England's batting coach, John Edrich – himself a former left-hander – to ask for specialist assistance. He came to Bristol, and spent a very valuable day with me, forcing me to hit the ball straighter, rather than squirting it square on both sides of the wicket in my usual fashion. I also spent hours with the bowling machine, working out how I was going to play the inevitable bouncers that would be coming our way from the South Africans. All that preparatory work was to prove vital when I provided full support to Mike Atherton's efforts in saving the Johannesburg Test a few weeks later.

9
A PLACE IN HISTORY

I started the South African tour on trial, fighting for my place every time I walked on to the field. I ended it a hero, having helped Mike Atherton save a Test as well as setting a new world record for dismissals by a keeper in a Test. All this and a place in England's World Cup squad a few weeks later, with Ray Illingworth praising me to the skies for my performances in South Africa. Now that really was a big turnaround from Illy, because I'd felt he was the one responsible for my insecurity at the start of the tour.

The remark from Ray Illingworth about my keeping that I had overheard during the Trent Bridge Test had confirmed to me that he was still unconvinced about my credentials as the number one keeper. He now had wider powers than previous chairmen of selectors, and it would be him rather than Mike Atherton that I would need to impress. Alec Stewart was fit again, and improving all the time behind the stumps as he worked at his game with his usual dedication. He had been a star at Lord's, catching a beauty to get Brian Lara at a time when he might have swayed that Test. It was the sort of catch that specialist keepers come up with, to justify their place in the side, and it turned that Test our way. So I knew I would have to be out of the traps quickly and impressively once we got to South Africa. I felt confident about my batting after some hard, concentrated work at Bristol with John Edrich. The new South African coach, Bob Woolmer, would know all about the way I batted, and where I scored my runs, and he'd have a run chart in his office, detailing all the favourite scoring areas of the English players. A meticulous planner, Woolmer would have worked out a plan of attack against all of us. His fast bowlers would be the key part of his strategy and here I was concerned about Allan Donald. Who isn't in world cricket? In county cricket, Donald seemed to have a jinx on me, the last time bowling me around my legs from around the wicket. I was playing slightly across the line to the faster bowlers, so Edrich got me to play straighter, trying to hit the occasional delivery straight back past the bowler. Because of my technique, that hadn't been a particularly favoured area for me in my career, so I hoped it would give Woolmer food for thought when I unveiled it. I must get the bat down quicker for the yorker – a Donald speciality – stop playing around my front pad, and learn to play defensively with soft hands. It's a shot that Graham Thorpe plays particularly well, guiding the ball down to third man, with the hands not pushing at the ball. With a bit of luck, the ball wouldn't carry behind the stumps if you played softly enough. I also practised my bobbing and weaving against the bowling machine at Bristol. We used rubber balls at high speed, and I was peppered a lot, but that didn't matter. It helped me get attuned to the sort of speed I'd be facing, sharpening me up for the time when a hard, leather ball would be pinging in at my ribs and head, including getting used to deliveries from around the wicket at the hands of Donald and the others. I wanted to give myself every chance before arriving in South Africa to be in a position where I could anticipate what they'd be trying at me. My last full tour with England hadn't been pleasant, and I was desperate to prove that the Caribbean experience was a one-off in my international career. I had to build on my pleasing return against the West Indies last summer, especially with the bat. Nothing must be left to chance.

When I walked out to bat in the first Test, at Centurion Park, I saw that Woolmer and Hansie Cronje had done their homework on me. They had a deep square leg right away, for my shovel shot that gets me a lot of runs, and my other areas had all been blocked off. I really struggled in the first hour, as they probed away at me. Craig Matthews kept nagging away at me, just outside the off-stump. So I started to adopt the 'leave' shot. I worked out that I had to make the bowlers bowl differently at me, otherwise I wouldn't get a run. If they bowled just outside the off-stump, I was now going to leave it, by playing across my body, bringing the bat towards legside in an exaggerated fashion. It wasn't in my mind going into bat, but I was cornered, and had to do something! The crowd roared every time I played the shot, thinking I had played and missed, then they started to barrack, telling me to make an effort at playing the ball. Good – if I was getting under the skin of the crowd, it wouldn't be too long before the bowlers got frustrated. They were bowling ideal wicket-taking balls, just outside the off peg and I was ostentatiously leaving them. I started to take the mickey out of them, and Brian McMillan especially got ratty. He ended up banging in a few short ones at me, which brought me a few runs, and broke up their pattern. It made Matthews bowl straighter at me, just to get me playing at the ball, so that allowed me to flick a few off my legs, and also play him straight down the ground. So I was winning the battle after scratching around in that first hour. The bowlers were made to deviate from their plan of attack by tactics they hadn't anticipated. I finished fifty not out when the rains came and washed away the match. Round one to me. I'm certain that this experience at Centurion Park was a vital learning process for me when it came to having to bat for hours at Johannesburg a few weeks later – certainly the 'leave' was used a great deal!

So my batting form wasn't a worry for me as we prepared for the second Test in Johannesburg. I was concerned, though, about my rustiness behind the stumps. Because of the rain at Centurion Park, I didn't get the chance to keep wicket, so I wanted to get match practice in the Free State game in Bloemfontein. If not, I'd be going into the Johannesburg Test having not kept wicket in a first-class match for eighteen days, since South Africa A in

Kimberley. That's too long a gap for any keeper who wants to be at his sharpest. When it comes to the physical demands of keeping wicket, match practice is essential, no matter how much fitness work you do instead. Yet Ray Illingworth didn't seem to understand this, as I pestered him for a game in Bloemfontein. He thought it was more important that all the batsmen apart from Graeme Hick had a game, which meant Alec Stewart would keep wicket. On the eve of the match, it was decided that the four days would be split between a three-day game, then a one-dayer, so we'd all get some match practice. A compromise of sorts, but fifty overs in a one-dayer would still leave me rusty. So I felt out of form going in to the Test, lacking rhythm, and my legs didn't feel strong enough, because I hadn't done enough work out in the middle in the past fortnight.

Illingworth's unsympathetic response to a specialist problem that he just didn't understand only served to increase my nervousness. I was still anxious about nailing down my place in the eleven, and I couldn't get it out of my head that he had publicly fingered me as one of the scapegoats for the 1994 West Indies tour, nor had I forgotten his views about my missed stumping of Sherwin Campbell at Trent Bridge. I had to live with all that, of course, but it wasn't easy knowing that our manager-coach who had power to overrule the captain didn't rate me. I had to cross the mental barrier of keeping wicket for England in an overseas Test for the first time since doing badly in the Caribbean. Hardly the ideal preparation for a Test in which I was to break a world record.

We were all very pumped up on the first day of that second Test. The captain had surprised many by putting South Africa in after winning the toss, and so we were really motivated for taking any half-chance that came our way. My first victim was a routine one, taking Hansie Cronje off Dominic Cork, to give me my hundredth Test catch. Then came the moment I'd been dreading. Darryl Cullinan slashed at one, and it flew fast, high and wide to my right. I would have backed myself to get that one nine times out of ten, but here I took it on the thumb. It spooned up towards Graham Thorpe at slip, but he had turned his back, and the chance was gone. When I'd pushed my legs for lift-off, nothing had happened, and so I was sluggish in my leap to my right. I was annoyed at missing that chance, and got even more angry as Cullinan and Gary Kirsten batted on safely enough, to get them to the tea interval with only two wickets down. By now, I had worked myself into a rare old state as I walked off at tea, convinced I'd let Athers down after he'd gambled on putting them in. At that stage, we were desperate for wickets and under pressure. No doubt Illingworth had filed away that missed chance as well. What would he be saying in the dressing-room, out of my earshot? When I walked in, I was swearing and generally inconsolable. As I blew my stack, at no one in particular, Illingworth said, 'Are you all right?' and I had to bite my lip. I felt like saying, 'Of course I'm not. I haven't kept wicket for almost three weeks because of you. My legs feel like jelly, because you haven't given me the chance to get work on them. We're also trying to cope with the high altitude. Why doesn't a keeper get the same understanding as others?' Instead, I just waved him away. I got the impression from him that he wasn't very sympathetic towards me. I might have been wrong, but it appeared to me that all he really wanted to ask was, 'How the hell did you miss that one?' At moments like that, you need a sympathetic response, something like, 'Don't worry, concentrate on the next one, you'll get it.'

As I walked back onto the field after tea, I couldn't get it out of my mind that Illy might be thinking or saying, 'Alec would have snaffled that.' I felt I needed to strike back quickly, otherwise I'd be on the way out again. Thank God I did – without any addition to the tea score. And it was Cullinan. I was very pleased with the catch off Graeme Hick's off-spin. Hicky makes the ball zip through unexpectedly at times, and I had prepared myself for it. Cullinan went for the drive, it took a big deflection and I was in the right place for it. That's better. Then Jonty Rhodes, playing away from his body, edged Dominic Cork to me. I was suddenly on a roll, getting Gary Kirsten, as he edged a rising delivery from Devon Malcolm, and Dave Richardson three balls later, off glove and helmet. At the close, they were 278 for 7, having been 211 for 2 at tea. I had taken five catches, and although only Cullinan's was more than a regulation effort, I was pleased to hang onto them after that bad miss in the afternoon. Next morning, I caught Clive Eksteen, and then a few people started to talk world records to me. Now every keeper knows that Bob Taylor had the record of ten in the 1980 Bombay Test, seven of them in the first innings, and by chance, Bob had flown out to Johannesburg to host a party of England supporters.

It would be too coincidental to break the record in front of Bob, wouldn't it? I put it out of my mind, because there were more pressing matters to consider. Like our bad batting in the first innings that led to a deficit of 132 runs to get the South Africans sniffing victory. So when we bowled again, we needed some early wickets to get back into the match. We soon had them 29 for 2, and I had two more catches, both of them routine – Gary Kirsten and Andrew Hudson, off straightforward nicks. Eight dismissals now, only three to go, and eight more South African wickets available. I started to feel tension in my arms, worried I'd cock up the chances. Then I caught Hansie Cronje – a good one, low down – almost as if the appointment had been made with the world record, and the fates would get me there automatically. I felt on a high, taking Dominic Cork's outswingers so wide, that we didn't have a first slip. I was going to claim those, so we saved on slip fielders! The catch to equal the world record was technically the best of my career. I know that Alan Knott agrees. He had worked hard with me on diving catches, and when I talked to him later about this one, he was as delighted as me. Angus Fraser was the bowler and Jonty Rhodes the batsman. Gus tends to bowl close to the wicket, angling the ball in towards the right-hand batsman, and this in turn pushes the keeper fractionally towards his left side. Rhodes leant back to cut the ball, so I was instinctively prepared to push off from my left, as far as I could to my right side. He got a lot of bat on it, and it flew fast and wide. There was no slip near me, so I could dive as far as possible. I just managed to get to it with my right glove, at full stretch. I jumped up and hurled the ball to the sky. I was so excited and thrilled at that catch. One to go now. History in the making? I was delighted that at least I'd equalled the record, that was something.

I had to bide my time until the next day, because Brian McMillan strangely accepted the umpires' offer of bad light and we trooped off. Big Mac had just hit Devon Malcolm for six, four and six in consecutive deliveries, which seemed to suggest he was seeing the ball reasonably well. We were perfectly happy to go off, because they now had a lead of more than four hundred, with plenty of time to spare. They would come to regret losing that time on the third evening, as we batted out for a draw on the final day, but no one was to know that when McMillan decided to play safe.

So now I was under pressure, but of a different sort. What if I dropped a catch next day, and failed to break the record? How could I cope with getting so near, then blowing it? It was impossible to escape the possibilities and just blank it out, because the media did various interviews with me at close of play on that third evening, and Bob Taylor came in to our dressing-room to congratulate me. Alec Stewart, who had been geeing me up all day, was particularly warm in his congratulations, and that meant a lot to me. So did a phone call from Alan Knott. With all that going on, you'd need to be a mental giant to be able to switch off from such an exciting prospect. I went back to my hotel room, hoping to get some sort of relaxation, and ordered my usual meal of chicken and rice, to get my carbohydrate levels up. I watched television, but couldn't settle, my head was swimming. No chance of sleep, and a massive electrical storm around 1.30 am at least gave me some entertainment. I made yet another pot of tea, opened the windows and watched the fireworks. There was another matter bugging me. A few weeks earlier, I had decided that I wanted Aileen to come out and join me for the first time on tour. I can't put my finger on why I was so insistent, perhaps I had a sixth sense that something momentous was going to happen and I wanted her there to see it. It's not as if she's ever been at many games involving me. She'd been to the county ground at Bristol just once in recent years, and that was only to drop off some gear that I'd left at home. But I had a real craving for her to be in South Africa, and I'd been getting frustrated at the delays in organising her flight. She'd never even been on a plane before, and it was proving to be a difficult exercise. Our liaison officer, Doug Russell, was trying to get it organised and I continually pestered him, with progress so slow. At the start of the Johannesburg Test, he assured me that everything was at last going smoothly, despite a delay over Aileen's visa. She wouldn't be able to get a flight until just before Christmas, in time for the Durban Test. That was still a fortnight away, though, and as I sat in my hotel room, on the brink of breaking the world record, I was sad that Aileen wasn't there to see me have a crack at it. That would've been something to tell the grandchildren about.

So I was hardly refreshed in the morning when I presented myself at the team bus. For some reason, I was first on! It's not every day you get the chance to break a world record, is it? When I got to the ground, I was overwhelmed by good wishes. I couldn't move at practice for people coming up to me and saying, 'Good luck, Jack' or 'Don't drop it, Jack.' And of course, I proceeded to do just that. Shaun Pollock slashed at a delivery from Fraser and the ball flew at head height, wide to my right. I could only get a finger to the chance. It would have been a top catch if I'd clung onto it, but that didn't console me. Graham Thorpe, at slip, tried some words of reassurance, but would I get another chance? There was now a real chance that the South Africans would declare, as they chased quick runs. It seemed that they'd declare as soon as McMillan reached his hundred, to give themselves as much time as possible to try bowling us out. By now I was expecting the declaration at any time, and when Pollock was lbw,

I half expected Hansie Cronje to call us in. I couldn't bear to look at their dressing-room. My arms were seizing up again with the tension, and I was trying like hell to concentrate for every ball.

At last – Clive Eksteen obliged. He chased one from Cork that swung just enough, and the edge nestled into my gloves. I was worried about rushing it, and throwing the ball up before it had arrived. What a relief! Mike Atherton and Graeme Hick tried to pat me on the back, but I whizzed past them, to grab hold of Cork. Even in that moment of complete euphoria, I was aware that I would never have broken the world record unless the bowlers had kept finding the edge. It's not like Brian Lara's world record with the bat, which was all his own work. A keeper is nothing without his bowlers. Soon after that moment, McMillan got his hundred, and South Africa declared. I suppose I also owe a debt to McMillan for refusing to stay out in the bad light the previous evening. The way he was motoring along, he would have reached his century fairly soon, and then I wouldn't have had the chance to get another dismissal. When I got back into our dressing-room, Bob Taylor was there very quickly, showing yet again what a great gentleman of cricket he has been. Bob may have been just a little disappointed at losing his record, but he never showed it. He was absolutely charming, saying how important it was that an Englishman should be the new record holder, telling the media that it was a great day for specialist keepers, rather than manufactured ones. Bob had been a great supporter of me over the years, an inspiration to me with his neat, classy work, and a wonderful advert for the game. That day in Johannesburg, he showed his character and I only hope I'll react in the same sporting manner if someone takes the world record away from me.

My efforts with the gloves would have been more than enough to qualify Johannesburg 1995 as my most memorable match – except there was more to come. We had been set a target of 479, which would have been a good one to win, but our best hope was a draw. That would mean a long, determined haul from us, especially after McMillan fired out Alec Stewart and Mark Ramprakash in one over. Overnight, we were 167 for 4, staring down the barrel of defeat, but at least our captain was still there. With him at the crease, we were never finished, and the South Africans knew that. Next morning, I came in after Robin Smith was dismissed by Donald, who was really motoring in now. There was about half an hour to go till lunch, and basically we needed to stay in for another four hours after that to save the game. We still had five wickets in hand, but I felt ours was the vital stand, and I mean no disrespect to Cork, Gough, Fraser and Malcolm in saying that. I simply had to stay there, supporting Atherton, otherwise we'd struggle. The opposition lost no chance to remind us of that. As soon as I came in, I was greeted with, 'Come on guys, Russell knows he's the last one', and the atmosphere was like a bullfight. The ground was packed, the home supporters were baying for our blood, looking for South Africa's first Test victory over England for thirty years. They were slapping their palms on the advertising boards around the boundary as Donald roared in. In short, we were up against it!

Yet as soon as I reached the crease, I was convinced that, whatever happened at the other end, Atherton wouldn't get out. He looked as fresh as a daisy, even though he had been on the field throughout, since Friday evening, when their second innings started. It was now coming up to Monday lunchtime, but he looked calm and composed. It looked to me as if he was loving every minute of it. The situation had brought out his stubborn streak, and I told myself, 'I've got to stay with this guy, we can do it.' At the start I just concentrated on playing it ball after ball, then hoping to get to lunch. I set myself to block all day. Within fifteen minutes, I could have been out before I'd scored. Caught near short leg off Brian McMillan. In attempting to shovel one to the legside, I scooped it just over short leg. When it first went up, I thought I was in trouble. Then a split second later, I could see that, as if by fate, it was going to land safely. As the ball reached its height, I relaxed and thought 'no one's going to catch that'. It felt like slow motion, a strange feeling. The ball landed one yard between both short leg and short square leg. Soon after that, still before lunch, Meyrick Pringle should have caught me off his own bowling, after I stopped my shot, lobbing the ball straight back in the bowler's direction. He dropped it, and nine times out of ten I would have been on my way. For me, that was the decisive moment of the day.

I plugged away, not even thinking about scoring. I kept motivating myself by remembering Barbados 1990 when I thought we had done all the hard work only to fold up when I was bowled by Ambrose. That wasn't going to happen again. There are no guarantees that anyone else can finish the job, and my task here was to stay with my captain. I used Barbados to remind me of the bitter taste of failure and defeat that could be avoided, and that spurred me on. Athers, meanwhile, found my constant references to Barbados amusing whenever we met up for a chat in between overs. He reminded me more than once that he wasn't on that tour, but I kept insisting 'Remember, Athers, we lost at Barbados by just fifteen minutes!'

Getting to lunch was important, and as well as that lucky break from Pringle I had to contend with a really fiery spell from McMillan. At Centurion Park, he was no more than medium pace, but here he was distinctly lively. He jarred my bat handle more than once, and with a few well-chosen words, and some glares, made it quite clear he didn't think much to my style of batting. When I got the 'leave' shot out of the bag, he was even less impressed. If I could continue to rile McMillan, and make him lose concentration, that would reduce his effectiveness. I was wearing dark sunglasses for the first time in a Test, and they proved a useful shield against the intimidation of their bowlers. I wanted to create a psychological barrier between us, so that if they couldn't see my eyes, there was no point in trying to stare me out. It wasn't that I was frightened of eye contact, quite the opposite, as Athers could confirm from that game at Cheltenham the previous summer, but this was an exceptional situation here.

I also wanted to antagonise the home supporters, and opponents, to get under their skin. Who does this Russell think he is? It pumped me up to think I was annoying them. The shades helped when I kept playing the 'leave', because I'd stand there, stock still, after letting the ball go and when the bowlers let rip at me with the verbals, they couldn't get a reaction from me because the shades blocked them out. And when the crowd started shouting 'Use the bat, Russell', that was music to my ears. We were getting there.

I only responded to the verbal intimidation once. The left-arm spinner, Clive Eksteen, had fielders surrounding me because I had set myself just to block him. I knew I was in danger of poking up a bat/pad catch by playing this way, so I started wondering about other options. I turned round to the legside and noticed that the fielder positioned for the sweep had been brought in halfway from the boundary, almost saving one. It was an open invitation from Hansie Cronje to relieve the pressure on me by trying to hit past that fielder. I said 'No!' to myself, but I was so wrapped up in my innings that I then said it out loud. Cronje overheard this and shouted, 'Go on, be brave. You know you can do it. Why don't you have a go?' It was almost hypnotic the way he said it and I had to shout violently 'Get lost!' It was important to snap out of a trance that was almost dragging me in.

But enough of my efforts that final day. I was just the support for one of the greatest innings I've ever seen. Atherton's performance was amazing, an awesome display of coolness, bravery, technique and concentration. His toughness was inspirational to me, because I knew I just couldn't let him down. All I did for him was to keep him going, on the odd occasions when he played a false shot or his feet didn't move into the right position. Against Eksteen, he came only half forward once or twice, and I shouted down to him 'Come on, keep moving. Keep working', as well as the inevitable reference to Barbados. He was so cool. Once Shaun Pollock beat him outside the off stump and he wandered down to me at the end of the over and said, 'Don't worry, Jack, I'm just keeping them interested.' Later, as they started to get really frustrated, Pollock gave him a real mouthful after he'd played and missed at one delivery. Atherton turned to the bowler and dryly remarked, 'Pardon me, I think I'm probably entitled to play and miss once in ten hours.' That was a brilliant way to deflate a bowler. When McMillan tried to stare him out, Athers didn't say a word, just held his eyes until McMillan backed off. He wasn't trying to be funny, just transmitting the message that he was in control and wouldn't buckle to anyone. That was a wonderful sight from the non-striker's end. His technique against such high pace was marvellous. They were bowling right at his head and I'd be thinking 'God, this one really is going to hit him' and at the last instant, he'd move his head slightly out of the way. He kept his eye on the ball and swayed out of danger with the slightest of movement. No fuss. That must have been very dispiriting to those guys, after roaring in, giving it everything except the kitchen sink, only to see all that effort wasted by the slightest twitch of the batsman's neck muscles. And all the time, that particular batsman is in total control and everybody out there knows it.

As the afternoon wore on, we got louder and louder in our vocal support for each other. Athers punched himself in the heart at times to gee himself up, as we got past the danger period, just before tea. If they had got another wicket then, the hutch would have been open, and after a rest in the interval, they would have had a major surge of adrenalin, needing only four more wickets. Then it was a case of getting through the first overs after tea. When Gary Kirsten came on with his off-breaks, we knew we were home. One more blast with the new ball after that, but their fast bowlers were out on their feet by now. Yet I was surprised when the game suddenly ended. Hansie Cronje walked over, and shook my hand, leaving me to wonder if this was some sort of bluff. Then McMillan did the same, and I realised we had done it. Then it was pandemonium. I grabbed a stump and a bail and paused for a quick word with the umpire, the Australian Darryl

Hair. I asked him to pass on my thanks to Ian Healy for his telegram congratulating me on my world record. Then I suddenly thought 'Where's Athers?' and we grabbed each other and ran off together in triumph. The feeling was just what I imagined Rorke's Drift must have been like, when just over a hundred British soldiers fought off several thousand Zulu warriors. The Zulus had eventually stopped attacking out of respect for British courage in defence against all odds. Stand firm, toe to toe and give no quarter. I had used the experience of Barbados 1990 to my advantage here and it was a great moment to have got there to the finishing line this time.

The faces of the South Africans afterwards told the story. They were absolutely drained, gutted. To us, it was a magnificent sight to see them so out of it. Their dressing-room was like a morgue and the post-mortems were due to rage for days. They must have regretted not staying out in the middle on the Saturday night, when McMillan was crashing the ball around, and Cronje looked shell-shocked as he conducted the usual captain's media interviews after the game. In contrast, we were on cloud nine, we felt as if we'd won the game. Atherton's innings had lasted 644 minutes and his 185 not out will stand the test of time as a monument of endurance, technical skill and guts. I've played with and against some nasty, aggressive cricketers but none tougher than this guy. That resilience and fortitude transmits itself to everyone, and I could see from close quarters how much it demoralised their bowlers. For me, to share the Man of the Match award with him was the most memorable experience so far in my career. It seemed to all of us as if we'd won the series.

The emotional highs weren't yet over for me that day. When we returned to our hotel, I was asked to do yet another interview, and I obliged, sitting on the steps outside the hotel. I couldn't understand why our manager, John Barclay insisted on staying there with me during the interview. Perhaps he was worried for my welfare, because he knew that I'd been rash enough to accept a dinner invitation that evening from Ian Botham. I love Both dearly, he's been of my major heroes, but I'd always managed to give him the social slip whenever he'd threatened to drag me out. One night out with him, and I'd have needed to recover in bed for a week! This time, though, he had collared me in the dressing-room after the game. 'You're coming out with me tonight, Jack, for the first time. No buts' was his message and I had buckled. So I had that on my mind, as John Barclay continued to fuss over me, carrying my bags upstairs for me. Now I know I had helped to save the Test, but wasn't this taking managerial gratitude a little too far? So when I finally got in to my room, I was looking forward to a nice, long soak in the bath, to mull over an historic match, then ring home before submitting myself to the rigours of an evening out with Ian Botham. As I let myself into my room, I was irritated to see someone else's personal belongings on the floor. 'That's all I need,' I thought, 'They've let my room out already, and I'm not leaving till tomorrow.' It was dark in the room, and I was just getting used to the light before deciding to ring the hotel manager to complain when the light came on. There was a flash of light, and someone had taken my photo. A female voice shouted out 'Surprise, surprise!' and it didn't sound like Cilla Black. The accent was much more familiar. It was Aileen. She'd made it in time for my historic Test. The management had kept it secret. So that's why she had told me not to call her the night before, having said she was going out with a friend, but instead she was on a plane for the first time coming to surprise me. The perfect end to a memorable five days for me. And I could dodge Beefy's hospitality again. My liver and career were saved!

10
ILLY AND ATHERS

The England players have to carry the can for the disappointing way we tailed off in South Africa, and our poor efforts in the World Cup a few weeks later. Nobody else can do it for us once we cross the boundary line, and if you need to be fully motivated when playing for your country, then you've got a problem. Yet I'm convinced we would have given a better account of ourselves if Ray Illingworth hadn't been our manager/coach. Although our morale and team spirit remained high in South Africa and in the World Cup, that was in spite of Illingworth. His job was to get the best out of every player, to get us focused on the job in hand, to make us feel we were tactically sharp, and to support the captain fully. In that case, Illingworth was a failure. By the end of the World Cup, he had lost our respect and he was a lame duck in the job. Giving Illingworth unprecedented powers as chairman of selectors, cricket manager and coach had been the wrong move for English cricket. His relationship with Mike Atherton, his captain, had become so difficult that the players had lined up in Athers' corner, leading to the feeling that we weren't all pulling in the same direction. That's the minimum you expect from your management on an England tour. Touring can be hard enough without the manager trying to undermine the captain, but that's what Illingworth did far too often, particularly in South Africa.

It's a fundamental that the captain should be in charge on tour, because he gets it in the neck if the team fails, or under-performs. Yet in my opinion Mike Atherton was treated like a schoolboy at times by Ray Illingworth, and when things went wrong, Illingworth was quick to place the blame elsewhere, even though he had said the buck was to stop with him when he was appointed supremo in the spring of 1995. I had the feeling that Athers felt he owed his job to Illy, after Illy had backed him over the 'dirt in the pocket' affair during the Lord's Test of 1994 against the South Africans. After Athers admitted he had not been wholly truthful to the match referee over what substance had been in his trousers, the chairman took over, squared it with the referee and then fined Atherton heavily. But he had helped save his job, and that may have been a factor in Atherton's mind, on the many subsequent occasions when Illingworth seemed to infuriate him. It amazed me that, right till the end of Illingworth's time as chairman of selectors, so many influential people kept peddling the line that the two got on. All this stuff about two tough northerners respecting each other because they talked the same blunt language wasn't the case, in my opinion. We're told that there's never been a single issue that they've fallen out over – that's rubbish. We're asked to believe that they obviously got on well, because Illy was always in the England dressing-room – but that's because he was the supremo and, on tour, the coach. It would be odd if he was nowhere to be seen. Who was going to hang up the sign saying 'Chairman of selectors not allowed in here'? It was significant that when David Lloyd was appointed coach for the summer of 1996, and Illingworth's powers were clipped, he was rarely in our dressing-room for the whole of that summer. He had been discredited in the eyes of too many players, and the captain just had to maintain an uneasy truce with him until he finally retired from the job that September.

On that South African tour, I was frustrated several times by Athers. Why didn't he tell Illingworth to stop meddling, making inflammatory, derogatory comments to the media, and lowering the morale of some of his players? If I had been in Athers' position, I would have made it clear early on that the team which represented England was the captain's choice, that he would take full responsibility, and that he wouldn't do the job any longer if that didn't suit Illingworth. But he kept his head down most of the time, and on occasions he was undermined in front of his own players by Illingworth. To me, that's a cardinal sin. Yet Athers refused to walk away, despite great provocation. The players were totally on his side, he had all of our respect, yet he didn't appear to force many issues with Illingworth. Perhaps he did in private, I don't know, but there was no real evidence that they had an understanding. Perhaps Athers was looking further ahead, knowing that Illingworth was retiring soon, and then he could have a new, constructive dialogue with his successor, with the Ashes summer of 1997 the focal point. Yet a better working partnership with Illingworth would have surely brought a clearer strategy and improved performances when we drifted into the World Cup. Instead, we were clearly behind the times tactically, lacking in form and confidence and listless, with the captain unable to raise players' games. After the momentum went out of the South African tour, the captain ought to have been able to galvanise us, but when we got to India and Pakistan a few weeks later, it was soon clear we were in disarray.

Right from the start of the South African tour, we had a taste of Illingworth's peculiar style of man-management. We had been told by the TCCB that public statements were to be closely monitored, and that no newspaper articles or diary pieces would be allowed, by the dictate of Illingworth. The day before we flew out, he was quoted in the press along the lines of being in full control of team selection on tour. He also said that in the previous summer, against the West Indies, he had been persuaded against his gut reaction to go along with a couple of selections. He said he wouldn't make the same mistakes again – the clear inference being that Atherton had got things wrong. A nice start, guaranteed to make Athers feel confident about his role. Then the Boycott and Illingworth tapes appeared in the *Sun*, a three-day feature with the chairman answering detailed questions about England's recent selection policy. It was packed with classified information that shouldn't have been aired – what Atherton thought of various players, who he rated and who he didn't. There was also a piece suggesting that Atherton had misled Illingworth about Alec Stewart's willingness to keep wicket in the Lord's Test and that Phil Tufnell was too much trouble for the captain, and that's why he wasn't likely to be picked by England in the near future. Throughout the feature, the implication was that when England had picked the wrong team, it was the captain's fault, yet when we had done well, it was because of the wise old head of Illingworth, pulling the strings in the background. All of this with the usual accompanying banner headlines, after Illingworth had decreed that no players could make comments such as these in the papers. When Athers was shown the articles after we'd arrived in South Africa, he was clearly unimpressed, but for the sake of unity, he shrugged them off publicly. After all, it was a long tour, and it was more important to the captain to make sure he and the players stood shoulder to shoulder.

Illingworth was at it again at our first public function in South Africa. At the press conference to launch the series, he stood up and introduced 'my team'. He talked about what he expected, with hardly a reference to Mike Atherton alongside him. The players were cheesed off by this, and Athers just had to sit at the same table, facing the media, knowing what everyone was thinking. It made me angry, and Athers looked small. It was ridiculous for the coach to put his views ahead of the captain at the start of such an important tour; can you imagine Illingworth standing for that when he was skipper of England? It was no better when we had our first team meeting. Illingworth's introduction was hardly inspiring. The gist of his message was, 'We've come here to win. I expect commitment and effort, otherwise I'm wasting my time here and I may as well go back to my villa in Spain.' He then announced a ban on wearing jeans in the hotel. That may seem a trivial point, but it was typical of Illingworth's style that he turned it into an order, rather than a suggestion. That was no way to win the respect of the players, you don't get that from international cricketers by treating them like kids. Of course, discipline is important, and that's shown in a pride in your appearance, but this was a needless instruction and way down our list of priorities. Illingworth should have given us the freedom to wear jeans, but then asked for our full commitment in return. I had experience of this dilemma when captaining Gloucestershire in 1995. We were playing up in Harrogate, and the lads wanted to wear T-shirts and jeans to the match. I left them a note saying it was okay this time, but to make sure we won. That way, I'd been seen to have given them some latitude, rather than being stubborn, and I could ask for something in return. Illingworth's line seemed to be that he'd given up his winter in Spain to be out in South Africa, and that we ought to be grateful. I know the bulk of the players on that tour shared my opinion about Illingworth.

On our first day of serious training, Illingworth didn't hang around to watch us go through our paces at the Wanderers Ground in Johannesburg. He went off instead to play golf with John Edrich. Now it was absolutely right that the important figure that afternoon was our physiotherapist, Wayne Morton, who would be assessing how we would react to our first workout in the high altitude, but surely the coach ought to have stayed on after the nets and monitored which players were coping best with the unusual conditions, and who needed extra work. I would have thought he could have left his golf clubs in the bag for just one more day. He had set his man-management standards already. There was to be more intimidation than encouragement. The players needed to be told that we were the priority, that he was only interested in our interests. What would have been ideal was something like, 'I'm here to support you in every way I can. If you have any problems, come and talk to me. If there is anything you want to discuss technically, come and see me. It's my job to help you play to the best of your ability. If you all play well, we'll win because you have the talent. Now let's prove it.' Instead we got, 'I've picked you. So you owe me a performance.' The response would have been different if Illingworth had made us feel he rated us all. I must stress I had no problems at all with him on this tour, he seemed to be happy with the way I did my job, but I could see how his negative attitude grated with so many of the players.

I believe the most glaring example of Illingworth's poor man-management was the way he treated Devon Malcolm. Now Devon was our wild card on that tour, the unpredictable element that we knew could unsettle the South Africans. Of course, he could be expensive and wild, but he was genuinely fast and dangerous. On his day, he could win us a Test and with it the series. The South Africans knew that too. On his last appearance against them, at the 1994 Oval Test, he had devastated them with 9 for 57, and some of their batsmen looked very apprehensive against his pace and hostility. Devon still had a hold over them psychologically. Athers knew it as well and was desperate to use that to our advantage. Devon was our trump card, if handled properly. That proved a big 'if'. Illingworth had to handle Devon properly, to make the most of his potential and unleash him in the Test series at the right psychological times. He failed abysmally, and by the end of the series, Devon was at his lowest ebb, and getting the blame for losing the final Test.

It was clear from the start of the tour that Devon wasn't seeing eye to eye with Illingworth or Peter Lever, our bowling coach. Devon had undergone a knee operation in the autumn, and he wasn't fully fit when we got out to South Africa. He should have been eased into the action gently, making sure he reached his physical peak at the meaningful time, a month ahead. Instead, Peter and Raymond were at him right away, trying to change his action. They couldn't get through to Devon – it may be that Devon dug his heels in, I don't know – but they soon made no secret of their frustration with our fastest bowler. Then Devon showed his stubborn streak, by failing to turn up for the day/night game against Eastern Transvaal, even though the captain had expressly asked those not picked for the match to come along and support the lads. That was wrong of Devon, but clearly this was his protest at the way he was being treated.

It got worse. Battle lines were drawn up when Illingworth and Lever went public about Devon's perceived inadequacies as a fast bowler and cricketer. Lever told a group of English cricket reporters that if they hung around for a few more minutes, he'd have something for them. He than sat around the hotel pool with Illingworth, and proceeded to run down Devon. They'd been trying to streamline Devon's action in the nets, but alleged he didn't want to know. Lever said, 'He has just one asset – pace. That apart, he is a nonentity in cricketing terms.' Illingworth then pitched in: 'At the moment, he wouldn't frighten you lot, never mind the South Africans.' Now some might say that was an attempt to gee up Devon, but that badly misjudges the way England cricketers should be treated. Whatever the problems existing between Devon and the management, they ought to have been settled in private, not in the newspapers. Devon's tour contract that prohibited him making public comments without the permission of the manager meant he couldn't have the right of reply, yet it was okay for Raymond and Peter to denigrate him. They showed a total lack of understanding in how best to deal with Devon. One of the game's gentlemen, Devon is both an intelligent and sensitive man – but he's also a proud man. As a cricketer, he may lack deep awareness, but that doesn't matter so much when you have his ability to bowl fast. You have to treat him with respect, don't talk down to him, or try to bully him, otherwise he'll shut up shop and you'll end up with nothing. You need to put your arm around Devon, explain things to him patiently, politely and cajole him, and then he'll give you everything. Devon's attitude to the management in South Africa was that he had taken more than a hundred wickets in 34 Tests, and it was a bit late to start trying to refine his bowling action. The captain wasn't happy, either, and I don't blame him. Messing with someone's technique on tour is dangerous. Half the time it just looks as if the coach or specialist is trying to do something for the sake of it, because it looks good and justifies their position. I like Peter Lever, he's very funny and a good man. He used to amuse me during morning practice on the outfield, trying to catch balls in his baseball mitt, and he took the ribbing in good spirit. In this matter though, Peter and Illy got it wrong. The end result proved that. They undid all the psychological pluses from Devon's great day at the Oval in the space of five minutes. They shouldn't have attempted to change him into something that made him feel uncomfortable, especially at that stage of his career. It was a disgrace. Bob Woolmer and his captain, Hansie Cronje, must have been loving all this.

I believe that impromptu press conference was a set-up, as if to say, 'Look, it's not our fault. If he doesn't win us the Test series, it's because we tried to refine his technique, but he just wouldn't listen.' The message coming out of our camp was that Devon wasn't going to be the danger the South Africans expected. What must the opposition have thought of it all? Here we had a proven matchwinner, a fast bowler feared by the South Africans, yet our management was berating him in public, more or less washing their hands of him. Why couldn't the matter be sorted out in private, instead of giving the opposition a psychological boost?

There was another aspect to this sorry episode – Nelson Mandela. As soon as we arrived in South Africa, Devon was at the centre of local attention, particularly from the black community. We were due to feature in the first game of first-class status to be played in Soweto, marking a brilliant effort to transform that wasteland into an excellent playing area. Their cricket board and politicians seemed determined to offer Devon as a role model to all the disadvantaged black kids in South Africa, and when we went to Soweto to play an Invitation XI, it was clear that Dr Ali Bacher, the South African Cricket Board's managing director, wanted Devon to play. He wasn't fully fit after his knee operation

It's the oldest, but truest maxim – watch the ball!

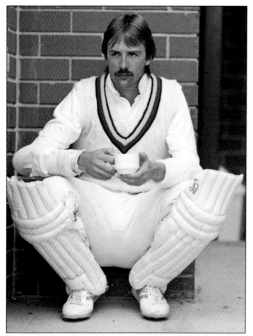

Above: The crab in action … or one way of getting a better sight of the ball.

Above: Russell's Rituals. Off the field, the inevitable cuppa tea is never far away from me.

Below: Giving Dickie Bird something more to worry about in his final Test, at Lord's, against the 1996 Indians.

Above: And they say it's all sunshine and glamour being an England cricketer! Training was tough at Lilleshall, December 1993, before the tour to West Indies.

Left: I've perfected the 'leave alone' shot that drives bowlers potty. Once I know they're frustrated by it, I'm winning the battle.

Below: No flies on me, at least, as I avoid being bitten at Alice Springs, Australia during an A-team tour. I thought about keeping with this net on...

I don't believe in leaving anything to chance when I go on tour, though the locals in St Vincent don't appear to be too impressed.

Taking a high one in the Lord's Test of 1990 against India. Flexibility is the key to my game.

Pakistan won the Lord's Test of 1992 by two wickets but not before we gave them a fright. Ian Salisbury's dismissal of Aamir Sohail started the alarm bells ringing. I look rather pleased!

Dodging a Courtney Walsh special, at Sabina Park, Jamaica, in 1994. He always seems to bowl quicker at me!

Above: One of the lowest points of my career, at Trinidad, as I'm out en route to England's all-out total of 46.

Left: A year later in the Trent Bridge Test of 1995, I should have stumped Sherwin Campbell. I never forget the mistakes, although I'm not so hard on myself as I used to be.

The 1995 winter tour to South Africa was an historic series. At Soweto, the England team was introduced to the great man, President Nelson Mandela.

Devon Malcolm was especially thrilled. Unfortunately, the crass handling of Devon by bowling coach Peter Lever and manager Ray Illingworth harmed our chances of winning that series.

One of my eleven victims that set the new world record for Test dismissals in one game. South African opener Gary Kirsten nibbles at one from Malcolm in the second Test at Johannesburg.

			SOUTH AFRICA	
HUDSON	c RUSSELL b FRASER	17	**314**	
KIRSTEN	c RUSSELL b MALCOLM	1		
CRONJE	c RUSSELL b CORK	48	WICKETS	
CULLINAN	c GOUGH b CORK	61	**9**	
RHODES	c RUSSELL b FRASER	57		
McMILLAN		80		
RICHARDSN	c RAMPKASH b MALCOLM	23	OVERS	97
POLLOCK	lbw b CORK	5	EXTRAS	18
EKSTEEN	c RUSSELL b CORK	2	LAST AT	314
PRINGLE	c HICK b FRASER	2	SA LEAD	446
DONALD		0	R/RATE	3.2

There for all to see. The scoreboard detailing my world record dismissals, Johannesburg, 1995.

The catch to dismiss Jonty Rhodes brought me level with Bob Taylor's world record, and from a technical point of view, it's the best catch I've taken standing back.

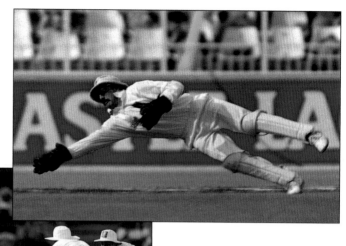

Above: That same Test match also included my most famous innings, just 29 not out. Defying the South African close fielders and blocking it out for a draw, alongside Mike Atherton, was a tremendous experience.
Right: Our elation was obvious at the end of the match.

Another memorable moment for me in that series. Stumpings for me in Tests are rare and to be treasured. Here, Darryl Cullinan is inches out off Richard Illingworth in the fourth Test in Port Elizabeth.

I maintained my batting form into the 1996 summer, when I managed more effective although unstylish runs towards my hundred in the Lord's Test against India.

Below: Here I am at the Imperial War Museum with a marvellous hero from the Second World War, Bill Sparks, who inspired me to paint the story of the Cockleshell Heroes which hangs in the museum.

Above: Drawing a crowd at the market in Peshawar on a day off during the 1996 World Cup.

Painting helped me escape from the realities of cricket, especially in Antigua on one of my most depressing tours to the West Indies in 1994.

At home with my wife and children. Since this was taken, we now have a fifth child!

Below: England v Matabeleland on the 1996 winter tour to Zimbabwe. I'm surplus to requirements again … and this picture just about sums it all up.

The late Willie Rushton loved his cricket and I'll always treasure this cartoon by him.

- Rushton's HEROES -

A JACK RUSSELL

and really ought to have been allowed to work on his rehabilitation instead, but the management relented and Devon was included. I got the impression then that Illingworth felt all the attention was going to Devon's head, and that he needed to be taken down a peg or two. This was nonsense. All the players could see how genuinely moved he was to be in South Africa at last in these special circumstances, and his delight overflowed when he met President Mandela during this game in Soweto. The atmosphere was electric that morning, when we found out he was coming just four minutes before he arrived. That man has so much presence and charisma. He looked like a Roman emperor, with an aura that few people on earth possess. We lined up to meet him and I'll never forget the moment. He said to each one of our party, 'Thank you so much for coming to our country, it's an honour to meet you', looking you straight in the eye, and gripping your right hand firmly. Nelson Mandela told me it was an honour to meet *me*! He didn't have to say that, it was one of the great occasions of my life. I was so thrilled that I then rang up my agent, Jim Ruston on my mobile phone, and said, 'Guess who's just shaken my hand?' If I was overwhelmed at meeting Nelson Mandela, what must it have meant to Devon Malcolm? He told Devon, 'I know you, you're the destroyer!' when they were introduced, and the fact that his hero knew all about his great bowling at the Oval moved him enormously. Then the President walked around the ground with Devon, a symbolic gesture that touched anyone with the slightest awareness of what Nelson Mandela had been through and what he wished for the new South Africa. Having read his autobiography on that tour, I could imagine the pride Devon must have felt that day.

I don't believe that Illingworth and Lever understood how emotional all of this was for Devon. They could have guided him sympathetically through that day, then got his mind attuned to the task in hand, which was to get him fully fit. Yet they thought it was more important to pack Devon off to the nets in Centurion Park, thirty miles away, where the first Test was due to be held.

They withdrew him from the Soweto match on the third morning, insisting he was better employed in the nets. That seemed like a public humiliation to Devon, who was hurt and getting rather depressed by now. My feeling was that the management thought Devon had been showboating during the Soweto fixture, because of all the attention, not least of all from Nelson Mandela. When the 'cricketing nonentity' quote came out next day, I was even more sure.

By now, the players were feeling sorry for Devon, and we all tried to keep his spirits up. I hoped that Mike Atherton would spend some time with him, because his spearhead was losing confidence the longer the tour went on. Devon clearly grieved in private, because it was only after he went public in a newspaper in January that we were aware of his depth of misery. With his team-mates on tour, he was fine, his usual affable self, but I wish now I had known how low he was. I know what it's like to get depressed on tour, and he could have cried on my shoulder any time if I'd had an inkling of how badly he believed he'd been treated. Meanwhile, the management appeared to have given up on a guy who had the potential to win us two of the five Tests if handled properly. He wasn't picked for Centurion Park, took six wickets in the Johannesburg Test, then was left out at Durban, which was a shame, because he had a big buzz about him on that first morning, a real spring in his step. I overheard Athers tell him he wasn't playing, and Devon was distraught. He couldn't believe it. He was very downcast when the vote went to Peter Martin and Mark Ilott, who were selected for their accuracy in conditions that the management felt called for line and length. For the fourth Test, on the slow wicket at Port Elizabeth, Devon wasn't considered, and that made sense. Better to get him fired up and raring to go for Cape Town, where again he was expected to be a handful on a lively wicket. The series was still all square, with the weather ruining two of the Tests, so the final one at Newlands would be the decider. Would Devon be our matchwinner at last?

Devon failed at Cape Town, but so did the rest of us. That's important to underline right from the start, when you consider Illingworth's emotional outburst in the dressing-room, when we'd been hammered by ten wickets, and he started looking for scapegoats, beginning with Devon. They beat us with two days to spare after we'd been bowled out for 153 on the first day, then 157 on the third. I wasn't aware that Devon had been picked for his batting! It's true that the last-wicket stand of 73 between Dave Richardson and Paul Adams was the pivotal period of the match which left us frustrated and the opposition on a high, and a vital lead of more than ninety runs. Agreed, Devon didn't bowl very well at this pair, but not as badly as Illingworth alleged in his book, *One-Man Committee*, that was published a few months later. He said that Devon showed no aggression against Adams, the last man, and that he should have ruffled him with a few bouncers. That was Illy's opinion. From behind the stumps, I saw it differently. Devon was very rusty after almost a month without match practice, and that was the management's fault for not picking him at Durban. Any fast bowler needs a match or two under his belt when his confidence is low and he lacks rhythm, and that was certainly the case here with Devon. Richardson and Adams played some excellent attacking cricket, and we all lost it for a time, not just our rusty fast bowler. Dominic Cork gave Adams a gift of four runs by attempting a run out with a throw that missed by some distance and wouldn't have meant a thing, because Adams was well in his ground in any event. Devon tried a couple of yorkers, only to see them misdirected, and they both flew off the pads to the long leg boundary. That happens when your fastest bowler gets the radar wrong, something that's always possible with Devon Malcolm, even when he's primed for action, with recent games under his belt. In any case, he only bowled four overs in that spell before he was taken off, so why weren't the other bowlers criticised by Illingworth? Next day, when we declined from 138 for four to 157 all out, was that Devon's fault?

The ructions in our dressing-room after the awards ceremonies were the fault of a breakdown in communication between

Atherton and Illingworth that was sadly typical on this tour. As we stood, waiting for the presentation ceremony to start amid gleeful South African celebrations, it was announced on the tannoy that we had agreed to play Western Province on this same ground, under the lights on Saturday night. This was to compensate all those who had forked out for tickets on what would have been the final day of this Test. We looked at each other in disbelief, and I could see that Atherton was seething. Clearly, he had no idea of the arrangement. Not many of his players would fancy a game so soon after this huge setback, but once the dust had died down, I'm sure we'd be aware of the massive disappointment our supporters must have felt, after spending a lot of money to come out from England to watch a Test that had finished inside three days. The match would be a chance for some of the guys who had been drafted into the one-day squad, and for the World Cup the following month. Yet it was galling to hear about it over the public address system. Atherton was at the end of his tether by now – anguished after such a bad defeat and drained after a stressful tour and the effects of that monumental innings at Johannesburg, which had taken a lot out of him. He was fuming that Illingworth had agreed to the Western Province game without consulting the captain.

When we finally got back to the dressing-room, Athers exploded, demanding to know what was going on. Illingworth explained that he had been approached by the local cricket board and had to make a quick decision, so that the crowd could be informed at the end of the match, before they melted away. With Atherton in the field, watching their openers get the winning runs, there was no way he could have been consulted. Athers made it clear he was far from impressed and with that, Illingworth lost his rag, slammed the dressing-room door and said, 'Right, let's get it all out in the open.' Give Illy his due, he wasn't going to shirk the issue. He said, 'Come on! Let's have it!' After a few general sideswipes, he went up to Devon and had a real go at him. Devon had to restrain himself, he must have wanted to deck him, but he just looked at Illy and started to whistle. That was the best way to counter such nonsense. When Illingworth said that to Devon, he lost what little respect the players might still have had for him. The rest of the tour went rapidly downhill after that.

Shortly after Cape Town, Illingworth gave an interview to a couple of Sunday newspapers, covering his tracks and pointing the blame at certain players. He thought that the Test careers of at least six of the tour party were over, including Robin Smith and Alec Stewart. Robin had made the highest score on either side in the Cape Town Test and he was incensed. It was particularly hard on Alec, who admittedly had not been at his best, but he was very worried at that time about his mother, who had just undergone surgery to remove a brain tumour. That was all he needed at this stage of the tour – the Chairman of the Selectors writing him off. The right way to encourage two such distinguished batsmen was to find a way to rebuild their confidence and technique, to tell them they were class players. That is what management is all about. I could feel for Robin and Alec, I'd gone through the same after the West Indies tour of 1994, when Illingworth made it quite clear publicly that I was on his hit list. Too often, we take the easy option of kicking out a quality player and then forgetting him. Occasionally, being dropped can be a good thing, but it should be part of a greater plan to maximise a player's ability and get him firing on all cylinders again. Who really expects a chairman of selectors to justify in detail why an established player has been dropped? It seemed to me that Illingworth was too busy keeping the media happy, rather than trying to get the England players fully motivated. He was never convinced by Angus Fraser, a bowler who has never let England down in my eyes – and Mike Atherton feels the same. Athers wanted Gus on the 1994–95 tour of Australia, but the chairman wouldn't have it. So when Gus was called into the tour after injuries and illness to Martin McCague and Joey Benjamin (both Illingworth choices), he had something to prove to a sceptical chairman. Gus took 5 for 73 in the Sydney

Test, which almost helped us to victory, but Illingworth wouldn't admit he'd been wrong, claiming that he had only one good spell in the series. Why not admit that Athers and Gus had proved him wrong, and good luck to them? If only Illingworth had realised that owning up to misjudgments increases respect for you among the players, then things might have been different. Illingworth, I felt, undermined his captain in Bloemfontein, just before the Johannesburg Test, when I heard him chatting to the media in the hotel. 'Well, you know the side I want to play, but Athers wants his mate Fraser.' I began to realise they weren't totally agreed on the makeup of the team, and that just chipped away at the captain's authority. I heard criticism of Atherton's field placing and tactics by Illingworth in front of other players. I felt this sort of thing didn't contribute to a harmonious relationship between captain and coach. There was a comment from Illy quoted in one of the national newspapers in which he said Martyn Moxon was technically the best opener in England. That made Athers furious. Maybe, by chance, it turned out to be a good psychological ploy because Athers went on to get a big score in that match. Athers is no fool, he knew what Illingworth thought about him. I got the feeling that Athers decided to keep his head down, and accept that Illingworth wanted to run the team as if he was the non-playing captain. That's a difficult task for the coach.

By the time we started a hectic round of one-day internationals in South Africa, after losing the Test series, we were going down the plughole. So many players were coming and going, with an eye on the World Cup, that there was no clear pattern of selection, no tactical initiatives. No wonder we lost 6–1, hardly the ideal preparation for the big tournament starting the following month. We ought to have played our best one-day side in the early matches against South Africa, then after honing our game plans, experiment in the later games. Instead we chopped and changed every game, throwing away good opportunities in some matches, but generally looking below par. Too many stupid mistakes, a lack of professionalism, and the captain looking shattered, getting no obvious encouragement from the coach. I had become a bit of a blue-eyed boy in Illingworth's eyes by then. He had taken to praising me readily to the media, referring to my gutsy batting, and describing my input on the field as the sort of role the senior pros used to offer the captain in his day. Well, that was all very nice, and it marked a pleasant change to hear that Illingworth had revised his opinion of me. I'm grateful to him but I was only supporting the captain in the way that any wicket-keeper should, vocally and tactically. I continued to bat well though in South Africa. In the one-dayer at Centurion Park, I hit 39 off 19 balls, feeling no one could bowl at me that day, I was so fired up. Ironically, at one stage, I was in line to score the fastest one-day fifty in international cricket. So I was ending the tour on a high note personally, happy that my form had held up, but I didn't expect to be picked for the World Cup. Despite Illingworth's public reservations about Alec Stewart's future, he was the sensible bet for batsman/keeper, so that there'd be room for another bowler in the party. Yet we both made the trip, although I heard about my selection rather unconventionally. I rang home, and mentioned in passing to Aileen that I still hadn't heard about the World Cup. 'You're going,' she said, 'it's just been on the *Nine o'clock News*.' That's an example of what a shambles the tour had become. There seemed no thought to gathering the players together and telling them the situation before the media heard about the squad.

In discussing my selection for the World Cup, Illingworth made some remarks about the value of my left-hand batting against possible spinners, and that it was a deserved reward for my performances in South Africa. When we got to Pakistan, I went to the house of Zaheer Abbas, my old team-mate from my early Gloucestershire days, and Illy was asked along as well. He knew 'Zed' from their international days, when Illy was the captain, and as they reminisced, the red wine flowed and Illy became a little indiscreet. He hinted to me that Atherton wanted Alec to keep wicket, but that he, Illy, had dug his heels in on my behalf to get me on the trip. I wasn't sure this was true. The gist of his support was that I shouldn't be penalised for the deficiencies of other players, and that I deserved to be there after doing well in South Africa. It may have been Illy's way of geeing me up, but it was wrong of him to suggest that the captain didn't want me out there, that I was relying on the support of the coach. Once more, he was undermining the captain.

Our entire approach to the World Cup was wrong and we got what we deserved. We arrived not knowing our best side after all the chopping and changing in South Africa, and we were behind the times tactically. The idea of the pinch-hitter – a selective hitter to open the innings – had been adopted successfully by other sides to take advantage of the fielding restrictions in the opening overs, but we still toyed with the idea, unsure of its value. You only had to take one look at the way the Sri Lankans approached the start of their innings to understand how valuable it was to get away to a roaring start. They really sandbagged us in the quarter-final, with Jayasuriya playing a devastating innings. Their plan was to smash the ball around at the start, whatever the situation, because it would be more difficult later on, when the ball got soft on the slow pitches and some fielders could be placed in run-saving areas, rather than in the circle. If a guy gets going early on on a good pitch, there's not a lot you can do about that. We were unable to match those kind of fireworks because so many of our punishing batsmen were out of form. Alec Stewart and Robin Smith had been publicly written off as international players by Illingworth, Neil Fairbrother just couldn't get a run, and was troubled by his dodgy hamstring, while Graham Thorpe struggled with his timing. On top of all that, our linchpin, Mike Atherton was also scratching around, his footwork sketchy, unable to get moving at the start of our innings. So invariably, we were behind the required rate early on, and could never build large enough totals. We couldn't generate momentum because we lacked confidence to play with the necessary freedom after the hangover from our 6–1 defeat in South Africa.

Our precise roles were never clearly worked out. It wasn't a great idea to expect Phil DeFreitas to make much of an impression as an off-spinner in the match against Sri Lanka, when he has been a seamer for most of his career. Predictably their batsmen climbed into him. Robin Smith told me a story that underlined our lack of preparation. When he finally got into the side after injury, he played as the pinch-hitter against Pakistan. It was going well for Robin when Graham Thorpe came in to join him. Thorpey called Robin over and told him where he would normally be looking for his 'tip and run' singles. It suddenly dawned on Robin how poor our preparations had been. All our main batsmen should have known each other's game inside out, to know exactly where they could gather quick, yet safe singles. It was a bit late now, in the final qualifying match of the World Cup, to be working out plans that ought to have been lodged in our minds right from the beginning of the tournament. Our team meetings were generally poor in the World Cup. The captain did his best to stimulate discussion, but the edge had gone, and Illingworth offered very little. In contrast to his earlier involvement in South Africa, he had moved to the periphery. Perhaps he realised he'd lost the last of any respect after his outburst in Cape Town, followed by Devon Malcolm's damaging revelations in a newspaper about the breakdown in their relationship. He'd said when we started our World Cup campaign that he didn't want to hear anybody complaining about touring India and Pakistan, and that we just had to get on with it. That was absolutely right – except Illy moaned and groaned his way throughout. If it wasn't the hotels, or the food, or the bad drivers, or the team bus, it was the practice facilities. There was always something for him to have a beef about, much to our amusement.

So we crashed out to Sri Lanka in the quarter-finals and we didn't deserve any better. We had fallen behind in a form of cricket that we had started more than thirty years ago. The feeling was that we should have come close because we play so much one-day

11
A SINGULAR
MAN

I know what many think – that Jack Russell, he's daft as a brush, he doesn't seem to do anything that's normal. They look at the way I bat, my crab-like shots, my wide open stance and then there's my stance as I keep wicket, looking out to mid-off as the bowler runs in, rather than the accepted method of looking straight down the pitch. My capacity for drinking pots and pots of tea gets a mention, and my diet, which is very much my own, a mixture of chocolate biscuits, chicken and bananas. On top of all that, I'm a painter! Not something you associate with a professional cricketer. I'm also obsessive about my privacy, I don't like anybody knowing where I live and I admit to going over the top at times to ensure that my family and I are left alone. Since childhood, I haven't really enjoyed the company of many people, because I'm shy. When I'm captain, I'm a different person. I know I'm on display when I'm in the company of the other players, and I only revert to being my usual self when I either go home or open my hotel room door. The change in my personality goes with the territory, you just have to be open and challenging, and try to get the best out of your players. I can lose myself in cricket – walking out in front of a packed house at Lord's is stimulating – but walking down the street can be a trial for me, in case I'm recognised and a stranger wants to talk to me. It's not that I'm unsociable, it's more that I'm a social misfit, a reclusive person. Howard Hughes fascinated me, because he had so much money that it brought him freedom, the freedom to indulge his own quirks, to be himself and to hell with what anyone else thinks. To some, his secrecy in his later years must appear ridiculous and unbalanced: I think he was brilliant at doing his own thing.

I don't want to be like everyone else, so it never bothers me when people say I'm mad. Eccentric is a better description, I think. You get called a fruitcake because others don't understand what you're doing. The village idiot who is slow in speech gets categorised, so does the disabled person who can't relate to others in conventional terms – but why do they get put in a box, and described in superficial terms? They are just different, and the world ought to be more tolerant about those who just walk to a different tempo in life. Many go on about my eccentricities, but to me most of them are logical and natural. Everything I do has a reason for it. A few had a good laugh at my expense when Aileen arranged to have the Queen's Speech played down the phone to my hotel room in Zimbabwe on Christmas Day, 1996. She managed to get the phone close to the television set back home, as Her Majesty spoke about the last year, and I could hear it loud and clear in Harare. Why wasn't I having a good time with the rest of the lads in the team room instead? I wasn't being unsociable to them, it's just that I'm a huge patriot, it means everything to play for my country and I always listen to the Queen's Speech wherever I am in the world. No one could ever criticise me for not giving everything for England when I go out on the field, and even though I wasn't going to play in the Test, starting the following day, I was still proud to be representing my country on tour. To me, it was worth the expense and the trouble to hear that broadcast. Is that nuts?

I will admit to being obsessional about my fads and habits. In business, cricket and family life, everything has to be in place, I don't like the normal order to be overturned, I don't react to changes in routine as flexibly as others. I've never had great self-confidence around other people, so I have to be aware that matters are mapped out logically and carefully, so that I'm not caught out. When I received my MBE at Buckingham Palace from Prince Charles in 1996, it was a fabulous, memorable day for me, but I was disconcerted early on, coming to terms with what was expected of me. As I walked through the Palace, I was taken aback when asked to go to the cloakroom. When I asked 'Why?', I was told that I needed to leave my top hat with the attendant. He gave me a disc, and to my horror, it was number 111 – the dreaded 'Nelson', the English cricketers' nightmare number. A daft superstition, I know, but I took it as a sign that things could easily go wrong on my big day unless I was very careful. It made me so nervous. I could see the headlines after I'd tripped and fallen against the Prince – 'RUSSELL DIVES FOR MEDAL'. This was unknown territory for me, so I started worrying that my trousers would fall down, or the medal clatter to the ground as I walked away. I went through the process of approaching the Prince and receiving the medal at least a hundred times in my brain. People were talking to me as we waited in the picture room to be presented, but I didn't take any of it in. For the next hour and half, I went over and over the procedure. What would an SAS soldier do in these circumstances? Get it exactly right, to the nearest inch, as if his life depended on it. It all went smoothly, the Prince was charming and informed about me, and the special day was complete when the National Anthem was played by the Grenadier Guards. I handed back my disc, marked 111, and all was well.

Basically I'm a perfectionist. That's why I've never taken up golf, I'd either get obsessional about playing it for hour after hour, aiming for the perfect shots, or the frustration of attempting such a difficult game would drive me potty. I like to plan things to the exact degree. I'm a big fan of Charles Dickens' works, and I remember Mr Micawber talking about something always turning up to get him out of trouble. Well, Mr Micawber ended up in prison. You can't do enough homework and preparation in life and your profession. Margaret Thatcher used to get a lot of stick for being so tireless and nagging at her Cabinet ministers, but she had to work so hard to make up for the weaknesses of others. Her head was on the block, so she worked harder than anyone else, and I admire that. When I first came into the England team, I was so dedicated to perfection that I kept a log of every day's play in a Test in which I kept wicket. I'd bring it up to date every night, logging the balls I had dropped, the stumpings and catches taken or missed, the degrees of difficulty involved, the byes conceded. It was my bible. I could tell you any time how many chances I had missed for England. It became yet another obsession with me, but one day I lost it. I'd left it lying around in my studio – always a chaotic place – and I just couldn't find it. Then I realised I didn't need that book anymore. I had become so dependent on striving for perfection that my mistakes had assumed too much importance. The next ball was the vital one, not the one that could never be replayed. So that was one of my obsessions laid to rest!

Now I will admit to being very particular and superstitious about my cricket gear. I hate to take on new pieces of clothing or equipment. My cricket clothes are used by me for as long as possible. Take the white handkerchief that's in my right hand trouser pocket. I copied this from Alan Knott, it seemed to help him. I stitched red cotton in one corner to identify it as mine, and I hung onto it for eight years. One day, on the tour in Australia, my trousers were sent to the hotel laundry and I forgot to remove the handkerchief. It was lost for good, despite endless phone calls and visits by me to various laundries. I was really sad, don't ask me why – it just seemed that part of my cricket career had disappeared. My hat has been worn in every first-class game, apart from my debut against Sri Lanka in 1981. There's hardly any of the original left, but I stitch bits on it all the time, using old cricket trousers. It's washed twice a season, and to dry it, I use a glass biscuit jar, a tea cosy and a tea towel. The hat fits on top of all three, and is then, after starching, placed in the airing cupboard, thereby keeping its shape. I almost lost it for good during the 1994 tour to West Indies. I was sharing with Graeme

Hick, and after putting the hat into a small oven, because it would dry quicker after starching, I clean forgot about it. 'Hicky' spotted the smoke coming out of the kitchen, shouted to me and I dived in to retrieve it, frantically beating it to put out the fire. I was almost in tears, what would I do? I know, I'd fly Aileen out with her sewing machine to patch it up. Hicky fell apart in hysterics and once the rest of the lads found out about it, I was unmercifully hammered. I threatened Hicky with all sorts of tortures if the press got to hear about it, and it remained the tour's best-kept secret. In the end I took pieces from another hat and stitched them on to mine. Inside the hat, there are still the scorch marks on the brim. Now I take no chances with my hat getting lost – it goes everywhere with me, along with my gloves, in a travel bag. I won't leave anything to chance with these precious items. They go in my hand luggage, and no one is allowed to touch them. I have a recurring nightmare that I misplace my hat and gloves. These 'tools of the trade' are my comfort zone, absolutely vital for my feel of the ball and vision. During the World Cup of 1996, I had to dig my heels in over a dictat by the organisers that I couldn't wear my usual floppy white hat. They decreed that I had to wear coloured headgear to go with our royal blue strip. I refused and threatened to walk out of the tournament. I would have compromised, by putting some stitched blue material on the hat, but no one was going to make me dispense with such a treasured possession. In the end, after frantic faxes between Calcutta and London headed 'Jack Russell Hat Crisis' our manager John Barclay saved the day, using all his diplomatic skills, persuading Sunil Gavaskar, the head of the World Cup technical committee, to let me have my own way.

As for my keeper's gloves, I used the same pair from 1985 until 1995, using them in every game until they just fell apart. At least four of the fingers and one thumb had fallen off at various times, and had to be restitched by me. I have a sandwich box, containing needles, thread, sticky tape, black dye and other things that'll patch up my gear for as long as possible. After a time, though, the old gloves just weren't working with me, they were working against me, so they had to go, in case they hampered my efforts at taking the ball. So I went to South Africa with a new pair of gloves, and broke the world record with them, for once acting ruthlessly to discard old gear paid off for me. Actually, I don't believe I'm all that quirky about my gloves; you'll find lots of keepers have their own little idiosyncrasies about them. There was never a more classical, orthodox keeper in my time than Bob Taylor, yet he had his distinctive approach to his gloves. He never used webbing between his index finger and thumb, nor did he have any padding on the palms of his gloves at all. He used just a thin layer of leather, with rubber on the palms, and nothing else. Bob liked the complete freedom of being able to feel the ball in the glove, not to have padding absorb the shock of the ball's impact. If you ever get the chance to look at Bob Taylor's hands, you'll see how little damage he picked up in almost a quarter of a century in the first-class game – a tribute to his superb technical skills. Yet Bob went his own way when it came to a vital part of the keeper's equipment. No one ever said Bob Taylor was odd.

Aileen is the only one allowed to wash my kit, and when I'm on tour or away from home in England, I do it myself. I hang my underwear from the lightshade to dry. I'm particularly protective of my shirt, which I've worn since 1988. It was modified by Aileen, with a double back which gives added protection against draughts when I'm crouched down behind the stumps for long periods. It's vital to have warm, dry gear and so I carry a tumbledrier around in the boot of my car when I'm on the circuit in England. When the other players first saw me taking the tumbledrier out of my car, they thought it was another typical Russell eccentricity. Strangely enough, quite a few of them now ask if they can use it. What could be more sensible than keeping your kit dry, avoiding a cold back and stiffness when you're supposed to be supple and athletic out in the field?

To me, there has to be a reason for doing something, and if the thinking behind the action is sound, I don't worry about how odd it may appear. That's why I decided to open up my stance towards mid-off when I crouch behind the stumps, standing back to the faster bowlers. Using the conventional method – with both shoulders more or less facing down the pitch – I found I was getting pushed too much towards my left side, as the ball moved back in off the seam to the right-handed batsman. So I was at times a shade unbalanced when trying to get to the offside on the right. The same applied to the left-handed batter. Opening up my stance gave me greater balance, allowing me to push off swiftly to either side. That was the main reason why I managed to catch Jonty Rhodes at Johannesburg in 1995, the dismissal that equalled the world record. The extra mobility achieved from facing slightly to the offside allowed me to push off at full stretch and take the ball in my right glove. It was one of the best catches of my career, in an area where I'd had to work hard to improve my catching. Alan Knott had been instrumental in brushing up my technique for diving catches in front of first slip, and he encouraged me to open up my stance. Some traditionalists tut-tutted about how strange it looked, but ignored the fact that it improved my technique. The same with my batting. When I started, I was fairly conventional, but Knotty encouraged me to try different things. His attitude was, 'It's not how, it's how many' when you bat, that the vacant areas of the field need to be explored, rather than hitting the fielders with orthodox shots. So I started shovelling the ball on the legside, developing a crab-like stance, and playing the 'leave' – all designed to frustrate the bowler, making him bowl differently, preferably at my legs, which is usually a productive area for the left-hander. It does disconcert some bowlers. One or two of them find it hard to stop laughing when they first see the crab stance, so I'm already one up on them.

Knotty always dared to be different in his brilliant career, but then he was a genius. Lesser mortals like me settled for taking in the knowledge that he generously shared. I used to look forward so much to our games against Kent, knowing that he'd happily spend hours chatting about cricket at close of play. I'm a slow changer at the end of play, because I like to unwind and mull over the day's cricket, but Knotty would be even slower. Sometimes, we would still be in the dressing-room three hours after the close, and I was fascinated by how methodical he was. He left nothing to chance. He'd have various items of clothing to protect him from chills or stiff necks, including an overcoat, blazer and trilby to keep his head warm, because you lose so much warmth through your head. It was an education to watch him sorting out his kit for the next day in such an organised, methodical fashion. I learned such a lot from him in terms of technique, attitude, concentration and preparation. He also drummed it into me that effectiveness counts far more than style. Be unorthodox if that gets you a head start and most importantly if it works. Right through my England career, Knotty's been there, preaching the gospel of individualism and although that's always been my attitude to life, it's been marvellous to have it confirmed so often by one of the most brilliant keepers of all time.

Knotty was very quirky about his food when playing for England, and I share that trait. There are so many stories about what he ate on tour – more particularly, what he wouldn't eat. He'd exist on nuts and bananas if necessary, because he was so fanatical about avoiding an upset stomach in places like India and Pakistan. It worked for him because he barely missed a game for Kent and England throughout a long career, and I view food in the same way. If I didn't have to eat to survive, I'd never bother with eating. I have two addictions, though – chocolate and tea. Wherever I find myself, I get the kettle on, and usually there's a cup of tea in my hand. On the rare occasions I'm in a restaurant, I'll be wading through a couple of pots of tea while the others are knocking back the wine. I just love the taste of tea, and it helps me relax. As for chocolate, I'll get through a packet of Jaffa cakes every day, plus one of McVities wholemeal biscuits. A bar of chocolate also gets the daily treatment. It would be wrong to call me a gourmet! My preferred meals when possible are mashed potato with milk and butter, mixed in with plain white rice, served up with Heinz baked beans over the mashed potato, topped off with a generous dollop of HP brown sauce. With that I'll have two slices of brown bread and butter and a glass of fresh milk. Occasionally I'll have a steak with the mashed potato and sauce, but the steak has to be on the cremated side of well done. Or I might have steamed breast of chicken or fish, but it has to be heavily doused in HP sauce or tomato ketchup. Nothing else, I can't face any other sort of cooked meal. I have eaten the same sandwiches for years – cheese and Branston pickle, four of them on brown bread. If I have to go somewhere, I'll take those sandwiches in tin foil, plus a banana and a flask of weak, milky tea that will give me at least ten cups. For breakfast it's cereal, which has to be soaked in milk for twelve minutes to get the consistency I prefer. I have breakfast cereal at lunch during a day's play, and whoever is twelfth man organises the timing of the milk in the bowl for me. It must be twelve minutes. That's exactly how I like it, it's no different from how someone wants their steak cooked or if they want their vegetables slightly undercooked.

So many go on about my strange eating habits, but as usual there's a reason for the way I view food. It's just a means to an end for me. The potato and rice helps me build up my carbohydrate load in the evening, the cereal gives me energy, and it's the same with bananas. On my first England tour to the West Indies in 1990, I used to eat bananas on the field during drinks intervals, and that raised a few eyebrows. Now you see all the top tennis players do it between games as they towel down. When Jack Russell does something like that it's eccentric, but when it's Boris Becker, well that's good sense. I drink lemon juice and water because it contains a lot of vitamins and force down carrots and broccoli. I don't really like vegetables, so I have to try. I just like to feel safe in the food I eat. That's why I ate steak (cremated) and chips for 28 consecutive days in India during the Nehru Cup tour in 1989, and why I did the same with chicken on our tour to the West Indies. Because eating is no big deal for me, I saw no reason to alter my pattern. I also didn't want to get a stomach bug that would rule me out of any cricket. So chicken it was, even on one night of our tour in Guyana, when I commandeered Geoffrey Boycott's meal from the hotel kitchen. 'Boycs' is almost as faddy as me when it comes to food, and he'd made sure that the last available piece of chicken was reserved for him that night. I got back from the ground before him, convinced the kitchen staff that Mr Boycott was eating out, so his portion was going spare. Geoffrey wasn't best pleased when he turned up for his evening meal! After all, he wouldn't have been as selfish as me, would he?

I do admit to being fanatical about my food, and the brand names have to be right as well. It has to be McVities biscuits, the sauce must be HP and the baked beans manufactured by Heinz. It's always been the same with me. Ask my Mum. When I was a lad, I used to have Heinz oxtail soup all the time – little else. One day, Mum served it up for me, and it tasted different. She swore blind it was the usual Heinz make, but I wouldn't have it. I went outside to the rubbish bin, scavenged inside for the empty tin and emerged triumphantly with an oxtail soup tin that didn't carry the Heinz trademark. I'd proved my point, I knew what I liked. Now that sounds daft, I know, a bit obsessional – but it shows I haven't changed much!

I do get uptight about my privacy, though. At home, I don't like to be disturbed by the phone if I'm painting in the studio or watching one of my favourite black and white movies. So only my wife, mother and agent have my personal phone number. Gloucestershire CCC have a number where they can reach me, and my fax number, so I can return urgent calls, but that's it. Aileen is the only one who has my mobile phone number. Hardly any of the Gloucestershire lads have been to my house, and that's because I want to switch off from that part of my life when I come home. One day, when I've got all the renovations and alterations done, I may invite them round to satisfy their curiosity, but they won't know exactly where I live. I'll pick them up in a mini van, blindfold them, and I'll do the driving. I'm serious! Why should someone know a great deal about me, just because we work together? I had a big dilemma when I needed to get the builders in soon after I moved to my present house. I was wondering how I could preserve my privacy and mentioned to my agent, Jim Ruston that I could blindfold them and drive them myself to the house. Jim thought that was a bit extreme, and he was probably right!

Maybe I'll end up a total recluse, someone like Howard Hughes or John Paul Getty when he was younger, before he discovered cricket. I really admire Mr Getty for the way he's gone about his later life, doing his own thing, preserving his privacy, but doing charitable work behind the scenes. I treasure the fax he sent me after my long Test vigil at Johannesburg, that helped Mike Atherton save the Test. He wrote 'Thank you for enriching my life. That was one of the bravest and most dogged innings ever played.' I suppose Mr Getty is lucky in that he is fabulously wealthy, but at least he seems to use it constructively, enriching other people's lives at the same time by thoughtful donations, especially to the world of cricket. Money is another of my obsessions, I suppose. I've been accused of being mean, but that might stem from the fact that I no longer stand in the bar with the other players, throwing alcohol down my throat, wasting money. Some of the Gloucestershire players I argued with about money a few years back are near the end of their careers without a great deal to show for it financially, and I hope that won't happen to me. That's why I won't gamble. I hate losing. If I stick a fiver on a horse and it loses, I would put a tenner on for the next race, and so on till I'd won back my money. It would be the same if I was in a casino, I'd end up sticking my house on number 23 on the wheel and lose the lot. Then I'd gamble the gallery to try winning back the house! If I gambled, my obsession about coming out on top would be my undoing.

I suppose another of my obsessions is wasting time. You earn your freedom in life by getting off your backside and working damned hard to make things happen for you. I honestly believe you can do anything you want if you try hard enough. I always give money to those guys who clean your car windows in London, whenever you stop at traffic lights; at least they're out there doing something worthwhile. Challenges in life and in cricket turn me on. I'll never just put my feet up on the table and say 'I've cracked it', there'll always be goals to attain. I'm very stubborn, nothing will stop me if I get something into my head. That's why Winston Churchill is one of my heroes, and not just for his leadership during the Second World War. He generated belief in our country when we really needed it, he faced the ultimate challenge and succeeded. He never seemed to waste a minute of his life, he was always working – either writing, painting, building extensions or making wonderful speeches. Churchill needed thirty hours a day, and I feel the same way.

All I'm basically doing is trying to survive in an enjoyable way. Sometimes I think it's a fight for survival, in my cricket, in my business and life generally. Nobody is going to tell me how to live my life and for that freedom, you need money. I'm lucky that I can earn that money doing things I love, playing cricket and painting – and that makes me happy. But I'm very cautious and closed in my relationships with anyone other than my family. David's tragic and premature death when I was just 23 has scarred me. I don't think I ever grieved for him properly, I just immersed myself in my cricket to bury the pain. I was so hurt at the loss of David that I subconsciously distanced myself from outsiders, didn't allow myself to get into personal relationships that would bring me pain if I lost them. Aileen is my closest friend. She's totally different to me – bubbly, chatty, sensible, a Yorkshire lass, and she and the children will eat anything put on the table, unlike me! Aileen doesn't get involved with cricket, other than get annoyed when I'm not in the England team, but that suits me. I like to come home to different interests and challenges. One obsessive in our family is enough!

I'm such a control freak that I've already organised my own funeral. Nothing must be left to chance, everything must be exactly in place, military precision and all that. I'll have my hands surgically removed, then embalmed, and placed in a glass case for display in my gallery. Would the Tate Gallery consider this modern art?! I want my coffin to be placed on top of a Second World War British tank, on my last journey from home to church. If no tank is available, then a horse-drawn carriage. Black horses. I don't mind who carries in the coffin, but it has to be done with 'Wandrin' Star' being played during the service. Sung by Lee Marvin, no other version will do; I loved his gravelly voice. Then a recording of the Agincourt speech from *Henry V*, the one about 'Once more unto the breach, dear friends'. That's such a stirring speech, so full of the camaraderie and bravery the best British fighting units possessed throughout our history. Someone like Laurence Olivier speaking the words, I think. After that, some music – 'Search For The Hero Inside Yourself' by M People. Great words, ideal sentiments – you've got to do it yourself, but you really can. David Lloyd used this as part of his musical compilation to motivate us in the England dressing-room when he took over as coach, and I love it. Also 'Over the Hills and Far Away' from the television series *Sharpe*, and 'A Cotswold Lad' by Johnny Coppin. Next, some Winston Churchill speeches. What an inspiration his words must have been in wartime. In my humble career as a cricketer, I've never given up and that's why it would be an appropriate message at my funeral, especially coming from one of my all-time heroes. To finish the service in the church, it would have to be 'Jerusalem'. Inspirational, moving and so British. As they carry my coffin to the graveside, I want a lone piper. Bagpipes are so moving, and that piper will bring everyone to tears. I want military music played by that piper, nothing obviously Scottish. Then it would be time for 'Land of Hope and Glory' and to end it all, a bugler playing 'The Last Post'. The piper and bugler would be in the red of the Grenadier Guards. I shall leave funds to pay for it all and hope everyone there sheds a tear or two and finds it moving. I certainly would. On my tombstone, I would like the following: 'I used to wander through graveyards like you, hoping that one day I would be more famous, so that people wouldn't wonder who I was. Life is too short for you to be stood here. Thank you for your interest – off you go and do something beneficial before you end up like me!' Oh, just one more request – someone from the Royal Family. I'm a big monarchist, but just one would do. If the Queen chose to attend, she might bring one of her dogs – a corgi to Jack Russell's funeral. Not too much to ask is it?

So am I barking mad? I'll admit to some eccentricities – certainly in my eating habits – but one cricketer's fad is another's superstition. In many ways, my obsession with an ordered, structured world is just a method of getting the best out of myself as an international sportsman. If I go off painting, that relaxes me and recharges my batteries for the fray. To me, that's much more constructive than hanging around a bar. My cricket gear has to be exactly right and familiar to me, because that helps me perform to my optimum. If I'm operating in familiar surroundings, I've simply got a better chance of doing my job satisfactorily. So a battered, white floppy hat does help me keep wicket well. So the team benefits as well. There has to be room for individuality in sport. It would have been counter-productive to expect Ian Botham to be cooped up early in his hotel room, concentrating on the task in hand next day. The same with David Gower. Not a guy to build up his stamina with long cross-country runs, but a naturally fit, hugely talented cricketer who could be left to his own devices and bat as entertainingly as anyone I've ever seen. It takes all sorts in sport. I really admired the man management skills of Brian Clough, Alex Ferguson and Bill Shankly, the leadership of Bobby Moore, the dedication of Nick Faldo, the consistency and good manners of Steve Davis, the grace and sportsmanship of Bobby Charlton, the rugged bravery of his brother, Jack. Could you ever imagine two such different footballers as the Charlton brothers? Yet they were both winners in their different ways. It's getting there that matters, not how you get there. I've managed to reach a certain status in my sport because of my individualistic streak, not despite it.

12
WHAT'S NEXT?

I know it's greedy, but I have just two wishes, two things that would make me so happy. One is that I could travel back in time in my own personal Tardis, so that I could be at Waterloo, at Balaclava, or Rorke's Drift, soaking in the atmosphere of those amazing battles, experiencing the courage of the combatants at close quarters, then re-creating all that on canvas. The second is that I could live for another hundred years. One of my big regrets is all the time I've wasted in my life before sorting out my priorities. If I added up all the hours and days in which I've done nothing – mostly when young – then I'd gain another couple of years at least. I can see myself on my deathbed, moaning about all the wasted time, wishing I'd done more. People annoy me when they say they're bored, and have nothing to do. I feel like saying 'Give me your twenty-four hours a day, so I can have forty-eight!'

I want to remain successful in whatever I do. That's a hard challenge, but it's rewarding when you carry it off. As a player, I'd like to go on for at least another ten years, emulating the great Bob Taylor, who was still good enough at forty-three to be the world's number one. My fitness shouldn't be a problem, hopefully, as long as I look after myself. As for my England future, it all depends on the make-up of the side, but I owe it to Gloucestershire to keep giving of my best for as long as possible. It would be wonderful to see England regain the Ashes and for Gloucestershire to become a big club, going into the 21st century.

One day, after I've retired, I'd like to be in charge of Gloucestershire's cricket. The timing has to be absolutely right, where I can sort out my commitments so that I can give enough time to the cricket – but I'd love to put my views into practice. There's still an opinion that wicket-keepers are like football goalkeepers – too individualist to be good managers or coaches. It's how much you think about cricket, plus the ability to communicate your ideas, that are important rather than what your role has been as a player. In any case, who is closer to the action than the keeper? Who has a better idea of who can cope with the mental pressure out in the middle? Who does the captain usually turn to for a second opinion? The wicket-keeper gets an overall impression of what's going on, and if you're out there in the thick of the action for so many years, you can't fail to take a lot in. Something like Director of Cricket at Bristol would appeal to me, as long as I could give it my full attention, and I was in complete control. I'd need to stand or fall on my own decisions, rather than hiding behind committees all the time. To me, committees are the dry rot of English cricket, they take up too much time, are not productive enough, and are a platform for too many egos. They also don't take responsibility, preferring to point the finger at the captain or the coach, when they could have been more supportive and professional. Committees, if they have to exist, ought to create the right managerial atmosphere for those in charge. I'm not sure that committee members do enough for the clubs they represent. Once you select your salaried people to run the cricket on and off the field, you should let them get on with it. There are often sound reasons why a player is out of the first team, and such matters should be sorted out in the dressing-room.

The experience of captaining Gloucestershire in 1995 really opened my eyes. I got a taste of the interlocking units in the machine that is the team, the need to get the best out of your players while treating them as individuals in a team context. I learned that you can't get the best out of your side by continually talking to them just as a team. You need to break down the engine and look at the component parts. It's like analysing the various skills of a commando unit. One is the specialist in explosives, another in communications, another deadly with the knife to the ribs, yet in a raid, they can all do each other's job without fuss and with total concentration. With a county team, you need to take particular skills for granted, otherwise they wouldn't have reached such a high standard, but the knack is to analyse each cog and making sure the skills flourish at the right time. For that to happen, the players must feel they are respected, encouraged to succeed with no jealousy and no back-biting if the methods used fail. That was one of the key ingredients in Warwickshire's remarkable success a year or two back. Their captain at the time, Dermot Reeve, cajoled the players into believing in themselves, by always playing positively and radiating a sense of enjoyment.

Communication with your players is absolutely vital. My experience with England at the hands of Graham Gooch made me realise that. When I first established myself in the England side, Goochy was tremendous with me, making me feel my input was important and that my performances were highly valued. During the 1990–91 tour to Australia, he started to steer away from that after I'd been dropped for the Adelaide Test, and that disappointed me. Eye contact became scarcer, my views weren't sought as often, and it appeared to me that Goochy's priority was to focus on those players actually in the first team, rather than those on the sidelines. To me, you don't need so much attention from the captain when it's going well for you, and you ought to have enough self-motivation and professionalism to profit from your good form or self-confidence. It's the struggling players who need extra attention, because a few disenchanted guys can alter the atmosphere and also the captain might need to call on any of them in the case of illness or a broken finger.

On the tour to Zimbabwe and New Zealand, I could see that at times, it was difficult for the younger guys, who weren't being picked at various stages. I knew exactly how they felt from previous experience and we'd get chatting about what it was like when training together during a match, or when working out in the gym. I'd tell them all about life in Pakistan on my first England tour, when I barely played, what some of the grotty hotels were like, and how important it must be to keep it all in perspective and remember you're representing your country. It was necessary to make them realise that getting emotional about being out of the side blurs your vision and your aims, leading to frustration. Overall, I reckon younger players like Chris Silverwood and Ronnie Irani did well to keep cheerful for most of the time on their first England tour. Andy Caddick also did very well to come back strongly in New Zealand after kicking his heels for long periods in Zimbabwe. He passed a big test of character.

When I captained Gloucestershire, I targeted those players who weren't doing well, who lacked confidence. I said things like, 'Now how do we get you back in the side?' so that they knew they still had something to aim for, that they weren't consigned to weeks of playing second-team cricket. I felt I knew my players better after we'd exchanged letters about our individual aims and hopes for the season. They were aware that I wouldn't ever consider the word 'defeat' until the game was over, that I expected everyone to give the mythical 110 per cent, but if that was forthcoming, they'd be fully supported by me. Writing those directives before the season, and in the midway point was important to me; the players deserved to know their captain could deal with them on a private basis, as well as talk to the team as a whole. I find it amazing that throughout my England career, I have never had a written directive from any of my captains. Phone calls, yes, encouraging words in hotel rooms, yes – but a letter or a note indicates extra care taken. You can't fail to get an extra buzz if the England captain drops you a line.

England have made some big mistakes in my time over their desire for conformity, for cloning the players. We seemed to have put some of our matchwinners in chains, robbing them of their capacity to damage the opposition by expecting them to be the same as everyone else. David Gower had a tendency to get himself out in dreamy fashion, but he was never going to change, so why waste time getting him in the nets where he was usually bored? He should have been treated as a mature individual, who knew what was right for him at that stage of his career, because David could win you the big matches. Get him on your side, and he'd do the cosmetic things like going to the team training sessions so that nobody would say he was being pampered. But it was wrong to have David netting day after day, and expecting him to go on long runs to build up stamina. It may have worked for another great player, Graham Gooch, but not for Gower.

Devon Malcolm was also handled badly in South Africa by Ray Illingworth and Peter Lever. We all know that Devon can bowl erratically at times, but when he gets it right, he can win you Test matches. The South African players knew that, but in my view our coaches on that tour didn't appear to agree. When you consider how short we have been in the past decade of bowlers who can win you Tests, it was stubborn and short-sighted to try to change Devon's technique at that advanced stage in his career. Phil Tufnell has been one of those England bowlers with matchwinning potential, but Gooch and Mike Atherton have been frustrated by him and then sceptical about whether he can change. He doesn't fit into the peg marked 'great trainer, dedicated practiser, fitness fanatic' but I feel that doesn't mean he can't be a matchwinner. If you keep him on the rails, talk to him when he's feeling low, boost his confidence, don't nag about his smoking, give him some space while spelling out what's expected – then you might just have a happier cricketer who can then do justice to his obvious talent.

At Bristol, I faced similar situations with two explosive batsmen, one at the start of his career and the other nearing the end. Monte Lynch has at times been one of the most destructive batsmen in county cricket over the past twenty years, and when he joined us from Surrey, it was clear he hadn't cured his tendency to get out on the hook, or hit one straight up in the air for no apparent reason. But Monte has won games throughout his career, and we allowed him his head. We didn't expect him to change his style just because he'd moved counties, we had to concentrate on him, using his assets to the best advantage. Andrew Symonds is a similar case. In 1995, he was inspired, often in partnership with Monte Lynch, and I wouldn't shackle the youngster. Time enough for him to come to terms with his game, his value for us was his positive approach, which in turn rubbed off on everyone, to the benefit of the side.

Talent needs to develop to be harnessed. It shouldn't be undermined, or the player written off because he's allegedly awkward or uncooperative. That deadlock often stems from an inability to manage the player in the right way. Of course, there are ground rules for success, things that need to be worked at, no matter how monotonous – but I don't believe that everyone should be treated the same. Good man-management involves treating players as individuals to the benefit of the team. Many have dismissed me and my ideas as eccentric, yet I have usually had a reason for whatever I've done. Instead of criticising me, dismissing my approach as that of an oddball, perhaps a more intelligent response should be, 'Hang on, it works for Jack, I wonder why?' One of the true qualities of man-management is to deal with all talents, of all ages, all characters and all attitudes – and get the best out of them. I admire Manchester United's manager, Alex Ferguson, for his vision of the future. He can blend in the youngsters with the successful seniors in a winning side, but he did the difficult bit by creating a confident, winning unit with the right older players. Their professionalism and individual flair makes it comparatively easier for the youngsters to come in and shine, because the foundations are right. I recall one of our committee members at Bristol saying to me, 'What about the youngsters? Why don't we play more of them?' My reply was, 'Well, we could but have they the experience to win?' It's no good youngsters growing up with the attitude of being in a losing side. It's best to breed them in a positive, winning environment. You can't do that, unless they're all highly talented. If the senior players are prepared to move with the times, and are still worth selecting because of their contributions, then they shouldn't be ousted just because it looks attractive and imaginative to be playing a lot of youngsters. I've heard coaches on the county circuit say, 'It's better to play all the youngsters', but perhaps they were thinking they're easier to control than senior players, and therefore a better option for the coach who may not be very good at man-management. Blend is crucial, and so is an open mind.

It's been frustrating to have missed out on team success in my time at Bristol. We have had so many good players, yet we haven't appeared to have that mental hardness, that winning habit. We ought to have won the Championship at least once in the mid-eighties, when we had such a good bowling attack, and when we've been in sight of a Lord's Final we've failed to do ourselves justice. I'm very conscious that Gloucestershire haven't won the championship for more than a century, nor a trophy since 1977, when we won the Benson & Hedges competition, but the players are just as frustrated about that as the supporters. I can't believe I'll retire without getting my hands on a trophy, and if we can break through that barrier, I do believe we'll go on strongly from there. After that, I'd love to get the chance to put my cricket principles on the line and see if I can motivate the new generation into becoming heroes of Gloucestershire. Nothing would give me more pleasure than seeing their photos on the wall at the County Ground, alongside W G Grace, Wally Hammond, Tom Goddard, Tom Graveney, Mike Procter and Zaheer Abbas. We've been one of the great names of county cricket since the last century, and I hope that in the twenty-first century, I'll be doing my bit to discover some major talent.

It may be that my cricketing ambitions don't materialise, but I'll always have my painting. I would still paint, even if I didn't sell another painting, because it's an addiction to me. I'm still searching for the perfect painting, and I hope I don't manage it because that means I might be tempted to stop. I was very pleased with the 'Moment of Victory', to commemorate the winning run for us in the 1990 Jamaica Test, and the colour note for my painting of the cricket ground belonging to John Paul Getty contains the best sky I've managed so far – but these are only isolated examples, I'm still trying to get there. So many people say to me, 'I wish I could do that' and I reply, 'Well, have you tried?'. They admit they haven't, so how can they say they're not up to it when they haven't even had a go? When I started in 1987, I had no intentions of showing anybody what I'd done, I was trying it out for my own satisfaction. Within me, there must have been some smattering of talent, but it's probably there for many more people, if only they'd try. I can't beat the words of the painter Tom Keating: 'I'm trying to encourage everybody to have a go. Anyone can pick up a brush, it's inhibition that stops even children. It just needs courage.'

My early inspirations were Constable and Rembrandt. I saw my first Rembrandt in the National Gallery one wet day in London when our match had been called off, and one picture stuck in my memory. It's called 'Syndics of Drapers' Guild'. It featured a red table, with a hand held out, and it was electric. The atmosphere was magnificent and the 3D effect stunning. Constable was a big influence on me, because I shared his love of the English countryside. I'm essentially a landscape painter and I could never get bored, especially with the variety that England has to offer. The landscape and wildlife specialist, David Shepherd is another hero of mine, and not just because his work is so stunning. He once described his work as 'three per cent talent and ninety-seven per cent hard work' and although that's an over-simplification of his particular abilities, I could relate to that. With me, it's almost exclusively hard work, but that gives me great pleasure because I'm getting rewarded for putting in the hours and for dedication. That should be the attitude of anyone in a profession. Work hard and enjoy the rewards, don't expect anyone to pick up the tab for you. Many so-called experts in the art world were dismissive of David Shepherd's abilities, but he took them on, backed his judgement and now he's incredibly successful and respected for what he's done with the World Wildlife Fund and the David Shepherd Conservation Foundation, raising awareness of the need to protect endangered species. And to think that David only had one small painting hanging in the National Gallery, and when his parents came to see it, they had to search for it. They eventually found it, near the door and just above the floor and they had to get down on their hands and knees to get a better look. When I drew a portrait of David which was printed to raise money, he was highly flattered and said he was honoured. When he was questioned about my painting by Brian Johnston on BBC Radio's *Test Match Special*, David was very complimentary about my sketch, and that thrilled me. The fact that it helped to raise money for his foundation through its sale was another happy sequel.

There are other artists I admire hugely, Raymond Harris-Ching – a brilliant wildlife artist, and Edward Seago – a landscape specialist from the early 20th century. The simple, almost naive work of L S Lowry, capturing so cleverly masses of humanity against the backdrop of factories, chimneys, schools and terraced houses in Lancashire – not glamorous at all, but breathing vitality and realism. Lady Butler's magnificent military paintings – especially one of the 28th at Quatre Bras, 1815, the Gloucester Regiment in Melbourne's City Art Gallery, and 'Scotland Forever' in the Leeds Gallery. Such atmosphere – you can smell the battle. There's an excellent modern-day impressionist called Trevor Chamberlain who lives in Hertfordshire and sold me a lovely painting of boats on the River Thames in subdued light. Loving river scenes as I do, I was full of admiration for the way he got the light and the reflections off the river so effectively. Compared to some of these painters I've mentioned, I'm just a naive amateur, trying merely to stretch himself, but it is a wonderfully therapeutic, rewarding pastime. As he often did, Winston Churchill got it right when he wrote, 'Painting is a companion with whom one may hope to walk a great deal of life's journey. Happy are the painters. For they shall not be lonely.' How true. I'm in a different world when I paint, and I'm convinced it's helped me become a better cricketer.

In 1994, my cricket was in a bit of a slump, after I'd been dropped by England, but it was a great year for my painting career, after taking the plunge and deciding to open my gallery in Chipping Sodbury. It's given me an extra incentive to improve my painting and develop my range. There's also some consolation in missing out on Tests when abroad on England duty – I can always go off and paint things you don't see in the Gloucestershire countryside! I ship work back to my agent, Jim Ruston, he handles the marketing and distribution and I can then concentrate on the sheer pleasure of getting out in the fresh air and retreating into a totally different world. The Gallery has given me the base from which to display my work, and it was a great day for me when we finally sealed the purchase. The negotiations dragged on and on during the 1994 summer, and we got to the Cheltenham Festival still haggling over various points. Right up to when I took the field one day at Cheltenham, Jim and I were still locked in discussions and we agreed on a signal if he managed to conclude the deal. Somehow I managed to hold onto my concentration behind the stumps, until I looked over to the tent as we changed ends. Jim gave me the thumbs-up, and I could relax. I love being in the Gallery. Parts of it date back to 1576, it's one of the oldest buildings in Chipping Sodbury, and at times I crouch down in a corner and just soak up the atmosphere, trying to imagine what it was like in there all those centuries ago. When we moved in, we demolished part of the chimney breast and we discovered a leather wallet that for some reason had been sealed away. Inside were pictures of some of the Gloucester Regiment having a drink just outside the Gallery before going off to the Second World War. Lineage and military history have always fascinated me, and it was remarkable to have such a piece of local history turn up just like that.

When I finally get the time, I'd like to do more research into my favourite military periods. The walls of my home are covered with military paintings – there are none of my paintings there – and I have some uniforms from various regiments. I'm sure it all drives Aileen crazy! Hopefully, I'll knuckle down to doing some proper research on the significant moments of our military history, and then do some travelling. I'd love to fly down to the Falklands one day, and try to recreate some of the heroic scenes which saw brave men like Colonel H Jones awarded the Victoria Cross. I sometimes go into the Victoria Cross room in the Imperial War Museum and I find it very emotional. The bravery involved in getting such an award hits me. I've spent hours in the Imperial War Museum, just transporting myself back to another age, a different form of combat. I'll clamber into the replica trenches and wonder what it must have been like when the whistle went and you had to go over the top, with oblivion just a bullet away. The rattle of the machine-guns, the whizzing shells, the smell of mustard gas – they were brave men. People tell me I've got a grisly fascination for war, but I'm the sort of person who is interested in experiences that are unfamiliar to me, I like to know what people feel, how do they cope? Bravery of any sort impresses me, and I go off into a trance when I sit in one of those trenches. One day, though, I perhaps took it too far. I'd immersed myself so deeply in my fantasies as people sidled through the trench that I must have looked like a dummy soldier. When I moved, I frightened the life out of one couple who'd been staring at me!

There are other ambitions away from cricket and art. I'd like to be a jockey. The character of horses has always interested me – I love painting them – and the kids have a couple of ponies, so they're not unfamiliar to me. I went to the Cheltenham Festival races one year, and I loved the sight of these magnificent beasts charging to the finishing line. I met Peter Scudamore, a legendary jockey who also happens to be a massive cricket fan, and we got talking. After he'd explained the finer points of horse riding, I said I fancied having a go at it. I'll have to wait until I've retired from professional cricket, because neither Gloucestershire nor England would allow me to get involved in something that's potentially dangerous, but I do fancy it. Hopefully, I'll be the right shape and weight for a start. The idea of teamwork between horse and rider appeals, and the physical bravery involved. It's you against the rest, like eyeballing a nasty fast bowler, with the adrenalin flowing and the crowd roaring you on.

Like all the Gloucestershire supporters, I dream of the county I love so dearly becoming a great team again, a major force in English cricket for a sustained period of five, ten or even fifteen years. It can be done, there's no doubt about it. The problem is, it needs a certain vision and commitment. I hope somebody will come along and take the county back to its former glory, and sustain it for a long period of time. It is a mammoth and difficult task; not one to be taken lightly, but a really tremendous challenge. In 1997, on my return from the winter tour, I offered to take up that challenge.

Due to commitments with the West Indies, Courtney Walsh was unable to come back and captain Gloucestershire in the 1997 season. So the club approached me to take on the job. After careful consideration (I even went to a secluded spot in Cornwall for a few days, to clear my head and give it undisturbed thought) I returned to Bristol to meet with club officials. I explained my plan, which included a captain's role with ultimate responsibility. I informed them that I was happy to take on total responsibility for all aspects involved with cricket, at all levels in the county, and that I was happy to sink or swim by my results. In effect, I said I would gladly put my head on the block, but I wanted to control the destiny of my own neck. I didn't think that was unreasonable. They were a little shocked, I think, by the boldness of my ideas, but I had a vision of creating a great club again, over a period of five years, initially, which, with the correct structure in place, could go on and dominate the English game for many years to come. It is possible. One man in charge, one man responsible – no hiding behind committees (there would be no need for a cricket committee); one person answerable to those at the top running the club, who are ultimately responsible to the members. After all, it is a members' club, and they have the ultimate say.

The club officials argued that international duties would interfere with my role. With the right structure and right men assisting, that could be overcome. A six or seven-month contract would be adequate, but they seemed to disagree, although I said in the meetings on at least three occasions that I would be happy to work 365 days a year and get the job done (including Christmas Day!) if I thought it would help the club become successful. But they seem to think a twelve-month contract was the only solution. Some people have said to me, 'Wouldn't they pay you enough money?' The discussions didn't get that far. It was the principles and authority to be able to direct operations both on and off the field that were the stumbling blocks. It would be difficult to influence the direction of Gloucestershire cricket if you don't have sufficient say. I was offered the post of manager/captain, but that was exactly the role I had in the year I was captain, with one of the coaches as my assistant. In other words, nothing new was on the table. I would be happy to put my neck on the block, but I think it's only fair to be allowed to determine the destiny of my own neck. Is that unreasonable?

The chairman and other club officials turned down my proposals. I was disappointed, I have to admit. Frustrated, but not bitter. They are the people in the position of power, with the future of Gloucestershire cricket in their hands, and it's their prerogative. They have their own plans for success, and that's fine by me. I'll have the ambitions for a while yet, I'm sure. I'm having a tremendously fascinating career, and it would be nice to spend a chunk of my life putting things back into the game. There are very few coaches, managers or directors of cricket that can influence the game directly on the field of play by actually being out there, playing in the First XI. The problems is, I won't be able to play forever, so my opportunities to take this kind of role, as I see it, are not infinite.

While I can still play, and together with my desire, knowledge, physiological and man-management skills, I would like to take up this challenging role one day. I love Gloucestershire. I love playing for the county, it's been my life ever since pulling that wishbone one Christmas when I was a youngster. I sincerely hope that one day I will be able to put everything I have got into Gloucestershire cricket. But, business is business, and if the opportunity for a challenge comes along, no matter where in the country, or around the world, I would be a fool not to consider it.

I've always relished a challenge, and that's the way I've lived my life. I've always wanted to be different and successful. You don't have to be selfish to make something of your life, just dare to be different and swim against the tide occasionally, especially if it's what you believe in. Go out and do it! If you don't fancy propping up the bar at night, don't do it. Save your money for other things that have more appeal. I've told myself that I'll always get there in the end even if takes ten years, and that applies to everybody. The responsibility for success rests solely on your own shoulders. When you finally achieve it, that brings the greatest satisfaction.

CAREER STATISTICS

Compiled by Wendy Wimbush

CAREER MILESTONES

1981   First-class debut aged 17 years 307 days – the youngest-ever Gloucestershire wicket-keeper, making eight dismissals, including 5 catches in the 2nd innings

1982   Selected as wicket-keeper for England Under-19 v West Indies Under-19

1984   Reached 1,000 first-class runs and 100 dismissals

1985   Capped by Gloucestershire

1986   Reached 200 dismissals

          August: First first-class representative match – TCCB v New Zealanders at Edgbaston

          September: Surrey at Oval – caught Stewart, Butcher and Lynch off successive balls, a feat not achieved since G O Dawkes (Derbyshire v Worcestershire) in 1958

1986–87   Toured Sri Lanka with Gloucestershire

1987   Reached 2,000 first-class runs and 300 dismissals

1987–88   First representative tour, to Pakistan, as second wicket-keeper to Bruce French. Played in first limited-overs international, a World Cup match against Pakistan at Peshawar

1988   Test debut at Lord's v Sri Lanka, scoring 94. Reached 3,000 first-class runs

1989   First Test v Australia, Headingley: conceded no byes in total of 601–7 dec, Fourth Test, Old Trafford. Scored first Test hundred, also his first first-class hundred, the fourth England player to

continued overleaf

do this in a Test and the first since S C Griffith at Port-of-Spain in 1947–48

Cornhill Player of the Series

Reached 4,000 first-class runs and 400 dismissals

1989–90	Fourth Test v West Indies, Bridgetown: 5ct in 1st innings, the first England wicket-keeper to achieve this feat
1990	20 July: Scored only limited-overs international fifty against India at Trent Bridge
	August: 50th Test dismissal – Manoj Prabhakar in his 16th Test (Old Trafford)
	September: Southampton against Hampshire – 500th first-class dismissal
	Reached 5,000 first-class runs
1990–91	December: Second Test v Australia, Melbourne, 6ct, a record for England in Tests v Australia
1991	Reached 6,000 first-class runs
	August: Took only first-class wicket (Carl Hooper) – Gloucestershire v West Indians at Bristol (Mark Alleyne took over as wicket-keeper)
	September: Took 500th first-class catch – Gloucestershire v Northamptonshire at Bristol
1992	7 July: Taken ill and missed the last day of the Third Test v Pakistan at Old Trafford (Stewart deputised)
	Reached 7,000 first-class runs and 600 dismissals
	Had his best season: 985 runs at 42.82
1992–93	Reached 8,000 first-class runs and 700 dismissals

continued next page

1992–93	4 August: Called to Edgbaston as cover for Stewart but was released to play at Cheltenham against Derbyshire. He scored 99* in the 2nd innings. In the next match he took 7 dismissals against Lancashire
	Captained Gloucestershire for the first time v Somerset at Taunton when Courtney Walsh was taken ill
1994	Reached 9,000 first-class runs
1994–95	Joined England team in Australia as cover for Stewart but made only one appearance, as substitute, at Bendigo against Victoria, 20–23 January
1995	Reached 10,000 first-class runs v Middlesex at Bristol
	Reached 800 dismissals
	Fourth Test v West Indies, Old Trafford: 100th Test dismissal – Ian Bishop; 5th England wicket-keeper with 100 dismissals
1995–96	Second Test v South Africa, Johannesburg: 100th Test catch – Hansie Cronje
	World record 11 catches in the same match
	Batted 277 minutes in the second innings, adding 119* for the 6th wicket with Michael Atherton to save the match. Took 27 dismissals in series – England record
1996	Reached 11,000 first-class runs and 900 dismissals
	Second Test v Pakistan, Headingley: 150th Test dismissal – Moin Khan

SUMMARY OF ALL FIRST-CLASS MATCHES

Season	Venue	M	I	NO	HS
1981		1	1	1	1*
1982		4	6	1	41
1983		24	32	9	64*
1984		21	27	6	63
1985		23	23	4	34
1986		27	31	9	71
1986–87	SL (Gs)	1	2	1	39*
1987^s		26	38	9	57*
1987–88	Pak	1	1	0	4
1988^s		24	36	8	94
1989		19	29	7	128*
1989–90	WI	8	15	5	55
1990		17	23	2	120
1990–91	Aus	8	13	1	36
1991^s		20	32	5	111
1991–92^s	NZ	7	8	1	57
1992		20	34	11	75
1992–93	Aus(EngA)	4	6	1	51*
1993^s		19	33	7	99*
1993–94	WI	8	12	2	62
1994		19	34	8	85*
1995		17	26	4	91
1995–96	SA	10	13	4	129*
1996		19	30	5	124
1996–97	NZ	1	2	1	61*
TOTALS		348	507	112	129*

^s Bowling   * Not out

Season	Bowling
1987	1.1–0–7–0
1988	1–0–12–0
1991	1.2–0–14–1
1991–92	1–0–5–0
1993	1.5–0–15–0

Russell's only wicket – Carl Hooper (WI) at Bristol 1991

Runs	Avge	100	50	Ct/St	St
1	-	-	-	7	1
81	16.20	-	-	4	2
507	22.04	-	3	46	17
513	24.42	-	1	26	9
253	13.31	-	-	59	6
585	26.59	-	2	56	4
51	51.00	-	-	1	1
798	27.51	-	4	54	10
4	4.00	-	-	-	-
870	31.07	-	6	57	12
586	26.63	1	2	51	7
269	26.90	-	1	24	2
794	37.80	2	3	45	1
168	14.00	-	-	27	4
627	23.22	1	2	48	4
242	34.57	-	2	22	1
985	42.82	-	5	40	3
103	20.60	-	1	3	1
863	33.19	-	5	56	7
268	26.80	-	2	17	1
901	34.65	-	4	58	1
977	44.40	-	8	50	2
520	57.77	1	3	39	5
858	34.32	1	7	48	3
61	61.00	-	1	3	-
11885	30.08	6	62	841	104

TEST MATCH SUMMARY

Season	Venue	M	I	NO	HS
1988	SL	1	1	0	94
1989	Aus	6	11	3	128*
1989–90	WI	4	7	1	55
1990	NZ	3	4	0	43
1990	I	3	3	1	35
1990–91	Aus	3	5	1	30*
1991	WI	4	7	0	46
1991	SL	1	2	1	17
1991–92	NZ	3	5	1	36
1992	Pak	3	4	2	29*
1993–94	WI	5	9	1	62
1994	WI	3	5	1	91
1995–96	SA	5	7	2	50*
1996	Ind	3	4	0	124
1996	Pak	2	3	1	41*
TOTALS		49	77	15	128*
	Sri Lanka	2	3	1	94
	Australia	9	16	4	128*
	West Indies	16	28	3	91
	New Zealand	6	9	1	43
	India	6	7	1	124
	Pakistan	5	7	3	41*
	South Africa	5	7	2	50*
HOME		29	44	9	128*
OVERSEAS		20	33	6	62
TOTALS		49	77	15	128*

Runs	Avge	100	50	Ct/St	St
94	94.00	-	1	3	-
314	39.25	1	1	14	4
139	23.16	-	1	14	-
84	21.00	-	-	7	-
59	29.50	-	-	11	1
77	19.25	-	-	9	1
73	10.42	-	-	5	-
29	29.00	-	-	3	-
135	33.75	-	-	8	1
56	28.00	-	-	6	1
195	24.37	-	1	10	-
199	49.75	-	1	9	1
140	28.00	-	1	25	2
162	40.50	1	-	8	-
51	25.50	-	-	9	-
1807	29.14	2	6	141	11
123	61.50	-	1	6	-
391	32.58	1	1	23	5
606	24.24	-	3	38	1
219	27.37	-	-	15	1
221	36.83	1	-	19	1
107	26.75	-	-	15	1
140	28.00	-	1	25	2
1121	32.02	2	3	75	7
686	25.40	-	3	66	4
1807	29.14	2	6	141	11

COUNTY CHAMPIONSHIP SUMMARY

Season	M	I	NO	HS
1982	4	6	1	41
1983	23	30	9	64 *
1984	20	26	5	63
1985	21	23	4	34
1986	24	31	9	71
1987$	24	34	7	57 *
1988	19	30	6	72
1989	10	15	3	41 *
1990	11	16	1	120
1991$	12	19	3	111
1992	16	28	9	75
1993$	17	30	7	99 *
1994	17	30	7	85 *
1995	14	21	3	87
1996	13	21	4	75
TOTALS	245	360	78	120

$ Bowling

1987	0.1–0–0–0
1991	0.3–0–10–0
1993	1.5–0–15–0

Runs	Avge	100	50	Ct/St	St
81	16.20	-	-	4	2
469	22.33	-	3	45	17
513	24.42	-	1	26	9
253	13.31	-	-	55	5
585	26.59	-	2	51	4
779	28.85	-	4	50	8
658	27.41	-	4	46	9
188	15.66	-	-	32	2
651	43.40	2	3	27	-
464	29.00	1	2	36	3
904	47.57	-	5	30	2
826	35.91	-	5	53	7
807	35.08	-	4	55	1
778	43.22	-	7	41	1
634	37.29	-	7	31	2
8590	30.46	3	47	582	72

FIRST-CLASS SUMMARY BY TEAM AND VENUE

	M	I	NO	HS
England	29	44	9	128*
Gloucestershire^s	266	385	86	120
TCCB	1	-		
MCC	2	2	1	12*
England A	1	2	0	11
Rest	1	2	0	9
UK/HOME	300	435	96	128*
England XI:				
in Pakistan	1	1	0	4
in West Indies	16	27	7	62
in Australia	12	19	2	51*
in New Zealand^s	8	10	2	61*
in South Africa	10	13	4	129*
Glos in Sri Lanka	1	2	1	39*
OVERSEAS	48	72	16	129*
TOTALS	348	507	112	129*

^{s} Bowling
Gloucestershire   5.2–0–48–1
England   1–0–5–0

DOMESTIC LIMITED-OVERS SUMMARY

	M	I	NO	HS
Sundays 1982–1996	182	138	33	108
Benson & Hedges 1983–1996	54	40	15	51
NatWest 1982–1996	36	25	7	59 *
Totals	272	203	55	108

Runs	Avge	100	50	Ct/St	St
1121	32.02	2	3	75	7
9037	30.22	3	49	621	81
-	-	-	-	3	-
19	19.00	-	-	4	-
11	5.50	-	-	2	-
11	5.50	-	-	-	1
10199	30.08	5	52	705	89
4	4.00	-	-	-	-
537	26.85	-	3	41	3
271	15.94	-	1	30	5
303	37.87	-	3	25	1
520	57.77	1	3	39	5
51	51.00	-	-	1	1
1686	30.10	1	10	136	15
11885	30.08	6	62	841	104

Runs	Avge	100	50	Ct/St	St
2443	23.26	1	9	146	27
633	25.32	-	1	54	10
434	24.11	-	1	47	8
3510	23.71	1	11	247	45

FIRST-CLASS HUNDREDS (6)

128* England	**Australia**	**Old Trafford**	**1989**
120 Gloucestershire	Somerset	Bristol	1990
103* Gloucestershire	Nottinghamshire	Trent Bridge	1990
111 Gloucestershire	Hampshire	Bristol	1991
129* England XI	Boland	Paarl	1995–96
124 England	**India**	**Lord's**	**1996**

PAIRS (3)

Gloucestershire	Northamptonshire	Bristol	1989
Gloucestershire	Worcestershire	Bristol	1989
Gloucestershire	Nottinghamshire	Worksop	1992

TOURS

Pakistan	1987–88
West Indies	1989–90, 1993–94
Australia	1990–91, 1992–93 (Eng A)
New Zealand	1991–92, 1996–97
South Africa	1995–96
Zimbabwe	1996–97

For limited-overs internationals only:

India	1989–90, 1995–96
Australia	1994–95
Pakistan	1995–96

Gloucestershire played one match in Sri Lanka in 1986–87
1994–95: Joined England team as cover for Stewart, but only made one appearance as a substitute.

FIFTIES IN LIMITED-OVERS INTERNATIONALS

50   India   Trent Bridge   1990

HUNDREDS IN DOMESTIC LIMITED-OVERS MATCHES

108   Worcestershire   Hereford   1986

FIFTIES IN DOMESTIC LIMITED-OVERS MATCHES

For Gloucestershire (9)

94*	Lancashire	Bristol	1986	JPSL
70	Worcestershire	Gloucester	1987	Ref
72*	Glamorgan	Bristol	1987	Ref
62	Essex	Chelmsford	1990	Ref
51	Worcestershire	Worcester	1991	B&H
56*	Somerset	Gloucester	1992	TCCB (Sun)
70	Surrey	Gloucester	1994	AXA
56*	Worcestershire	Gloucester	1995	AXA
59*	Suffolk	Bristol	1995	NW
76*	Surrey	Oval	1995	AXA

INTERNATIONAL LIMITED-OVERS MATCHES SUMMARY

Season		M	I	NO	HS
1987–88	Pak	1	1	1	2*
1988	SL	1	-		
1989–90	Nehru Cup	5	4	4	10*
1989–90	WI	6	3	0	28
1990	NZ	2	2	1	47*
1990	Ind	2	2	0	50
1990–91	WSC in Aus	3	3	0	13
1990–91	NZ	3	3	0	13
1991	WI	3	1	0	1
1995–96	SA	5	5	1	39*
1995–96	W Cup	6	4	0	12
1996–97	NZ	1	1	0	2
	Pak	3	3	2	7*
	SL	3	2	1	10*
	Aus	2	1	0	13
	Ind	3	3	1	50
	WI	10	5	1	28
	NZ	9	9	1	47*
	SA	6	6	1	39*
	UAE	1	-		
	Holland	1	-		
HOME		8	5	1	50
OVERSEAS		30	24	6	39*
TOTALS		38	29	7	50

Runs	Avge	100	50	Ct/St	St
2	-	-	-	3	-
		-	-	-	-
35	-	-	-	3	2
49	16.33	-	-	4	-
60	60.00	-	-	2	1
64	32.00	-	1	-	1
25	8.33	-	-	6	-
25	8.33	-	-	4	1
1	1.00	-	-	4	-
93	23.25	-	-	6	-
27	6.75	-	-	7	1
2	2.00	-	-	2	-
13	13.00	-	-	6	1
19	19.00	-	-	1	1
13	13.00	-	-	1	-
74	37.00	-	1	1	2
58	14.50	-	-	8	-
101	12.62	-	-	13	2
105	21.00	-	-	9	-
		-	-	1	-
		-	-	1	-
125	31.25	-	1	6	2
258	14.33	-	-	35	4
383	17.40	-	1	41	6

INDEX